MURRAY
WALKER'S

1995 Grand Prix Year

**Photography by
LAT Photographic**

PUBLISHER
Richard Poulter

EDITOR
Simon Arron

ART EDITOR
Mike Askew

PRODUCTION MANAGER
Steven Palmer

BUSINESS DEVELOPMENT MANAGER
Simon Maurice

SALES PROMOTION
Clare Kristensen

**Murray Walker's
1995 Grand Prix Year**
is published by Hazleton Publishing
3 Richmond Hill
Richmond, Surrey
TW10 6RE, England
Produced in association with *Shell*

Colour reproduction by
Masterlith Ltd, Mitcham, Surrey

Printed in England by
Ebenezer Baylis & Son Ltd, Worcester

ISBN: 1-874557 56X

DISTRIBUTORS

UNITED KINGDOM
Bookpoint Ltd
39 Milton Park
Abingdon
Oxfordshire
OX14 4TD
Tel: 01235 400 400
Fax: 01235 861038

AUSTRALIA
Technical Book and
Magazine Co. Pty. Ltd,
295 Swanston Street
Melbourne VIC 3000
Tel: (03) 9663 3951
Fax: (03) 9663 2094

NEW ZEALAND
David Bateman Ltd
PO Box 100-242
North Shore Mail Centre
Auckland 1330
Tel: (9) 415 7664
Fax: (9) 415 8892

NORTH AMERICA
Motorbooks Int.
PO Box 1,
729 Prospect Avenue,
Osceola,
Wisconsin 54020, USA
Tel: (1) 715 294 3345
Fax: (1) 715 294 4448

SOUTH AFRICA
Motorbooks
341 Jan Smuts Avenue
Craighill Park
Johannesburg
Tel: (011) 325 4458/60
Fax: (011) 325 4146

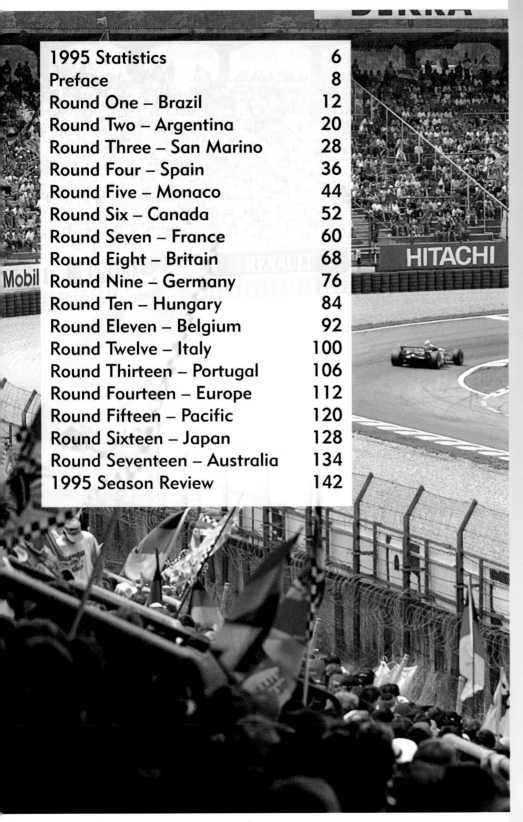

Contents

1950, Giuseppe Farina, Alfa Romeo.

1951, Juan Manuel Fangio, Alfa Romeo.

1952, Alberto Ascari, Ferrari.

1961, Phil Hill, Ferrari.

1962, Graham Hill, BRM.

1964, John Surtees, Ferrari.

1985, Alain Prost, McLaren.

1986, Alain Prost, McLaren.

1988, Ayrton Senna, McLaren.

162 GRAND PRIX WINS, 18 WORLD CHAMPIONSHIPS ON SHELL. CONCLUSIVE PROOF NOT ALL FUELS ARE THE SAME.

1953, Alberto Ascari, Ferrari.

1956, Juan Manuel Fangio, Lancia-Ferrari.

1958, Mike Hawthorn, Ferrari.

1968, Graham Hill, Lotus.

1970, Jochen Rindt, Lotus.

1984, Niki Lauda, McLaren.

1989, Alain Prost, McLaren.

1990, Ayrton Senna, McLaren.

1991, Ayrton Senna, McLaren.

SHELL'S SPONSORSHIP OF McLAREN ENDED IN 1994

DURING 1995...

- Five-times World Champion Juan Manuel Fangio, generally acknowledged to have been the greatest of them all, died at his home in Balcarce, Argentina, at the age of 84.
- A 500cc reduction in engine size to three litres was introduced, together with other speed-reducing and safety-enhancing aerodynamic and construction regulations.
- Formula One returned to Argentina after an absence of 14 years.
- The Pacific Grand Prix in Japan was delayed for eight months, due to the Kobe earthquake.
- Benetton, McLaren, Jordan, Ligier, Pacific, Arrows and Sauber changed their engine suppliers.
- Nigel Mansell made a brief two-race return to Grand Prix racing with McLaren at Imola and Spain, but declined to continue thereafter in what he considered to be an uncompetitive car.
- The historic Lotus team foundered, as did the French Larrousse and British Simtek teams.
- Major changes were made to the Imola circuit following the tragic deaths there in 1994.
- The Italian Grand Prix was in doubt until last minute agreement by the government to implement FIA circuit safety demands involving the removal of trees.
- Michael Schumacher and David Coulthard, first and second in the Brazilian Grand Prix, were disqualified for fuel irregularities but later re-instated by an FIA appeal court.
- Jean Alesi, Johnny Herbert and David Coulthard won their first Grand Prix after, respectively, 91, 71 and 21 starts.
- The FIA introduced sophisticated electronic systems for monitoring jump-starts and pit-lane speeding.
- Andrea Montermini drove in the San Marino Grand Prix five days after the removal of his appendix.
- The Benetton team, with Michael Schumacher, demonstrated a repeated race-winning mastery of re-fuelling strategy considerations.
- Renault achieved its 100th Grand Prix victory.
- In Canada Rubens Barrichello and Eddie Irvine gave the Jordan team its first-ever double-podium finish.
- The World Championship comprised 17 races instead of the traditional 16.
- Michael Schumacher won the drivers' World Championship for the second year in succession and became the first German to win his home Grand Prix since Rudolph Caracciola in 1939. He also won his second home Grand Prix at the Nürburgring.
- After five seasons with Benetton, world champion Michael Schumacher announced that he would move to Ferrari in 1996, taking the coveted 'Number One' with him.

1995 DRIVERS – CAREER STATISTICS

Driver	Nat	Team	Starts	Wins	Poles	Fastest laps
Jean Alesi	F	Ferrari	102	1	1	2
Luca Badoer	I	Minardi	29	-	-	-
Rubens Barrichello	BR	Jordan	48	-	1	-
Gerhard Berger	A	Ferrari	180	9	11	18
Mark Blundell	GB	McLaren	61	-	-	-
Jean-Christophe Boullion	F	Sauber	11	-	-	-
Martin Brundle	GB	Ligier	142	-	-	-
David Coulthard	GB	Williams	25	1	5	4
Jean-Denis Delétraz	F	Pacific	3	-	-	-
Pedro Diniz	BR	Forti	17	-	-	-
Heinz-Harald Frentzen	D	Sauber	32	-	-	-
Bertrand Gachot	F/B	Pacific	47	-	-	1
Mika Häkkinen	SF	McLaren	63	-	-	-
Johnny Herbert	GB	Benetton	80	2	-	-
Damon Hill	GB	Williams	51	13	11	15
Taki Inoue	J	Footwork	18	-	-	-
Eddie Irvine	GB	Jordan	32	-	-	-
Ukyo Katayama	J	Tyrrell	18	-	-	-
Pedro Lamy	P	Minardi	16	-	-	-
Giovanni Lavaggi	I	Pacific	4	-	-	-
Jan Magnussen	DK	McLaren	1	-	-	-
Nigel Mansell	GB	McLaren	187	31	32	30
Pierluigi Martini	I	Minardi	119	-	-	-
Andrea Montermini	I	Pacific	17	-	-	-
Gianni Morbidelli	I	Footwork	60	-	-	-
Roberto Moreno	BR	Forti	42	-	-	1
Olivier Panis	F	Ligier	33	-	-	-
Massimiliano Papis	I	Footwork	7	-	-	-
Mika Salo	SF	Tyrrell	19	-	-	-
Mimmo Schiattarella	I	Simtek	7	-	-	-
Michael Schumacher	D	Benetton	69	19	10	22
Aguri Suzuki	J	Ligier	64	-	-	-
Gabriele Tarquini	I	Pacific	38	-	-	-
Jos Verstappen	NL	Simtek	15	-	-	-
Karl Wendlinger	A	Sauber	41	-	-	-

1995 RACE STATISTICS

Race	Winner	Pole	Fastest lap
Brazil	Michael Schumacher	Damon Hill	Damon Hill
Argentina	Damon Hill	David Coulthard	Michael Schumacher
San Marino	Damon Hill	Michael Schumacher	Gerhard Berger
Spain	Michael Schumacher	Michael Schumacher	Damon Hill
Monaco	Michael Schumacher	Michael Schumacher	Jean Alesi
Canada	Jean Alesi	Michael Schumacher	Michael Schumacher
France	Michael Schumacher	Damon Hill	Michael Schumacher
Britain	Johnny Herbert	Damon Hill	Damon Hill
Germany	Michael Schumacher	Damon Hill	Michael Schumacher
Hungary	Damon Hill	Damon Hill	Damon Hill
Belgium	Michael Schumacher	Gerhard Berger	David Coulthard
Italy	Johnny Herbert	David Coulthard	Gerhard Berger
Portugal	David Coulthard	David Coulthard	David Coulthard
Europe	Michael Schumacher	David Coulthard	Michael Schumacher
Pacific	Michael Schumacher	David Coulthard	Michael Schumacher
Japan	Michael Schumacher	Michael Schumacher	Michael Schumacher
Australia	Damon Hill	Damon Hill	Damon Hill

The amphibious Footwork FA16 (above) was fitted with Brian Hart's compact new V8; Gianni Morbidelli was retained as lead driver.

Brits abroad: six UK drivers (right) were signed to top seats, although Martin Brundle's would be in the commentary box for the first three races. From the left, Messrs Coulthard, Hill, Herbert, Irvine, Brundle and Blundell smile for the camera. Blundell would stand in for Nigel Mansell, while McLaren built a car to accommodate a pair of seven-million dollar hips.

"Did I ever tell you about the time I stalled a Formula One car?" Damon Hill (top) listens to a few useful tips.

And you thought Nigel Mansell had trouble getting in his car...(above)

While it had the aesthetic appeal of a Routemaster bus, McLaren's MP4/10 (below) certainly provided a few pre-season talking points.

Without doubt, 1994 had been one of the saddest and most contentious Grand Prix years of all time. The tragic deaths of Ayrton Senna and Roland Ratzenberger; bans; exclusions; fines; accusations of cheating; political machinations; seemingly endless regulation and circuit changes; the potentially disastrous pit fire at Hockenheim; the hotly debated Schumacher/Hill collision in Australia which decided the World Championship...

Their combined effect had numbed enthusiasm and tarnished a great sport. Everyone had been glad to see the end of it and was looking forward to what was optimistically expected to be a very different, much more competitive and exciting season.

The final implementation of the FIA's regulation changes had necessitated major innovations by the teams. Three-litre engines, instead of 3.5; smaller wings; a 50mm downforce-reducing 'step' in the monocoque floor; a 10mm composite skidblock: they all dictated that the cars would lap more slowly, and have less grip, though they should be easier to drive and more spectacular to watch. Wider cockpit openings, tough new side-impact tests, smaller fuel tanks and revised fuel rigs would increase safety margins, while new FIA checking procedures, using specialised equipment, would make for much improved policing and enforcement of the technical regulations.

With every team having to grapple with new aerodynamic problems by producing all-new cars, the competition was expected to be much closer, especially as there had been major contractual moves during the winter. Not only had drivers been switching camps, so had the engine builders.

Thus Benetton was now to use Renault power; McLaren had dumped Peugeot, after only one season, and had dramatically switched to Mercedes-Benz's V10 (designed and produced by Ilmor in Britain); Jordan had achieved a major coup by linking with Peugeot; Arrows switched to Brian Hart's excellent V8; Ligier was to be powered by Mugen (backed by Honda, which was determined to win again as it had so often done in the past with Williams, Lotus and McLaren); the Sauber team had cheerfully inherited the works Ford deal abandoned by Benetton.

In fact, of the leading teams only Williams-Renault, Tyrrell-Yamaha and Ferrari were maintaining engine continuity.

But if the new constructor/engine relationships were exciting, the top teams' closely-matched driver pairings were equally so.

Williams had spurned Formula One returnee Nigel Mansell, the 1992 world champion, in favour of David Coulthard, the young Scot who had adapted so impressively to Formula One when he was called in to replace the late Ayrton Senna in 1994. As a result, and against all expectations and predictions, Nigel had joined the blindingly quick Mika Häkkinen at McLaren. Johnny Herbert had at last got the top drive he had so long deserved, joining reigning world champion Michael Schumacher at Benetton. After a very disappointing season with McLaren, Martin Brundle had rejoined Ligier to partner talented Frenchman Olivier Panis in selected races, whilst Finland's Mika Salo, who had impressed so much with Lotus in the last two races of 1994, had joined Ukyo Katayama at Tyrrell.

Understandably, there had been no changes at Ferrari, with the daunting combination of Gerhard Berger and Jean Alesi, or at Jordan, which retained both Rubens Barrichello and Eddie Irvine. With the welcome return to Formula One of Karl Wendlinger, happily recovered from his crash at Monaco, to accompany the excellent Heinz-Harald Frentzen, the Sauber team returned to the strong line-up it had initially used during 1994.

Karl Wendlinger (above) was back at Sauber, having missed most of 1994 in the wake of his Monaco practice accident. The Austrian had still to prove his full race fitness, however.

Would the Ferraris (below) finally come out of their shell? Pre-season testing had looked good, in-between accidents...

Things can only get better. Pacific spent more money designing the PR02 than it had on the whole 1994 season, though the budget didn't stretch to buying somewhere comfortable for Bertrand Gachot (above right) to sit.

So with 16 top drivers fighting for points in, apparently, closely matched cars, an exciting and unpredictable battle for World Championship honours looked to be on the cards.

Sadly though, as ever in the ruthlessly competitive world of Formula One, there had been casualties over the winter, most notably the demise of the once-great Team Lotus. After 36 years of Grand Prix racing, with six drivers' and seven constructors' World Championships and unforgettable achievements by Jim Clark, Graham Hill, Jochen Rindt, Emerson Fittipaldi, Ronnie Peterson, Mario Andretti and Ayrton Senna, amongst others, the team had, over 10 years after the death of founder Colin Chapman, finally failed to keep up with the financial demands of Formula One. Its purchase by David Hunt, brother of the late, great James, and its merger with the fledgling Pacific team had kept the name alive but sadly the name was seemingly all that was left.

Things looked equally fraught for the French Larrousse team, which was struggling to survive.

Drivers had suffered, too. After a distinguished 14-year career in Formula One, Michele Alboreto had failed to secure a seat, as had Mark Blundell, Andrea de Cesaris, Christian Fittipaldi, David Brabham, Eric Bernard, JJ Lehto, Erik Comas and Alessandro Zanardi. For one reason or another they had all lost out.

Inevitably there were venue changes. We were going back to Argentina, after a 13-year absence, at the expense of Hungary which was listed as a 'reserve' event. And the lacklustre MkII Nürburgring in Germany, a very pale shadow of its magnificent predecessor, was to stage the European GP in place of Jerez, Spain. There would be major changes to Imola after the tragic events of the 1994 San Marino GP, while the modifications demanded at Monza would undoubtedly remain a bone of contention until it was almost too late.

Doubts were also raised about the Pacific GP at Aida, in Japan, after the terrible earthquake at nearby Kobe.

On the plus side, the magnificent Eau Rouge complex at Spa in Belgium would be back to its former glory and Silverstone would be enhanced by major changes to pits and paddock and a more open approach to the first corner, Copse.

So, as the teams prepared for their first GP of the season at the superb Interlagos circuit in Brazil, there was an expectant buzz: six British drivers, all of them with top teams and a real chance of winning races; performance-enhancing internal rivalries between Hill and Coulthard, Schumacher and Herbert, Berger and Alesi, Katayama and Salo, Barrichello and Irvine, Mansell and Hakkinen, Brundle and Panis, Frentzen and Wendlinger; the promise of closer racing and enhanced overtaking opportunities thanks to the revised regulations; the intrigue of diverse refuelling tactics.

Would the 41 year-old, but super-fit and extra-hungry, Nigel Mansell have the speed and stamina to overcome his younger rivals? Could Damon Hill get the job done in his third season of Grands Prix? How would the Benettons go with Renault power?

Could Mercedes-Benz triumph again in F1, with McLaren?

Could Jordan continue its upward momentum? Would 1995 be the year when Ferrari returned to the top after only one win from the last four seasons? Could Williams make 1995 another championship year? Could Ligier and Tyrrell become a threat again? Could Sauber, with Ford power, join the elite? How many new winners would there be? Hakkinen? Herbert? Barrichello? Irvine? Coulthard? Alesi? Brundle? Panis? How would the smaller teams, Minardi, Simtek, Pacific Team Lotus and debutant Forti, perform?

All these questions, and more, were about to be answered!

ROUND 1

26 March 1995
Circuit: Interlagos

We went to Brazil eagerly anticipating a bright new dawn for Formula One. Competition amongst the new three-litre, aerodynamically hobbled cars was going to be closer and safer and the new regulations would create stability. But it wasn't like that at all. At an overcast and low-key Interlagos, where the absence of the late, great Ayrton Senna would be most apparent, it was just as argumentative as 1994 had been in parts.

The battle was still between Benetton and Williams, the top men were still Schumacher and Hill, the concern about refuelling was still very much there and, with frenzied speculation about rumoured fuel irregularities, allegations that some drivers' weights weren't all they seemed and contention over the drivers' super licences, the off-track wrangling was undiminished.

What's more, 'Our Nige' wasn't there. Following Mansell's surprise signing for McLaren-Mercedes, pre-race testing had established that the ugly new MP4/10 was too small for him. At great expense a new monocoque was frenziedly being made, but Nigel would not be competing until the third race. That was a great disappointment for everybody except Mark Blundell, who was recalled from the sidelines to take his place.

Normally Interlagos, on the outskirts of São Paulo, a vast industrial sprawl on the Brazilian coast that you wouldn't hurry back to, is a great place to start a season. But not this time. The track surface, always bumpy, had been worsened by inept resurfacing work and was now downright dangerous. At times the cars were well-nigh uncontrollable, the drivers' feet were being thrown off the pedals, their vision was being impaired by the bumps and their cars were being subjected to enormous stresses. Always a race of attrition, Brazil '95 was going to be even worse.

At 09.30 on Friday the cars accelerated out of the pits for the first 'free' (it doesn't count towards grid positions) practice session. Now we were going to see how relevant winter testing times had been. The new Williams-Renaults of Damon Hill and David Coulthard were in a class of their own and, as the teams fine-tuned chassis to suit the bumpy track, it was the Williamses they were trying to match. When the grid was formed on Sunday afternoon Damon Hill was in his fifth pole position, 0.3s faster than his 1994 rival, and world champion Michael Schumacher. For Damon, Friday and Saturday had been trouble-free but for Schumacher they had been anything but. He had a gigantic off on

Benetton unleashes a stream of irregular, but legal, Elf into Schumacher's fuel tank (above). After three pit stops and an FIA court appearance, the German was eventually declared the winner.

But for suspension failure, Damon Hill (left) would have started 1995 on a winning note.

Friday when a steering joint broke and on Saturday he again shot off the wet track. David Coulthard – accused of being a poor qualifier – was third, an outstanding achievement considering that it was his first time at Interlagos and that he was recovering from tonsillitis. Johnny Herbert, at last starting a full season in a car worthy of his talent, was an equally praiseworthy fourth. Wisely, he had not been allowed out during Friday's qualifying whilst Benetton investigated the reason for Schumacher's accident. Fifth and sixth were the Ferraris of Berger and Alesi, a second off Hill's pace, followed by Mika Häkkinen's much-maligned McLaren-Mercedes and Eddie Irvine's Jordan-Peugeot. Down in a lowly 16th spot after myriad problems in the second Jordan was Brazil's new hero, the downcast Rubens Barrichello. Rubens had been aching to do well in honour of his own hero, Ayrton Senna, whose helmet colours he had adopted for the weekend.

After two days of wet/dry weather it was fine for the race, but just minutes before it began there was a sensational announcement from the stewards: Schumacher and Coulthard, second and third on the grid, were racing under appeal! Samples of their Elf fuel taken during the meeting had been "different" from those approved by the FIA and if their race fuel also differed their results would be in jeopardy. Scarcely had the startled congregation absorbed this thunderbolt than the race was off. A fine way to start the season...

Super-starter Schumacher catapulted his Benetton ahead of Hill's Williams at the Senna S, the downhill left/right complex at the end of the main straight, but there was no question of him clearing off. Damon was glued to his gearbox with Coulthard making it a trio as

A nation still in mourning (above).

Government Elf warning: fuel chemistry can temporarily damage your race results (right).

Pedro Diniz made his F1 debut on home soil in the Forti (below), which was not demonstrably faster than the F3000 Reynard from which he had graduated.

they pulled away from the rest, led by Häkkinen, who had already passed Alesi, Berger and Herbert. Twice Damon made a determined lunge for the lead in the opening laps, but each time Schumacher closed the door. Somehow, though, it seemed just a matter of time before Hill took the lead. Delighted with his car he looked calm and comfortable; Michael was under very considerable pressure.

By lap 10 Schumacher and Hill, as one, were five seconds ahead of Coulthard who, concerned about his stamina, sagely decided to pace himself. Häkkinen was seven seconds further behind but well ahead of a terrific battle for fifth between the two Ferraris, just led by Gerhard Berger.

With smaller fuel tanks being deployed to take advantage of the revised regulations, refuelling tactics were going to be critical. So what would the various strategies be? Last year Benetton had usually opted for three stops, so when Schumacher came in on lap 17 it was clear that they would be doing the same in Brazil.

15

He was fifth when he rejoined, and now Damon was in front. With a clear track he put the hammer down. When he pitted on lap 21 he was 23s ahead of Schumacher, enough to allow him to pit and stay ahead. Of the top six, Berger was the last to stop, on lap 27, and when he rejoined the top three read Hill, 3s ahead, Schumacher and Coulthard. To everybody's delight, but no great surprise, Mika Salo was fourth in the Tyrrell-Yamaha with just 1.5s covering himself, Alesi and Häkkinen.

In his first GP, for Lotus in Japan last year, Salo had made a major impact. Now, in the impressive new Tyrrell-Yamaha, he was emphasising just how good he really was.

On lap 31 a collision with Suzuki's Ligier ended a poor-starting Johnny Herbert's race and disaster struck Damon Hill. Exiting the Senna S his Williams stepped sideways, and he slid on to the grass and out of the race. Driver error? Something on the track? Or a car problem? "Suddenly the thing just locked up and I went off," said Damon. At the time he thought it had been a gearbox failure, but it later transpired that a rear suspension pushrod had broken. Whatever, a race over which he appeared to have complete control was over. Once again, he had demonstrated that he was Schumacher's equal. But with Michael now back in the lead Hill was going to be 10 points down in the championship. Or so it seemed.

When Schumacher came in for his second stop on lap 36, Coulthard took control. Despite his relative inexperience and his secondary physical condition, not having been able to train for two weeks, he was driving superbly, and he led for 11 laps until he made his own second – and final – stop. But Michael still had a third stop to come, so he had to build a big enough lead, at least 20s, to compensate. Eyes down. This was going to be exciting!

Meantime, after two long-running battles with team-mate Alesi, Berger had clawed his way up to a

For Rubens Barrichello (above), it was a tough weekend physically and emotionally.

Despite finishing a lap down, Gerhard Berger (above right) was declared the winner several hours after taking the chequered flag. And then undeclared again a couple of weeks later...

Unable to catch the attention with his performance in the cockpit, Taki Inoue (below) resorts to other methods.

distant third after a fumbled first stop which lost him at least 12s, his right front wheel having nearly came off as he left the pits. Everyone else had been lapped. Häkkinen was fourth, Alesi fifth, Salo sixth and Morbidelli close behind. What had happened to the flying Salo? After being a brilliant third for seven laps he had developed such bad cramp in one arm that he spun. Having deftly kept his Yamaha V10 alive and rejoined he was now doing the best he could – and very good it was. Morbidelli was another man to watch; his excellent Arrows with its Hart V8 engine had hardly run before it got to Brazil, but for nine laps he was in the points. Sadly he was to retire, but not before he had demonstrated the car's obvious potential. When Gianni disappeared, his fine sixth place was taken by Mark Blundell, grasping his unexpected opportunity with both hands. Ninth on the grid, he had been grappling with gear selection problems for most of the race but was coping magnificently, to prove that you must never, ever underestimate McLaren.

On lap 53, having set the fastest lap of the race two laps earlier (1m 20.921s, 119.563 mph), Schumacher led Coulthard by 21s as he made his third and last tyre/fuel stop. On lap 54, he was only 3.4s ahead of the Williams and from then on he gradually increased his advantage to win his 11th Grand Prix by 8s and rack up 10 invaluable World Championship points.

We thought.

With Coulthard a superb second, for the second time in his first nine Grands Prix, Berger a lapped third, Häkkinen fourth, Alesi fifth and Blundell an excellent sixth, it had been an interesting and satisfying opening race of the season. But there was a sting in its tail. Whilst Schumacher, Coulthard and Berger delightedly sprayed their champagne from the podium, gave their thoughts to the world at large and went their different ways, the media agonised about whether the post-race fuel analyses would change the result.

They did.

Six hours after the race had finished, whilst Schumacher was on his way to holiday on the coast and Coulthard was at 35,000 feet, flying home, a bulletin announced that, because of alleged fuel irregularities, both Schumacher and Coulthard bad been disqualified. The facts were unclear and both Benetton and Williams were to appeal but Gerhard Berger was declared the winner (a record 105th for Ferrari), with Häkkinen second, Alesi third, Blundell fourth, Salo a magnificent fifth and Japan's Aguri Suzuki a startled sixth for Ligier.

This one was going to run and run but irrespective of whether you thought it was an administrative cock-up or a positive demonstration that the FIA was in charge it was a messy and unhappy way to start a new season.

Eventually, an FIA Court of Appeal decreed that, while the fuel samples did indeed differ to those submitted for pre-season analysis, the drivers had gained no advantage. As a result, Schumacher and Coulthard were re-instated, though both teams were fined, and neither was allowed to score points in the constructors' championship.

Hopefully things would not be so fuzzy in Argentina.

Benetton-Renault

After problems with new gearbox in both testing and practice, things come good in race, but turn sour afterwards. Schumacher has big off on Friday, due to worrying steering failure and also goes off in wet on Saturday. Both he and Herbert have gearbox problems and Johnny not allowed out by team on Friday after Michael's crash. But Schumacher takes second on grid with Herbert fourth, only 0.4s slower than Michael, despite limited laps. Schumacher outdrags Hill at start and fights to hold off aggressive Damon until lap 17 pit stop. Back to lead (laps 31-34) after Hill retirement, until second stop, lap 35. Runs second to Coulthard until retaking lead, lap 47. Stays there, including third stop, lap 53, and wins 11th GP, with fastest lap. Disqualified for alleged use of irregular Elf fuel. Team appeals and confidently expects ruling to be reversed, which it eventually is – though team receives $200,000 fine and is docked constructors' points. After poor start Herbert drops to 10th. Has clutch and speed limiter problems at lap 20 stop. Retires from ninth, lap 31, after colliding with Suzuki's Ligier.

Tyrrell-Yamaha

Despite both spinning twice on appalling Interlagos surface, Katayama and team newcomer Salo qualify 11th and 12. Ukyo uses spare car after warm-up problems. With major oversteer, spins out of eighth on lap 16. Salo has superb first race for Tyrrell. Battles for seventh with Irvine, laps 5-14, before first stop, from sixth, lap 21. Runs superb third, laps 31-37, but spins due to arm cramp, lap 38. Rejoins eighth, after early second stop, and finishes seventh despite limited use of arm. Temporarily up to fifth after disqualifications.

Williams-Renault

Relaxed and confident, Damon Hill takes fifth pole of his career (with Friday time), but in Sunday warm-up is fractionally slower than outstanding team-mate David Coulthard, who overcomes "poor qualifier" image to start excellent third. Hill beaten to first corner by Schumacher but harries him until Michael pits, lap 17. Damon then confidently leads until spinning out (rear suspension failure), lap 31, with victory seemingly certain. Coulthard leads magnificently, laps 37-46, despite lack of training (tonsillitis), but has to yield to Schumacher after second pit stop. Finishes fine second, eight seconds down and with third fastest lap of race.

McLaren-Mercedes

Mark Blundell replaces non-starting Nigel Mansell whilst McLaren frantically builds new car to fit their new star. After much-needed handling improvements to the MP4/10, Mika Häkkinen and Mark take seventh and ninth on grid. Both acquit themselves well in the race, but lose time with refuelling problems. Mika to fourth, past Alesi, Berger and Herbert, on lap one. Pits when second, lap 23, after which a bird damages his rear wing. Takes third from outstanding Salo before second stop, lap 43 and finishes fourth, seven seconds behind Berger. Blundell selects neutral at start and drops to 14th. Makes excellent recovery despite gear selection difficulties and paces himself to finish fine sixth. McLaren not so badly off as its deriders had suggested.

Arrows-Hart

Although virtually untested, new FA16 with Hart V8 engine shows great promise. After being ninth fastest on Friday morning Morbidelli has damper problem but qualifies 13th. Japan's Taki Inoue, on steep learning curve, starts 21st. Morbidelli drives outstanding race, battling for fifth with Alesi after second pit stop, but retires, lap 62, when fuel pressure fails. Inoue spins and stalls after hitting Wendlinger, lap 32. Rejoins after push start and visits pits but, like Gianni, has fuel pressure failure. Retires from 12th and last, lap 49, as car catches fire.

Simtek-Ford

Team arrives with untested new car. After multitude of problems Jos Verstappen qualifies 24th and Domenico ("Mimmo") Schiattarella 26th, after heavy off on Saturday. Mimmo out lap 13 (faulty steering). Jos retires from 14th, lap 17 (clutch).

Jordan-Peugeot

Local hero Rubens Barrichello uses special helmet design to honour Ayrton Senna's memory. Eddie Irvine eighth fastest on Friday but Rubens only 16th after sharing Eddie's car due to engine problem. Neither improves position on Saturday and both retire early. Irvine from seventh, lap 15, with gearbox O-ring failure, Rubens from 12th, lap 17, with broken gearbox actuator. Great disappointment for team, especially Rubens, after very successful pre-race testing.

Pacific-Ford

Encouraging debut for totally untested, Frank Coppuck-designed PRO2 after best-forgotten 1994. Despite new car problems, Gachot qualifies 20th and last-minute signing Andrea Montermini 22nd. Bertrand retires from 15th, lap 24 (stuck in fifth). Andrea gives team first GP finish despite broken floor and fuel-rig release problem. Finishes ninth, six laps down.

Larrousse-Ford

Team fails to arrive after succumbing to its financial problems. But team owner Gerard Larrousse says that, having now secured a budget, it will be at Imola. In which case, a substantial `no-show' fine awaits.

Forti-Ford

Italian team graduates from Formula 3000 with barely tested, bulky-looking car and two Brazilian drivers: veteran Roberto Moreno and newcomer Pedro Diniz, who qualify 23rd and 25th. Roberto spins out of 11th place (of 14 survivors), lap 48. Pedro, still running at end, finishes tenth and last, seven laps adrift.

Minardi-Ford

Disgruntled team has to re-design car to use customer Ford ED engine after being jilted by Mugen-Honda. With virtually no testing, Pier-Luigi Martini qualifies 17th and GP returnee Luca Badoer 18th. Both retire with gearbox failure, Piero on first lap and Luca from 10th place, lap 48.

Ligier-Mugen Honda

Benetton clone Ligier JS41 (team owned by Flavio Briatore and masterminded by Tom Walkinshaw) looks great and, with Mugen-Honda V10, goes well, driven by the excellent Olivier Panis and Japan's Aguri Suzuki who will share second car with Martin Brundle. Panis qualifies 10th, and is impressive fourth in Sunday warm-up, but is barged out of race at very first corner. Ironic, for he had covered more racing miles than any other driver in 1993. Suzuki starts 15th. Pits from eighth on lap 31 for new nosecone, after tangling with Herbert. Races reliably to finish eighth, two laps down.

Ferrari

Team arrives with relatively little testing of new 412 T2, but it all comes right at Interlagos. In two-pedal (hand clutch) car Gerhard Berger qualifies fifth despite suffering from heavily blistered hands in narrow cockpit. Jean Alesi starts sixth. The two race together, fifth and sixth, until Alesi pits, lap 17. Gerhard stops later when fourth, lap 27, and loses time with botched front-wheel replacement. Back together, with Jean sixth, lap 29. Gerhard to third at Jean's second stop, lap 44, and stays there to end of race. Exhausted Alesi finishes fifth; both are one lap down. Berger gets to taste victory champagne after fuel disqualifications, but eventually has to accept original result.

Sauber-Ford

Now with Ford power, Sauber has an unhappy time, largely due to poor aerodynamics and resultant nervous handling over Interlagos bumps. Heinz-Harald Frentzen starts 14th with Karl Wendlinger, seemingly fully fit after 1994 Monaco crash, unhappy 19th. Neither finishes. H-H out from 12th on lap 11 ("the engine just stopped"), Karl from 14th, lap 42, after long pit stop to fix melted battery wire.

BRAZIL RESULTS AND STATISTICS

Autodromo Jose Carlos Pace, Interlagos, São Paulo

Subida do Lago — Curvo do Sol — Descida do Sol — Ferra Durra — Mergulho — Pinheirinho — Bico de Pato — Subida dos Boxes

26 MARCH 1995

Circuit length 2.687 miles/4.325 km

STARTING GRID

SCHUMACHER (Benetton B195) 1m 20.382s	**HILL** (Williams FW17) 1m 20.081s
HERBERT (Benetton B195) 1m 20.888s	**COULTHARD** (Williams FW17) 1m 20.422s
ALESI (Ferrari 412 T2) 1m 21.041s	**BERGER** (Ferrari 412 T2) 1m 20.906s
IRVINE (Jordan 195) 1m 21.749s	**HÄKKINEN** (McLaren MP4/10) 1m 21.399s
PANIS (Ligier JS41) 1m 21.914s	**BLUNDELL** (McLaren MP4/10) 1m 21.779s
SALO (Tyrrell 023) 1m 22.416s	**KATAYAMA** (Tyrrell 023) 1m 22.325s
FRENTZEN (Sauber C14) 1m 22.872s	**MORBIDELLI** (Footwork FA16) 1m 22.468s
BARRICHELLO (Jordan 195) 1m 22.975s	**SUZUKI** (Ligier JS41) 1m 22.971s
BADOER (Minardi M195) 1m 24.443s	**MARTINI** (Minardi M195) 1m 24.383s
GACHOT (Pacific PR02) 1m 25.127s	**WENDLINGER** (Sauber C14) 1m 24.723s
MONTERMINI (Pacific PR02) 1m 25.886s	**INOUE** (Footwork FA16) 1m 25.225s
VERSTAPPEN (Simtek S951) 1m 26.232s	**MORENO** (Forti FG01) 1m 26.269s
SCHIATTARELLA (Simtek S951) 1m 28.106s	**DINIZ** (Forti FG01) 1m 27.792s

RACE CLASSIFICATION

Pos	Driver	Nat	Car	Laps	Time
1	Michael Schumacher	D	Benetton B195-Renault	71	1h 38m 34.154s
2	David Coulthard	GB	Williams F17-Renault	71	1h 38m 42.214s
3	Gerhard Berger	A	Ferrari 412 T2	70	1h 38m 44.151s
4	Mika Häkkinen	SF	McLaren MP4/10-Mercedes	70	1h 38m 50.995s
5	Jean Alesi	F	Ferrari 412 T2	70	1h 39m 34.668s
6	Mark Blundell	GB	McLaren MP4/10-Mercedes	70	1h 38m 44.460s
7	Mika Salo	SF	Tyrrell 023-Yamaha		1 lap behind
8	Aguri Suzuki	J	Ligier JS41 Mugen-Honda		1 lap behind
9	Andrea Montermini	I	Pacific PR02-Ford		5 laps behind
10	Pedro Diniz	BR	Forti FG01-Ford		6 laps behind

Retirements	Nat	Car	Laps	Reason
Gianni Morbidelli	I	Footwork FA16-Hart	62	Fuel pressure
Taki Inoue	J	Footwork FA16-Hart	48	Fire
Luca Badoer	I	Minardi M195-Ford	47	Gearbox
Roberto Moreno	BR	Forti FG01-Ford	47	Spin
Karl Wendlinger	A	Sauber C14 Ford-Zetec	41	Electrics
Damon Hill	GB	Williams FW17-Renault	30	Seized gearbox
Johnny Herbert	GB	Benetton B195-Renault	30	Collision/clutch
Bertrand Gachot	B/F	Pacific PR02-Ford	23	Gearbox
Rubens Barrichello	BR	Jordan 195-Peugeot	16	Gearbox
Jos Verstappen	NL	Simtek S951-Ford	16	Clutch
Ukyo Katayama	J	Tyrrell 023 Yamaha	15	Spin
Eddie Irvine	GB	Jordan 195-Peugeot	15	Hydraulics
Mimmo Schiatteralla	I	Simtek S951-Ford	12	Steering
Heinz-Harald Frentzen	D	Sauber C14 Ford-Zetec	10	Electrics
Olivier Panis	F	Ligier JS41 Mugen-Honda	0	Accident
Pier-Luigi Martini	I	Minardi M195-Ford	0	Gearbox

Fastest lap

Damon Hill   GB   Williams FW17-Renault   lap 25   1m 20.982s (192.264mph)

Results and Data © FIA 1995

DRIVERS' CHAMPIONSHIP

Michael Schumacher	10
David Coulthard	6
Gerhard Berger	4
Mika Häkkinen	3
Jean Alesi	2
Mark Blundell	1

CONSTRUCTORS' CUP

Ferrari	6
McLaren-Mercedes	4

Argentina

**9 April 1995
Circuit: Autodromo
Oscar Alfredo Galves**

Following his disappointment in Brazil, Damon Hill (above) made amends with a thoroughly convincing triumph in the second – and final – South American race of the year.

What Buenos Aires looks like...when it's not raining (top left).

From podium to parliament: the politics Carlos Reutemann learned at Ferrari have stood him in good stead in his new role as a state governor in his native Argentina. The winner of 12 GPs demonstrated a 1994 Ferrari (left) with aplomb.

Not many of us knew much about Argentina. It was the 'bit' below Brazil, the land of the Pampas, home of the Gauchos, polo and the tango. They ate a lot of meat, the musical *Evita* was about ex-dictator Juan Peron's wife and we'd gone to war with them over the Falklands. But we also knew it had produced some truly great racing drivers, including Juan Manuel Fangio, arguably the greatest of them all, and a figure whose passing marked one of the saddest moments of the motor racing year. We had heard, too, that there was a terrific racing circuit in Buenos Aires. So it was with a genuine air of excitement and anticipation that we flew to BA, and we weren't disappointed when we got there.

They say that Buenos Aires is the most European of Latin American cities. Situated on the River Plate, just across the water from Uruguay, it's big – some eleven million people live there – and it is very impressive, with its wide, tree-lined, eight-lane highways, fine architecture, modern offices and shops, open spaces, parks, memorials and statues.

Everything they say about the size of the steaks is true. The atmosphere is relaxed and the restaurants are superb.

They weren't quite right about the circuit, though. About 20 minutes from the city centre, it is a much-revised and shortened version of the daunting 3.7-mile track which had last been used for the 1981 race (won by Nelson Piquet in a Brabham-Ford). Some 2.65 miles long, newly-surfaced and with all-new grandstands, garages and excellent media facilities, everyone basically liked it, although the drivers felt it to be too much like Hungary. Point and squirt. Lots of slow second gear corners. On and off the accelerator and brakes. Very difficult to overtake. At 72 laps, it would be a long, hard race, and qualifying well would be as important as it is in Monaco.

The sunshine which greeted our arrival had given way to torrential rain for the two familiarisation sessions on Thursday. On Friday and Saturday it was just as bad. Only on Saturday morning did conditions allow teams to work on dry set-ups, in the hope that raceday would be rain-free.

The man who coped with it best to take a brilliant pole position – the first in his nine-race Grand Prix career – was David Coulthard. Fastest in the wet on Friday, by over half a second, he repeated the feat on Saturday driving his Williams-Renault calmly, confidently and seemingly totally at ease with everything, including the bitter fact that he would not know whether he had officially finished second in Brazil until the FIA appeal court sat in Paris five days later. With Damon Hill alongside him, it was the first all-Williams front row since France 1994. Eddie Irvine was on row two, alongside Michael Schumacher, so there were three British drivers in the top four. Heartening, too, was the fact that the Ferrari revival was clearly gathering speed. With a new, high-torque V12 engine

Apparently, driving the Sauber C14 is one of the world's most cherished jobs. Heinz-Harald Frentzen (above) considers his good fortune.

Great while it lasted: Jos Verstappen (right) drove with verve for Simtek.

The bridesmaid again: Jean Alesi (below) added to his growing collection of second places.

Jean Alesi had been sensational. Fastest on Thursday and Friday mornings, second fastest in Friday qualifying...but only sixth on the grid, behind Häkkinen's McLaren, because he had mistimed his quick lap in the wet.

But, when we looked out of the hotel windows on Sunday morning, it was dry!

The start was a shambles. Charging hard for position before the first corner, Alesi lost the Ferrari, spun in the jostling pack and caused chaos as cars and drivers slammed into each other. Out came the red flag and, half an hour later, the race was re-started with several drivers, notably Alesi, Herbert, Barrichello and Panis, in their spare cars.

Coulthard had superbly taken the lead at the first start and he did so again, with Schumacher surging ahead of Hill. Mika Häkkinen had blasted up to third at the first start but this time he got it all wrong. Slicing across the track, just as he had done at Hockenheim in 1994, he broke Irvine's front wing, shredded his own rear tyre and immediately took himself out of the race.

At the end of the first lap Coulthard was, incredibly, already two seconds ahead of a battle between Schumacher and Hill with Tyrrell's new boy Mika Salo a superb fourth, from seventh on the grid. Because of the passing difficulties, re-fuelling strategies were going to shape the race and we were expecting the first stops around lap 17. But right now all eyes were on the leaders as Coulthard pulled away and Hill harried Schumacher every inch of the way. Suddenly, on lap six, already leading by four and a half seconds, Coulthard's Williams faltered. His electronic throttle was misbehaving. In a flash Schumacher and Hill were past but David's problem didn't last for long. Down to third and 3.7s behind the leaders on lap seven, he was right behind them on lap nine. Incredible! As the three of them circulated nose-to-tail it was Schumacher who looked least happy. All through practice he had struggled with the set-up of his Benetton and now both Williams drivers looked to have his measure. On lap 11, Damon took the lead and on lap 16 Coulthard passed the German as they both lapped Martini's Minardi. Michael was under massive pressure! But on lap 17 this was eased as poor Coulthard, briefly back in the lead as Hill pulled in for his first tyre stop, trundled off the track to retire. This time the problem was terminal; rotten luck but he had made his point. And with a vengeance.

With Schumacher following Hill in on the next lap, Jean Alesi, on a two-stop strategy to the others' three, led the race for eight glorious laps followed by Hill, Schumacher, Herbert (who had started 11th), one-stop Frentzen and Jos Verstappen.

Jos Verstappen? In the Simtek? Yes! The young Dutchman who had driven for Benetton with great distinction in 1994 was really flying in a car which no one would have thought was a potential points scorer. On loan from Benetton, Jos loved the car and the Simtek

team loved him. They were doing a sensational job together but, in what was indeed turning out to be a race of attrition, Verstappen was out on lap 22 with a broken gearbox. Like Coulthard, he had made his mark.

It was wonderful to see a Ferrari going so well, and it was a consequence of merit, not default. When Alesi made his first stop on lap 26, Damon Hill had been tucked up behind him for four laps, but when he rejoined he was still second, 24s behind Hill and just less than a second ahead of Schumacher. Great stuff. Schumacher could hold the Ferrari but he couldn't get past it and when he pulled in for his second stop on lap 35 he was still third, now a massive 32s behind race leader Hill.

Was he in trouble? The affirmative response was down to tyre wear. For some reason the Goodyears were behaving inconsistently. Aguri Suzuki actually came in for new tyres five times whilst Schumacher found that two of his four sets had not been good. Incompatibility between tyre and track, it was said. Whatever, Michael was out of the running as far as victory was concerned. The battle was between Hill's Williams-Renault and Alesi's Ferrari, and only the top three were destined to go the whole race distance.

On laps 49 and 50 Alesi and Hill made their second and third stops, and on lap 51 there was a mere 4.1s between them, and they were both on fresh tyres and fuelled to make the finish. This was going to be great!

At this point, however, Mika Salo, who had been driving a superb race in his Tyrrell-Yamaha, fifth behind Johnny Herbert for the last 16 laps and catching the Benetton, made another attempt to get past the unhelpful Suzuki's Ligier, which had been lapped several times. The collision which ensued took them both out and, in the pit lane afterwards, there was a Finnish/Japanese punch-up as tempers ran high. One's sympathies had to rest with Salo, who had been consistently baulked and had lost two certain championship points.

At the front, Hill was driving a copybook race as he revelled in what he later described as a perfect car. Alesi was spectacularly driving the wheels off his Ferrari, but Damon drew away until, on lap 58, with 14 to go, he was 11s ahead. With Schumacher an incredible 43s behind the Williams, the top three were settled. Some consolation to Michael was the fact that his fourth set of tyres was good, and allowed him to celebrate the fastest lap of the race on lap 55 (1m 30.552s,

105.251mph). But he was fairly and squarely beaten by Damon who, on lap 11, had passed Schumacher on the track in a race for the first time. It was his 10th career win and Damon had not put a wheel wrong. He felt it had been his best drive yet; no one was disagreeing. But, four days later, Schumacher led the championship after the FIA appeal court reversed the Brazilian GP stewards' decision and returned points to Michael and David Coulthard. Most people felt that they had done the right thing although Berger, Alesi and Ferrari were far from pleased.

So victory for Hill, 6.4s ahead of Alesi, with Schumacher third, a lapped Johnny Herbert fourth, scoring his first 1995 points for Benetton, Frentzen fifth and Berger sixth.

As ever, there had been other outstanding drives. Rubens Barrichello, for instance, had started from the pit lane in the spare Jordan originally set up for Eddie Irvine. He had forced his way up to seventh by lap 23, only to retire when his Peugeot engine developed an oil leak. Coulthard had been superb. Verstappen had impressed enormously, and so had Olivier Panis, who finished seventh, after giving Berger a hard time.

Although the appeal court had reinstated Schumacher and Coulthard, it had denied Williams and Benetton their points from Brazil. Heading for its home GP at Imola, Ferrari thus led the constructors' championship...

Ebullient as ever, Jean Alesi (above) looks to pass Olivier Panis around the outside as they return to play 'Hunt the Spare' after the multiple pile-up which forced the original race to be aborted.

Welcome to sunny Buenos Aires...Upon arrival in Argentina for the first time since 1981, Grand Prix drivers had to put up with this (left).

Recovering from his gearbox trouble, David Coulthard puts the squeeze on Michael Schumacher (above). The pole-winning Scot showed every sign of being able to win a Grand Prix. If only his Williams was able to last one...

Benetton-Renault

After Interlagos disqualification and nearly drowning during a holiday break between races, Michael Schumacher arrives in Buenos Aires in sombre mood…and with a tarnished image, having been accused of manipulating his weight to confer him with an advantage during races. Only ninth fastest on wet Friday but improves on Saturday to start relieved third. Battles with Hill and Coulthard until lap 17 tyre/fuel stop when rejoins third behind Hill and Alesi. Finishes third, 33s down, blaming inconsistent tyres for inability to challenge. Still sets fastest race lap. Johnny Herbert qualifies 11th after spinning both days. Collides with Barrichello after first start. Races spare car to fourth place (one lap down). He too is unhappy with tyres. Post-race FIA appeal court restores Schumacher's Brazil win and points but confirms team's penalty, plus fine of $200,000. Schumacher thus heads drivers' championship.

Tyrrell-Yamaha

Team has difficulty balancing car in qualifying but Salo, with new seat to overcome cramp problems, lines up best-yet seventh. Hit by Herbert at first corner but, in repaired car, makes superb second start. Races fourth, laps 1-6. Passed by Alesi, hits Moreno's Forti for new nose, lap 13. Recovers to excellent fifth, catching Herbert, but is consistently baulked by already-lapped Suzuki who takes Mika out on lap 48. Furious punch-up ensues in pits. Katayama, now overshadowed by Salo, starts depressed 15th after set-up problems. Slow puncture necessitates three stops. Runs midfield to finish eighth, three laps down. Team and Mika lose points from Brazil following Paris appeal court decision.

Williams-Renault

Great Argentina for team. David Coulthard, fastest in both waterlogged qualifying sessions, brilliantly takes first GP pole. Hill is second on first all-British/all-Williams front row since France 1994 (Hill and Mansell). Coulthard leads from both starts and is over four seconds ahead of Hill/Schumacher battle when errant electronic throttle zeroes itself. Down to third. Incredibly wipes out three second deficit in two laps and then calmly passes Schumacher to second, lap 16, only for throttle problem to recur and force retirement, lap 17. Hill loses second to Schumacher at second start. Forcefully harries Michael until lap 11, when he takes the lead which lasts until lap 16 tyre/fuel stop. Regains lead from Alesi, lap 26, and retains it to end despite very real challenge from Jean's impressive Ferrari. Joy from Damon's 10th win compounded when post-race FIA Paris appeal court restores Coulthard's lost Brazilian points (although team still denied theirs).

McLaren-Mercedes

After further suspension and engine changes Häkkinen starts contented fifth. Mark Blundell unhappy 17th for last scheduled McLaren GP (Mansell returning for Imola); blames set-up problems. Mika sears to third past Schumacher and Irvine at start but race stopped. In contentious repeat attempt hits Irvine's Jordan at second start and is immediately out with shredded rear tyre. Interviewed by stewards but no action taken. After blasting to eighth at first start, Blundell races ninth, laps 1-6. Past Katayama to eighth, laps 7-9 but out by lap 10 (oil loss/cracked gearbox casing). Both drivers (and team) lose points from Brazil following FIA Paris appeal court decision.

Arrows-Hart

Morbidelli qualifies well in 12th. Impressively up to seventh but retires, lap 43 (electrical failure). Inoue stops Friday qualifying and incurs $20,000 fine for team when marshals unable to remove spun-off car. Starts 26th after crashing in pit lane. Spins out, lap 41.

Simtek-Ford

Euphoria! Despite loss of vital course-learning and setting-up laps due to varied problems, Jos Verstappen incredible 12th fastest on Saturday and starts 14th. With Mimmo Schiattarella 20th on grid, team has both cars in top 20 for first time. Even better in race. Verstappen sensational sixth, laps 17-22, but retires with broken gearbox after lap 22 tyre/fuel stop. Schiattarella races reliably and well to finish ninth (four laps down) to equal Simtek's previous best. An huge fillip for a very hard-trying team.

Jordan-Peugeot

With revised gearbox actuators following Brazil problems, Irvine and Barrichello impress in qualifying (running first and second for part of Saturday). Eddie starts fourth but Rubens down to 10th after losing Saturday set-up time (engine change). Irvine assaulted by wild Häkkinen at second start. Stops for new nose. Resumes a lap down but retires with an oil leak, lap nine. Barrichello hit by Herbert and Badoer in shambolic first lap. Takes second start from pits in spare car hastily rejigged after being set up for such taller Irvine. Drives blinder of a race, progressing to seventh by lap 23. Then retires, lap 34, also leaking oil.

Pacific-Ford

An awful weekend. In still new and undeveloped car both drivers have gearbox and handling problems. Montermini has big off on Saturday afternoon. Andrea starts 22nd, Bertrand Gachot 23rd. But neither go far as Karl Wendlinger collides with, and eliminates, both cars at start.

Larrousse-Ford

Still missing, but renewed promise of two cars at Imola, to be driven by Eric Bernard and Christophe Bouchut.

Forti-Ford

New car too slow, needing better aerodynamics. With traction and balance problems, Moreno and Diniz qualify 24th and 25th. Both race reliably but, nine laps down, neither is classified as a finisher.

Minardi-Ford

After testing McLaren-style high mini-wing Badoer and Martini qualify 13th and 18th. Badoer unavoidably rams Salo at first start, then clobbers Barrichello's Jordan. Car irreparable so, with no spare, Luca is out. Pier-Luigi hit by Panis at start and resultant underbody damage adversely affects handling. After unplanned tyre stop, lap eight, advances to 10th, lap 35, before spinning out, lap 45. On plus side team delighted that hard work with X-Trac technicians solves Brazil transmission problem.

Ligier-Mugen Honda

Oliver Panis blots his copybook by clouting the wall on both Thursday and Friday before cautiously qualifying a lowly 18th. Hits Martini at first start and re-starts in spare car set up for Suzuki. Races hard and well after early stop with presumed puncture (it wasn't) to finish seventh, two laps down. Suzuki makes an Argentinean porridge of it. Qualifies 19th. Does well to race up to 11th, laps 1-6, but then stops five times for new tyres due to handling problems before eliminating both himself and Salo, lap 49. Punch up follows in garage. Aguri loses his Brazilian point after FIA appeal court decision.

Ferrari

Ferrari renaissance accelerates with new high-torque V12. Jean Alesi positively scintillates in wet with usual all-action driving style. Fastest on Thursday, second on Friday but starts sixth due to completing permitted 12 Saturday laps before soaking track conditions start to ease. Causes multiple collision shambles at start by spinning in first corner traffic. Switches to spare car for second start. On two-stop strategy takes lead, laps 18-25, and then holds fighting second to Damon Hill, 6.4s down, delighted with competitiveness of his car. Gerhard Berger, now with most Ferrari GPs of all (81), starts only eighth after problems with hand clutch in wet. Punctures tyre on first-start debris, thinks it is shock absorber failure and comes in to retire. Chief mechanic Nigel Stepney spots problem, tyre is changed and off goes Gerhard after losing over a minute (subsequently to discover that his shock absorber was, in fact, faulty!). Finishes sixth (two laps down), staving off determined charge by Panis. FIA decision takes points from both Berger and Alesi but does not promote team, which nevertheless now leads constructors' championship by three points.

Sauber-Ford

After Interlagos problems, Ford-inspired damping revisions improve handling. Frentzen does well to qualify ninth. Wendlinger, lacking confidence in wet, does badly to qualify 21st. Heinz-Harald stops once, and drives unspectacular but worthy race to finish fifth (two laps down). Wendlinger heightens misery by eliminating himself and both Pacifics in second-start collision. Will he last the season? Formula One can be a hard world.

RACE 2

ARGENTINA

9 APRIL 1995

Autodromo Oscar Alfredo Galves

Ascari
Ombú
Esses
Senna S
Confiteria Curve
Hairpin
Curve 1

Circuit length 2.646 miles/4.259 km

STARTING GRID

HILL (Williams FW17) 1m 54.057s	**COULTHARD** (Williams FW17) 1m 53.241s
IRVINE (Jordan 195) 1m 54.381s	**SCHUMACHER** (Benetton B195) 1m 54.272s
ALESI (Ferrari 412 T2) 1m 54.637s	**HÄKKINEN** (McLaren MP4/10) 1m 54.529s
BERGER (Ferrari 412 T2) 1m 55.276s	**SALO** (Tyrrell 023) 1m 54.757s
BARRICHELLO (Jordan 195) 1m 56.114s	**FRENTZEN** (Sauber C14) 1m 55.583s
MORBIDELLI (Footwork FA16) 1m 57.092s	**HERBERT** (Benetton B195) 1m 57.068s
VERSTAPPEN (Simtek S951) 1m 57.231s	**BADOER** (Minardi M195) 1m 57.167s
MARTINI (Minardi M195) 1m 58.066s	**KATAYAMA** (Tyrrell 023) 1m 57.484s
PANIS (Ligier JS41) 0m 00.000s	**BLUNDELL** (McLaren MP4/10) 1m 58.660s
SCHIATTARELLA (Simtek S951) 1m 59.539s	**SUZUKI** (Ligier JS41) 1m 58.882s
MONTERMINI (Pacific PR02) 2m 01.763s	**WENDLINGER** (Sauber C14) 2m 00.751s
MORENO (Forti FG01) 2m 04.481s	**GACHOT** (Pacific PR02) 2m 04.050s
INOUE (Footwork FA16) 2m 07.298s	**DINIZ** (Forti FG01) 2m 05.932s

RACE CLASSIFICATION

Pos	Driver	Nat	Car	Laps	Time
1	Damon Hill	GB	Williams FW17-Renault	72	1h 53m 14.532s
2	Jean Alesi	F	Ferrari 412 T2	72	1h 53m 20.939s
3	Michael Schumacher	D	Benetton B195-Renault	72	1h 53m 47.908s
4	Johnny Herbert	GB	Benetton B195-Renault		1 lap behind
5	H-Harald Frentzen	D	Sauber C14 Ford-Zetec		2 laps behind
6	Gerhard Berger	A	Ferrari 412 T2		2 laps behind
7	Olivier Panis	F	Ligier JS41 Mugen-Honda		2 laps behind
8	Ukyo Katayama	J	Tyrrell 023-Yamaha		3 laps behind
9	Mimmo Schiattarella	I	Simtek S951-Ford		4 laps behind
NC	Pedro Diniz	I	Forti FG01-Ford		9 laps behind
NC	Roberto Moreno	BR	Forti FG01-Ford		9 laps behind

Retirements	Nat	Car	Laps	Reason
Mika Salo	SF	Tyrrell 023-Yamaha	48	Accident
Aguri Suzuki	J	Ligier JS41 Mugen Honda	47	Accident
Pier-Luigi Martini	I	Minardi M195-Ford	44	Spin
Gianni Morbidelli	I	Footwork FA16-Hart	43	Electrical
Taki Inoue	J	Footwork FA16-Hart	40	Spin
Rubens Barrichello	BR	Jordan 195-Peugeot	33	Engine
Jos Verstappen	NL	Simtek S951-Ford	23	Gearbox
David Coulthard	GB	Williams FW17-Renault	16	Electrics
Mark Blundell	GB	McLaren MP4/10 Mercedes	9	Engine
Eddie Irvine	GB	Jordan 195-Peugeot	6	Engine
Andrea Montermini	I	Pacific PR02-Ford	1	Accident
Mika Häkkinen	SF	McLaren MP4/10 Mercedes	1	Accident/tyre
Bertrand Gachot	B/F	Pacific PR02-Ford	1	Accident
Karl Wendlinger	A	Sauber C14-Ford Zetec	1	Accident
Luca Badoer	I	Minardi M195-Ford		Did not restart

Fastest lap	Nat	Car	
Michael Schumacher	D	Benetton-Renault	1m 30.522s (169.377kph)

Results and Data © FIA 1995

DRIVERS' CHAMPIONSHIP

Michael Schumacher	14
Damon Hill	10
Jean Alesi	8
David Coulthard	6
Gerhard Berger	5
Mika Häkkinen	3
Johnny Herbert	3
Heinz Harald Frentzen	2

CONSTRUCTORS' CUP

Ferrari	13
Williams-Renault	10
Benetton-Renault	7
McLaren-Mercedes	4
Sauber-Ford	2

ROUND 3

30 April 1995
Circuit: Imola

What a difference a year makes. Following the tragic deaths of Ayrton Senna and Roland Ratzenberger, the 1994 San Marino Grand Prix weekend had been one of the blackest in the history of motor racing. But, 12 months later, the 1995 meeting was a complete contrast. The sun shone, the racing was exciting and safe, the crowd was large and wildly enthusiastic and the atmosphere was upbeat. No one was unaware of what had gone before, but the agony of the past had faded in anticipation of better times ahead.

Before Imola, off the autostrada between Bologna and Rimini, we were apprehensive, knowing as we did that the track had been massively revised with safety in mind. Had they spoilt what had been one of the best circuits of them all? No, they hadn't. In some ways it was even better. The daunting sixth gear, 190mph, left/right sweep through Tamburello and Villeneuve, where Ayrton and Roland had perished, had been interrupted by sensible third gear chicanes. The niggling Acque Minerali corners had been intelligently revised

Damon Hill (left) drove with the tactical judgment formerly associated with Alain Prost, his controlled performance giving him the World Championship lead for the first time in his career.

In honour of a departed idol: the drivers assemble (below left) to remember Ayrton Senna, one year on.

Concrete bungle: Michael Schumacher (below) walks away from what used to be a raceworthy Benetton.

to create two open right-handers. The double-left at Rivazza had been replicated further back to increase the run-off area and the Variante Bassa, where Rubens Barrichello had crashed so heavily in 1994, had also been eased. The result was a circuit which was much safer but which still flowed, was popular with the drivers and even better for the spectators and viewers. A necessary job had been very well done.

To the delight of the fanatical Ferrari-loving Tifosi, the Prancing Horse team from nearby Maranello was looking strong and one of their heroes, Nigel Mansell, was back in a McLaren-Mercedes specially built to fit him. But they were understandably aggrieved by the fact that, to the disadvantage of Ferrari, Gerhard Berger and Jean Alesi, the FIA appeal court had reinstated Michael Schumacher and David Coulthard to first and second places in Brazil. So there was plenty to speculate and argue about as Formula One prepared for its first European Grand Prix of the year.

There were two special familiarisation sessions on Thursday, and with a fired up Jean Alesi fastest the Tifosi went home satisfied. But after Friday's qualifying they were ecstatic; Gerhard Berger was second on the grid, only 0.008s slower than Michael Schumacher's Benetton-Renault with Alesi fifth and only half a second covering the top five – Schumacher, Berger, Coulthard, Hill and Alesi.

It had been a tense and exciting battle which left Damon Hill disappointed that he had not been able to

Bank robbers anonymous: Benetton prepares for a pit stop (top).

Berger (above) titlillated the Tifosi by qualifying on the front row and leading...until he stalled at his first pit stop.

Short but sweet (right): Verstappen belied the fact that the Simtek had barely tested until this race, but proved it with a lack of reliability

take pole position in a Williams-Renault which he knew was capable of it. But there was always tomorrow… except that Saturday was much hotter, and lap times were mostly slower. The grid stayed the same, so there was going to be a big crowd on raceday.

There was gloom on Sunday morning though as heavy rain swept the track. The pre-race half-hour warm-up was a shambles. I had never seen so many spinning cars. Oil from the newly laid tarmac combined with the rain to make a surface like sheet ice which claimed driver after driver, including Schumacher (who had gone off and removed a wheel on Saturday), Hill, Coulthard, Irvine, Verstappen, Panis and Frentzen. There were others, too, but fortunately all of them escaped without harm.

The weather had improved as the two o'clock start came around, but the track was still wet in parts and very damp in others. So, grooved tyres or slicks? Wets would be best, but if the track dried as quickly as it usually did they would rapidly become an overheated liability. But slicks would be hazardous in the wet, and if it didn't dry out they'd have to be changed. In the event only six drivers started on wets: Schumacher, Berger, Coulthard, Hill, Alesi and Barrichello. They were the only ones who were right…

As Häkkinen and Mansell, who started sixth and ninth, struggled for grip with the rest of their slick-shod rivals, the correct-guessers on wets pulled away. Schumacher had Berger tucked up behind him;

Coulthard and Hill were together; Alesi was a close fifth and by lap two Barrichello was sixth. For five glorious laps Schumacher and Berger fought for the lead ahead of the warring Coulthard and Hill, but then in came Gerhard, the first to change to slicks. He rejoined in fifth place but was immediately two seconds a lap faster than he had been before. He had done the right thing, so in came Schumacher and Hill. Michael rejoined third, behind the new leader David Coulthard (yet to stop) and Berger. But not for long. Suddenly, at the approach to the fast left at Piratella, the TV screen showed the rear view of a shattered Benetton with both its right side wheels missing. It was Schumacher's! "It's not clear why I went off but I felt the car was a little bit unstable at the rear." Few people had any doubt that it was a case of too fast, too soon on new tyres on a damp track. Whatever, Schumacher was out with no championship points. With Coulthard now having stopped for slicks you only had to look at the euphoric Tifosi to see who was leading – Gerhard Berger!

For 11 laps he stayed there as a thrilling fight between Hill, up to second, Coulthard and Alesi gradually drew closer. On lap 12 the gap was 14s; on lap 21 it was 6.7 as Gerhard drew in for his second tyre stop – which destroyed any chance he had of winning. He stalled his engine, and the resultant delay cost 20s and dropped him to fourth behind Alesi. Now, the Hill/Coulthard/Alesi battle was for the lead. And what a battle it was, better than any we had seen for a very

long time. Less than a second covered the three of them as Coulthard, with Alesi swarming all over his gearbox, looked for a way past Hill. It was too good to last. Sure enough, more tyre stops broke it up. Alesi came in on lap 25 whilst Coulthard stayed out. Two laps later David spun, came in for his second stop and rejoined right in front of Alesi. After Hill's second stop (lap 29) the order was the same but Damon, driving a superb thinking race, had broken the opposition. He was seven seconds clear of the resumed, and ferocious, duel between Coulthard and Alesi – and pulling away. There were only four men on the same lap now, and the fourth was Berger, ahead of Nigel Mansell, going reasonably well on his return to Formula One, Eddie Irvine, Mika Häkkinen and Heinz-Harald Frentzen's Sauber.

On lap 35, Coulthard and Alesi spectacularly banged wheels on the 185 mph approach to Rivazza, just as news filtered through that the Scot had been penalised ten seconds for speeding in the pit lane. Having damaged a front wing endplate when he spun he had been graining his tyres, losing some two seconds a lap and needed to change his nosecone. But the rules forbade him to do so during a penalty stop. So now Alesi was second, some 16s behind Hill and 22 ahead of Coulthard with Berger fourth. Still fifth, Mansell had got nothing to be ashamed about for he was the highest of those who had started on slicks. His downfall was soon to come. On lap 44 his McLaren swept into the pits for a new nosecone, the original having cracked when Nigel drove into the unfortunate Gianni

Morbidelli's Arrows-Hart at the start. On the very next lap Mansell was in again, after a "misunderstanding" with Eddie Irvine which resulted in Nigel's left rear wheel treading on the Jordan's front wing. Pit stops were necessary for both of them; up to fifth and sixth places moved Häkkinen and Frentzen.

In the pits, it had been all action. As Mansell was having his nosecone replaced, so was Coulthard. David's fourth stop let Gerhard Berger through into third place and now the storm – and fun – was over.

After his third and final stop on lap 46, Damon Hill led the charging Alesi by 10s, Berger by 47 and Coulthard by 58. No one else was even on the same planet.

Damon won his 11th Grand Prix by 18s after a really magnificent drive which raised his wins-per-race percentage to nearly 30 per cent, a superb record. "I needed to think hard, use all my tactical ability and try to read the race. In all honesty, I was able to keep the thought that this was the place where we saw such terrible times last year out of my mind and get on with the job most of the time. However I think today was a good race and I think Ayrton would have approved of it."

So do I. It was very fitting that the great man's teammate of 1994 should have won at Imola in a Williams in 1995.

The Tifosi certainly thought so. Amongst the many banners was one poignantly reading 'Damon – win for Ayrton'. They went home very happy indeed. Not only had the spectacular Jean Alesi finished second for the second race in succession, but Gerhard Berger had finished third and posted the fastest lap of the race (1m 29.568s, 122.257 mph). Ferrari now shared the lead in the constructors' championship with Williams. "This is a really great result for Ferrari," said Sporting Director Jean Todt. "With more work and progress we will win soon. I am sure of that." Jean Todt may have been pleased; Jean Alesi wasn't. He had been desperate to win at his team's home track, was bitterly disappointed only to start fifth and fiercely criticised David Coulthard's forceful driving which had bent one of the steering arms of Jean's car during their brush at Rivazza. To be honest, it looked fair enough to me and David cleared the air in a subsequent visit to the Ferrari motorhome.

After a race in which Hill, Alesi, Berger, Coulthard, Williams and Ferrari had covered themselves with glory others were entitled to feel quietly satisfied too. Nigel Mansell had played himself in well on his return to Formula One; Rubens Barrichello had led everything except the Williamses and Ferraris until he had to retire; Jos Verstappen had again shone in the Simtek (an excellent eighth before his gearbox broke); and, as an aside, it was amazing that Andrea Montermini had been in the race at all – his appendix had been taken out only five days earlier! On the other hand the downcast Michael Schumacher's luck had certainly taken a downturn. Now six championship points behind Hill, would he be able to recover the deficit in Spain, two weeks hence?

Recurring theme: wherever you park a Benetton truck, a woman with striking dress sense will never be far away (above).

The on-track dispute between Coulthard and Alesi (left) continued in the Ferrari motorhome after the race.

Hard times: Nigel Mansell is just about visible as the red-and-white speck chasing Frentzen, Herbert, Salo, Katayama and Verstappen (below).

Benetton-Renault

With RS7A evolution of Renault V10 Michael Schumacher takes seventh career pole position by a whisker from Berger's Ferrari. "For the first time this season we have got the balance right," he says...but he still goes off on Saturday morning, removing a front wheel. Starts on wet-weather tyres and just leads until Berger stops for slicks, lap five. Michael changes tyres, lap nine, with 2.4s lead over Coulthard. Rejoins third but goes off heavily, lap 11. Loses championship lead to Damon Hill.

Johnny Herbert struggles to find good set-up amidst rumours that he is not getting full team co-operation. Qualifies eighth and makes wrong decision by starting on slicks. Spins down to 14th, lap two, but finishes seventh with fifth fastest lap, after three stops. Under-pressure Benetton team now 16 points behind Williams and Ferrari in constructors' championship.

Tyrrell-Yamaha

The 023 chassis reacts badly to characteristics of 'new' Imola. Team also breaks several high-mileage Yamaha V10s. Salo, who dislikes "five chicanes every lap", qualifies 13th. Katayama 15th. Mika tyre-stops from eighth, lap 18, but retires next lap when engine fails, having felt strange from the beginning. Katayama rockets up to ninth, lap two. Progresses impressively to sixth, lap 16. Rejoins ninth after lap 18 tyre stop but spins and stalls, lap 24, whilst trying to pass Eddie Irvine.

Williams-Renault

A great race, using new evolution Renault RS7A V10, with superb victory which honours memory of Ayrton Senna. Hill disappointed to qualify fourth behind Schumacher, Berger and Coulthard in a car "which is capable of pole". In wet warm-up both Damon and David spin repeatedly. With compromise set-up for drying conditions both start on wet-weather tyres - the correct decision. Coulthard/Hill to second and third, lap six, when Berger stops for slicks. Then, following Schumacher crash and stops for slicks, laps nine (DH) and 10 (DC), they join Alesi in pursuit of Berger. This becomes a fight for the lead after Gerhard's botched stop on lap 21. Coulthard spins when second, lap 27, and breaks front wing end plate. Then given 10s penalty for pit lane speeding. But Hill drives masterly, thinking race to take 11th career victory and, for first time, World Championship lead. After fourth stop for new nosecone, Coulthard finishes fourth, last to go full distance. Has post-race 'chat' with Alesi to clear air after Jean's forceful criticism of David's alleged blocking tactics. Team now shares constructors' world championship leadership with Ferrari.

McLaren-Mercedes

Nigel Mansell makes McLaren race debut in rush-built wide-bodied MP4/10B. "Don't expect anything for at least three races," he says. Qualifies ninth after losing Saturday set-up time when oil cooler splits. Häkkinen starts sixth. Team shoots itself in foot by starting both drivers on slicks in still damp conditions. Mansell hits Morbidelli at start and drops to 13th. At first tyre stop Mika is fifth, Nigel sixth. Mansell up to fifth by lap 32 but stops for new nosecone (Morbidelli incident), lap 42, and then for new rear tyre, lap 43, after tangling with Irvine's Jordan. Despite troublesome fuel stop, Häkkinen finishes fifth, one lap down. Mansell is 10th, two laps adrift. "Nothing in the race reflects the steady progress we are making with the car," says Ron Dennis.

Arrows-Hart

Morbidelli starts 11th on slicks. Hit by Mansell at start and loses a lap with slow drive to tyre stop. Subsequently races at rear of field to finish 13th, four laps down. Inadequate Inoue starts 19th but, racing on slicks, spins out of last place, lap 13.

Simtek-Ford

Another super, but short-lived, drive by Jos Verstappen in car benefiting from improved set-up. From 17th on grid is 13th on lap one but incurs 10s stop/go penalty for jump start. Tenth by lap five, and eighth at lap nine tyre-stop. Then sadly out, lap 15, when gearbox again gives up. Mimmo Schiattarella starts 23rd and tyre-stops from praiseworthy 12th, lap 26. Hits kerb and retires when 13th, lap 35. But team well-pleased with progress of car and drivers – especially Jos.

Jordan-Peugeot

With new livery and revisions to Peugeot engine, team hopes for first 1995 finish - and gets it (but still no points). Irvine again out-qualifies Barrichello, starting seventh to Rubens' 10th following the latter's second major practice at Imola in two years. Irvine starts on slicks and does well to be fifth at first tyre stop, lap 21. But stops at Ligier pit! Sixth behind Nigel Mansell at second tyre stop, lap 41. Collides with Nigel upon resuming battle and stops for new nose, lap 43. Spins on lap 55 but finishes eighth, two laps down. Barrichello is one of only six to start on wets and is sixth when stops for slicks, lap eight. Climbs to fifth but retires lap 31.

Pacific-Ford

Andrea Montermini has emergency appendix operation on Tuesday but qualifies on Friday! Starts 24th after missing Sunday warm-up with gearbox problem. Runs 19th after early spin but retires, lap 16, stuck in gear after lap 14 tyre stop. Bertrand Gachot 22nd on grid. Tyre-stops from 19th, lap 17, before retiring from 12th, lap 36, with Pacific's Achilles Heel - gearbox trouble. Despite all this, team pleased with general progress.

Larrousse-Ford

Following Argentine GP Gerard Larrousse announces that his team will not now be competing during 1995, as a result of his inability to generate sufficient funding. Regrettable, but unsurprising.

Forti-Ford

Moreno and Diniz start 25th and 26th on slicks in overweight, under-developed car. Both finish (PD 15th/RM 16th), albeit seven laps adrift.

Minardi-Ford

Team starts legal proceedings against Mugen for alleged failure to honour supply agreement. After hydraulic and engine problems, Martini qualifies 18th, Badoer 20th. Both race reliably to finish four laps down despite unplanned stops with punctures and a 10s pit lane speeding penalty for Badoer. Martini 12th and Badoer 14th.

Ligier-Mugen Honda

Aguri Suzuki unexpectedly retains drive for third race and qualifies 16th. Spins twice on slicks in opening laps but finishes 11th, three laps down, after two tyre stops. Olivier Panis starts 12th, also on slicks, and stops three times, including 10s penalty for pit lane speeding. Baulked at start and drops to 19th but recovers to finish 12th, two laps down.

Ferrari

To the extreme delight of the over-the-top Tifosi, team revival continues apace with further improved V12 for home race. After 'perfect lap' Gerhard Berger qualifies superb second, only 0.008s slower than Schumacher. With a fired-up Alesi a disappointed fifth ("traffic") but two seconds faster than anyone else in Sunday's wet warm-up, Ferrari looks good for race. Both correctly start on wets. Berger pushes Schumacher hard for lead whilst Alesi ceaselessly challenges Coulthard and Hill for third. Berger makes first stop for slicks, lap five, followed by Alesi, lap seven. Gerhard leads until second stop, lap 21, at which he stalls. Resumes fourth, now behind Alesi who is agitatedly trying to pass Coulthard. Resultant wheel-banging bends Ferrari steering arm, following which Coulthard pits and Alesi advances to second behind Hill - for second successive race. Berger benefits from Coulthard's four stops to finish full-distance third. A good race for Gerhard and Jean, but both had their road-going Ferraris stolen! Alesi fiercely criticises Coulthard's driving but post-race visit by David calms things down. Ferrari now ties with Williams for lead of constructors' championship.

Sauber-Ford

New high nose, but understeer persists. Wendlinger's worrying lack of form continues. Off in Thursday session and again on Friday. Qualifies 21st and hits Badoer on lap three. In for new nose and again for 10s pit lane speed penalty. Retires from 12th, lap 44, when wheel jams on at third stop. Much better for Heinz- Harald Frentzen. Starts 14th on slicks but, with two-stop strategy, finishes sixth, one lap down. But with much car development still needed, engine-supplier Ford not happy.

30 APRIL 1995

SAN MARINO RESULTS AND STATISTICS

Autrodromo Dino e Enzo Ferrari

Piratella
Tosa
Villeneuve
Acque Minerale
Variante Alfa
Tamburello
Traguardo
Rivazza
Variante Bassa

**Circuit length
3.04 miles/4.89 km**

STARTING GRID

SCHUMACHER (Benetton B195) 1m 27.274s	**BERGER** (Ferrari) 1m 27.282s
COULTHARD (Williams FW17) 1m 27.459s	**HILL** (Williams FW17) 1m 27.512s
ALESI (Ferrari 412 T2) 1m 27.813s	**HÄKKINEN** (McLaren MP4/10) 1m 28.343s
IRVINE (Jordan 195) 1m 28.516s	**HERBERT** (Benetton B195) 1m 29.530s
MANSELL (McLaren MP4/10B) 1m 29.517s	**BARRICHELLO** (Jordan 195) 1m 29.551s
MORBIDELLI (Footwork FA16) 1m 29.582s	**PANIS** (Ligier JS41) 1m 30.760s
SALO (Tyrrell 023) 1m 31.035s	**FRENTZEN** (Sauber C14) 1m 31.358s
KATAYAMA (Tyrrell 023) 1m 31.630s	**SUZUKI** (Ligier JS41) 1m 31.913s
VERSTAPPEN (Simtek S951) 1m 32.156s	**MARTINI** (Minardi M195) 1m 32.445s
INOUE (Footwork Fa16) 1m 32.710s	**BADOER** (Minardi M195) 1m 33.071s
WENDLINGER (Sauber C14) 1m 33.494s	**GACHOT** (Pacific PR02) 1m 33.892s
SCHIATTARELLA (Simtek S951) 1m 33.965s	**MONTERMINI** (Pacific PR02) 1m 35.169s
MORENO (Forti FG01) 1m 36.065s	**DINIZ** (Forti FG01) 1m 36.624s

RACE CLASSIFICATION

Pos	Driver	Nat	Car	Laps	Time
1	Damon Hill	GB	Williams FW17-Renault	63	1h 41m 42.552s
2	Jean Alesi	F	Ferrari 412 T2	63	1h 42m 01.062s
3	Gerhard Berger	A	Ferrari 412 T2	63	1h 42m 25.668s
4	David Coulthard	GB	Williams FW17-Renault	63	1h 42m 34.442s
5	Mika Häkkinen	SF	McLaren MP4/10-Mercedes		1 lap behind
6	Heinz-Harald Frentzen	D	Sauber C14-Ford Zetec		1 lap behind
7	Johnny Herbert	GB	Benetton B195-Renault		2 laps behind
8	Eddie Irvine	GB	Jordan 195-Peugeot		2 laps behind
9	Olivier Panis	F	Ligier JS41-Mugen Honda		2 laps behind
10	Nigel Mansell	GB	McLaren MP4/10B-Mercedes		2 laps behind
11	Aguri Suzuki	J	Ligier JS41-Mugen Honda		3 laps behind
12	Pier-Luigi Martini	I	Minardi M195-Ford		4 laps behind
13	Gianni Morbidelli	I	Footwork FA16-Hart		4 laps behind
14	Luca Badoer	I	Minardi M195-Ford		4 laps behind
NC	Pedro Diniz	BR	Forti FG01-Ford		7 laps behind
NC	Roberto Moreno	BR	Forti FG01-Ford		7 laps behind

Retirements	Nat	Car	Laps	Reason
Karl Wendlinger	A	Sauber C14-Ford Zetec	43	Jammed wheel
Bertrand Gachot	B/F	Pacific PR02-Ford	36	Hydraulic leak
Mimmo Schiattarella	I	Simtek S951-Ford	35	Broken suspension
Rubens Barrichello	BR	Jordan 195-Peugeot	31	Gearbox
Ukyo Katayama	J	Tyrrell 023-Yamaha	23	Spin
Mika Salo	SF	Tyrrell 023-Yamaha	19	Engine
Andrea Montermini	I	Pacific PR02-Ford	15	Hydraulics
Jos Verstappen	NL	Simtek S951-Ford	14	Gearbox
Taki Inoue	J	Footwork FA16-Hart	12	Accident
Michael Schumacher	D	Benetton B195-Renault	10	Accident

Fastest lap				
Gerhard Berger	Ferrari 412 T2	lap 57	1m 29.568s (122.257 mph)	

Results and Data © FIA 1995

DRIVERS' CHAMPIONSHIP

Damon Hill	20
Michael Schumacher	14
Jean Alesi	14
David Coulthard	9
Gerhard Berger	9
Mika Häkkinen	5
Johnny Herbert	3
Heinz-Harald Frentzen	3
Mark Blundell	1

CONSTRUCTORS' CUP

Williams-Renault	23
Ferrari	23
Benetton-Renault	7
McLaren-Mercedes	6
Sauber-Ford	3

14 May 1995
Circuit: Barcelona

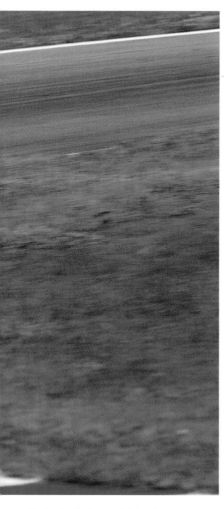

Having finished second with only one gear available in 1994, there was to be no stopping Schumacher (above) with a full compliment of ratios.

Bust Williams: the final lap having taken almost as long as the previous 20 or so, Damon Hill (left) abandons ship.

Whatever it was that happened in the Benetton garage on the Friday night of the Spanish Grand Prix dramatically changed the 1995 pecking order. In Brazil, Argentina and Italy the Williams-Renaults had been the class of the field, with Ferrari showing ever increasing promise. Benetton had been struggling to overcome twitchy handling but, in the Saturday qualifying session at Barcelona, Michael Schumacher blew the doors off the opposition. And he did so again on Sunday, very ably supported by Johnny Herbert. Nothing stays the same in Formula One for long.

We hadn't expected it. Williams had won every race at the new track on the outskirts of Barcelona since it had opened in 1991. And after successive wins in Argentina and at Imola, Hill was expected to make it three in a row to preserve the Williams record and extend his lead in the world championship. Such expectations were to be confounded.

The superb 2.9-mile, 13-turn circuit had been made even better by the elimination of the controversial 1994 tyre chicane, hastily erected at the behest of the drivers to bypass the 150mph Nissan Curve. The result was praise all round. "The track is perfect," said Hill, and Schumacher concurred. "I am now a veteran driver," said Nigel Mansell, "and years ago circuits like this were only found in one's imagination."

So, what did you need to go well?

In a word, it was balance. Cars required a set-up to satisfy the conflicting needs of the long 180 mph straight, the series of high speed corners which followed it and the other second and third gear bends. Ferrari seemed to have the best answer on Friday, Alesi fastest and Berger second, followed by Coulthard and Schumacher. But with only four-tenths covering then it wasn't going to take much to alter the status quo. Significantly though Damon Hill was only fifth, 1.2s slower than Alesi. The problem? "I can't find a balance. All the laps are very messy – locked wheels, oversteer and such stuff. I have got to work on the set-up." Schumacher may not have been in such dire shape but said the Benetton was unpredictable. So out came the computer traces and into a huddle they all went.

And that was where Benetton cracked it, amidst an atmosphere of suspicion…Rumours had been circulating that the excellent Johnny Herbert, unable to match Schumacher's scorching pace since joining the team,

was being denied vital information. It seemed unlikely, and Benetton hotly denied it, but Johnny had now decided to stop trying to master Michael's settings and to work with race engineer Tim Wright evolving a set-up more suited to his very different driving style. The decision was to pay dividends.

On Saturday, with revised settings, Schumacher caused alarm – and despondency – elsewhere with a pole position time that was a massive six-tenths faster than the Ferraris of Alesi and Berger, and nearly a second faster than the Williams-Renaults of Coulthard and Hill. In Sunday's warm-up he was again 0.6s faster than Jean and Gerhard, so with a clear track in front of him and his main rival, Hill, two rows behind him on the grid, Michael was in great shape. Herbert was seventh behind Eddie Irvine's Jordan, having been baulked on both his fast runs, but he felt the car was more drive-able. As we were to see.

The story of the battle for the lead of the Spanish GP is quickly told: there wasn't one. With a perfect start Schumacher was never headed during the whole 65 laps – not even during his two pit stops. Not only was his car's handling back to the razor- sharpness of the 1994 Benetton-Ford but, even at the beginning of the race, the combination of Schumacher and his Benetton-Renault, which was due to make two fuel and tyre stops, was able to pull away from its lighter, three-stop rivals. By lap five, in a class of his own, Michael was five seconds ahead of the gutsy Alesi. Behind them Damon Hill was up to third because David Coulthard

The last goodbye? Nigel Mansell's uneasy relationship with McLaren (top) looked irreparable after the former world
champion simply gave up in disgust. His second drive for the team proved to be his last.

Never one to give up, Martin Brundle (above) switched from his temporary role as TV pundit to return to the driving seat with Ligier.

Rubens Barrichello leads Mika Salo on his way to what should have been sixth place... until an injury time throttle problem dropped him out of the points (right).

(suffering from tonsillitis, as in Brazil) had understandably been caught out when the lights failed to turn to green, whilst Gerhard Berger, also ahead of Damon on the grid, had got away badly too.

Incidentally the starting lights fiasco was ironic because the new FIA jump-start electronic detection system was being officially used for the first time…

At the time, of course, we didn't know what the teams' pit stop strategies were going to be. Hill came in first on lap 13 for a 10.3s stop which dropped him to ninth. Then Coulthard came in from fourth place a lap later. Then Berger from third on lap 16, followed by the second-placed Alesi (now nearly 10s adrift) on lap 19. But Schumacher was still out there, making it crystal clear that, yet again, the Benetton strategy was going to be different. So often in the past Benetton had chosen three stops to its rivals' two. This time it was to be the reverse.

Finally he came in, on lap 21, emerging 7.5s ahead of Alesi with Hill third, three seconds behind the Ferrari, Coulthard fourth, Berger fifth and Johnny Herbert, happy with his Benetton's handling, sixth. Now all the top six had stopped once. So had Mika Häkkinen, who was seventh, but his team-mate Nigel Mansell was out and McLaren was well and truly in the mire. Häkkinen could just about cope with his unpredictable car; Nigel couldn't. After a bad start he had fought for 13th place with Katayama's Tyrrell-Yamaha until his lap 15 pit stop. On its new tyres the McLaren became "virtually impossible to drive". On his out lap Nigel understeered, out of control, across a gravel trap and on the next, watched by the downcast Mercedes-Benz management, he drove out of the race into the garage, giving up in disgust. The already flawed Mansell/McLaren partnership was looking even rockier.

On lap 26 Schumacher's iron grasp tightened even further when Alesi retired. As his Ferrari screamed its glorious war cry past the pits at some 180mph, just ahead of Hill's Williams, its V12 engine erupted in a vast cloud of smoke and that was it for Jean. It was the team's first retirement of the year and yet another blow for the unlucky Frenchman. "It's a real shame. The car was going well and I think I could have put Michael under pressure." That much I doubt, but now Schumacher led Hill by 11s with the knowledge that he would only be stopping once more to Damon's twice. With Coulthard third, six seconds behind Hill and seven ahead of Berger it wasn't, to be honest, turning out to

Gerhard Berger (top) admitted that it hadn't been one of his better afternoons, but he still finished the day on the podium.

As Schumacher gets the jump on Alesi and Hill at the start, Brundle – to the far right – appears to be heading for Barcelona city centre (above).

United cullers of Benetton: Schumacher and Herbert (top right) celebrate the team's first one-two in over four years.

Three Williams FW17s at rest (right). One of their drivers, David Coulthard, was in a similar state, being confined to bed by five o'clock each evening, as a result of tonsillitis.

be the most exciting Grand Prix we had ever seen, even if the unexpected domination of Schumacher was so noteworthy.

So what was happening behind the top four? Johnny Herbert was in the points – fifth – and lapping consistently faster than Berger's Ferrari. The hitherto unreliable Jordan-Peugeots of Eddie Irvine and Rubens Barrichello were still there in seventh and eighth whilst Martin Brundle was going well in the Ligier-Mugen in his first GP since Australia 1994.

Time for some light relief, although it could have been far from funny. In came Herbert for his second stop, only to leave at colossal velocity with the rear jack still attached to his Benetton. "Stop! Stop!" screamed his crew through the radio. "What?" Herbert queried, and as he did so the jack detached itself. "Go! Go!" came back the reply. Johnny's confusion was understandable. Soon afterwards something potentially even more serious happened as Bertrand Gachot's Pacific left the pits with its fuel tank valve jammed open, and petrol slopping out. The rear of his car ignited, but fortunately Bert spotted the fire and stopped safely. With Jos Verstappen's 1994 German GP pit lane fire in mind, the possible consequences didn't bear thinking about.

When Schumacher rejoined the fray after his second stop on lap 43 he was still nearly eight seconds ahead of Damon Hill. The race was in the bag, reliability permitting. Damon set the fastest lap of the race on lap 46 in his efforts to close the gap and actually got it down to 3.5s – only to have to make his third stop on lap 47. So Williams took a drubbing, the more so when David Coulthard, with four points for third place in prospect, retired on lap 54 when his gearbox gave up. But the sting of the Spanish Grand Prix was in the very last lap.

With Schumacher having given the perfect reply to those who felt that he was cracking under the pressure of Hill and the Williams, we waited for Damon to claim the six points for second place which would sustain his

championship lead. But the next man home was… Johnny Herbert! Damon had slowed to a crawl, jammed in fifth gear and with his Renault on tickover thanks to a hydraulic failure. Gutted by his misfortune, he finished fourth behind Berger. That last lap was misery for Rubens Barrichello too. In sixth place behind his teammate Eddie Irvine, his throttle broke to let a delighted Olivier Panis score Ligier's first point of 1995.

Woe for Williams. Muted enthusiasm from Ferrari, who still led the constructors' championship. Real satisfaction for Jordan and Ligier. Unbridled joy for Benetton. First and second places from Schumacher and Herbert had not only seen Michael retake the championship lead and demoralise the opposition, but had seen Johnny on a well-deserved Grand Prix podium for the first time in his career. It had been the team's first one-two since Japan 1990 and, from the way Michael and Johnny had gone at Barcelona, it wouldn't necessarily be the last.

Benetton-Renault

Crushing success puts team back on top. Schumacher under pressure following two successive Williams wins. Fourth fastest on Friday but takes second successive pole position, a demoralising 0.6s clear of Alesi, after overnight car changes. Underlines superiority on Sunday. With two-stop strategy, leads throughout to take second win in four races and retake championship lead. "If people think I am under pressure, I like to answer in the best way possible. I have done that." Great race for Johnny Herbert too. Goes his own way on set-up amidst strongly denied rumours that he is not being given access to Schumacher's data. Qualifies only seventh after being baulked. Makes poor start but up to sixth, lap three. Third at second stop lap 40, and creates drama by racing off with rear jack attached! Runs excellent third behind Hill from lap 55 but inherits second on last lap when Damon slows. Johnny's first-ever F1 podium gives team its first one-two since Japan 1990 (Piquet and Moreno) and lifts it to within four points of Ferrari in constructors' championship.

Tyrrell-Yamaha

Team struggles with set-up in effort to find grip. Salo starts 13th with Katayama 17th after blowing engine on Saturday and having to qualify in ill-fitting Salo car ("everything was too far away!"). Mika has "boring" race, running alone to finish 10th (one lap down) after two stops. Ukyo battles with Mansell for 13th until lap 15 pit stop where he stalls when trying to avoid a Ligier mechanic. Retires, lap 56, with loss of air pressure. Still no points despite strong car/driver package.

Williams-Renault

Team arrives on a high, leading both championships and having won the last two races, but leaves on a low. Unable to balance cars properly Coulthard with tonsillitis, and Hill qualify a worrying fourth and fifth behind Schumacher and both Ferraris. Hill starts well and races third with Alesi. To second, lap 26, when Jean retires. Unable to live with Schumacher's speed, mentally settles for six vital points only to have hydraulic failure on last lap which affects gearbox and throttle. Bitterly disappointed, limps home fourth having lost championship lead. Fastest lap of race (1m 24.531s, 125.09mph) is no consolation. With confusion about green light, Coulthard makes bad start and drops to seventh. Passes Häkkinen and Irvine to fifth. To third after Alesi retirement but retires, lap 55, when gearbox fails. Loss of 10 potential points costs team lead in constructors' championship. Hill stresses that there's much work to be done before Monaco.

McLaren-Mercedes

Ghastly meeting in presence of Mercedes top brass. "The car has a fundamental handling problem," says Nigel Mansell, "which is magnified by my driving style and the fast corners here." With limited experience of new car, Mansell qualifies only fractionally slower than Häkkinen but, in ninth and 10th, they are 2.5s off the pace. Mika fourth in Sunday warm-up. Makes super start and is brave third during first round of stops. Engine starts cutting out when sixth, lap 40. Retires, lap 54, when lapped ninth after second stop. Following bad start which drops him to 14th, depressed Mansell battles against Katayama until lap 15 stop. Iffy handling deteriorates further on new tyres and Nigel understeers into gravel trap, rejoins and retires in disgust, lap 18, raising doubts about future with team.

Arrows-Hart

After overcoming major understeer problem, Morbidelli starts 14th and Inoue best-yet 18th. Gianni happy to finish 11th after understeer returns and gearbox fails on last lap. Inoue retires with loss of drive and minor fire when 18th on lap 43.

Simtek-Ford

Software problem with throttle blipper which synchronises engine revs during gearchanges destroys gear ratios and prevents work to balance car. Verstappen qualifies 16th, Schiattarella 22nd. In trying circumstances team delighted that both drivers finish - JV 12th (two laps down) despite clutch failure and MS 15th (four laps down) with race-long understeer and loose track rod.

Jordan-Peugeot

Following good test at Imola which improves floor, aerodynamics, engine and dampers, Irvine does well to start sixth, with Barrichello eighth after losing time with engine problem on Friday. Eddie up to fifth at start but passed by Coulthard, lap seven. Battles with Häkkinen for most of the race. Passes Mika to take sixth, lap 47, and finishes fifth, one lap down, after Coulthard retires. Rubens has disappointing race. Is sixth for much of the race but throttle fails on last lap. Finishes seventh, one lap down. Team encouraged by first points and first double finish of year in front of Peugeot boss Jacques Calvet.

Pacific-Ford

Underfunded team suffers from lack of testing and development. Montermini/Gachot qualify 23rd/24th. Andrea improves to encouraging 17th in warm-up but is unable to start when gearbox hydraulic pressure fails during formation laps. Gachot races last but one until lap 43 retirement at end of pit lane with car on fire due to jammed fuel tank valve. A potentially disastrous mishap of great concern to all the teams, especially as several others also report fuel rig problems.

Forti-Ford

The team says it is improving but it's hard to see. Moreno/Diniz start 25th/26th, nearly eight seconds off the pace. Diniz out from last, lap 18 (gearbox). Moreno out from last, lap 40 (water pump).

Minardi-Ford

Revised suspension and aerodynamics; but still struggling. Martini 19th/Badoer 21st after nearly colliding on Saturday. Then race together to 16th/17th until lap 19 stop for Badoer who retires, lap 22, stuck in fifth. Martini soldiers on with understeer to finish 14th (three laps down).

Ligier-Mugen-Honda

Very encouraging return for Martin Brundle, who replaces sponsor-supported Aguri Suzuki for his first race since Australia 1994 (his last for McLaren). Despite lack of mileage in very different car, qualifies 11th, four places ahead of highly-rated team-mate Olivier Panis. Up to fifth after "one of the best starts of my career" only to be bundled out at first corner. Tenth at first stop, lap 19, but then down to 19th after fuel rig refuses to deliver. Climbs to 10th lap 54 and then to ninth after Coulthard retires. Panis drives commendably strong and reliable race to give team its first 1995 point by inheriting sixth after Barrichello stops on last lap.

Ferrari

Getting better all the time, but still not quite there. Alesi and Berger take provisional front row on Friday but slip down to second and third on Saturday. Again second and third in warm-up, but again 0.6s slower than superfast Schumacher. Alesi runs second to Schumacher, just ahead of Hill, but is 9.5s behind Michael at lap 19 stop. After Schumacher's first stop is further two seconds behind the Benetton when his V12 erupts in a cloud of smoke. Exit Alesi; the team's first retirement of 1995. Berger has bad start and is passed by Hill. Worried by poor tyre performance, debates two- or three-stop strategy and opts for two. Third at first stop, lap 16. Fourth at second, lap 33. Still fourth at third, lap 50. Passed by Coulthard, lap 51, but regains fourth when David retires and then takes third on last lap when Hill slows. Keeps record of having scored points in every race so far, but is unimpressed. "We are still not good enough in race trim and our race engine loses power after half distance. But we know what to do and I expect us to be with Benetton and Williams by Canada." The good news is that team leads constructors' championship.

Sauber-Ford

Promising tests at Imola with new floor and diffusor, new differential and lighter gearbox improve lap times by over one and a half seconds. "The car is now much better," says Heinz-Harald Frentzen, who qualifies 12th, albeit 3.4s slower than Schumacher. H-H picks up rubber in race and cannot match warm-up times. Races 10th/11th, mostly with Panis, and finishes eighth, one lap down. Wendlinger is again sadly not up to it. Starts 20th, 5.5s off pace and races reliably to finish 13th, two laps down. But although his first finish since Imola 1994 (when he was fourth) does a lot for his confidence, will he still be with Sauber for the next race at Monaco, one year after his serious accident there?

SPAIN RESULTS AND STATISTICS

Catalunya circuit – Barcelona

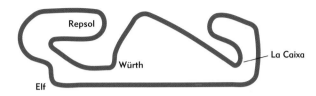

Repsol
Würth
La Caixa
Elf

Circuit length
2.949 miles/4.747 km

STARTING GRID

SCHUMACHER (Benetton B195) 1m 21.452s	**ALESI** (Ferrari 412 T2) 1m 22.052s
BERGER (Ferrari 412 T2) 1m 22.071	**COULTHARD** (Williams FW17) 1m 22.323s
HILL (Williams FW17) 1m 22.349s	**IRVINE** (Jordan 195) 1m 23.352s
HERBERT (Benetton B195) 1m 23.536s	**BARRICHELLO** (Jordan 195) 1m 23.705s
HÄKKINEN (McLaren MP4/10) 1m 23.833s	**MANSELL** (McLaren MP4/10B) 1m 23.927s
BRUNDLE (Ligier JS41) 1m 24.727s	**FRENTZEN** (Sauber C14) 1m 24.802s
SALO (Tyrrell 023) 1m 24.971s	**MORBIDELLI** (Footwork FA16) 1m 25.053s
PANIS (Ligier JS41) 1m 25.204s	**VERSTAPPEN** (Simtek S951) 1m 25.827s
KATAYAMA (Tyrrell 023) 1m 25.946s	**INOUE** (Footwork FA16) 1m 26.059s
MARTINI (Minardi M195) 1m 26.619s	**WENDLINGER** (Sauber C14) 1m 27.007s
BADOER (Minardi M195) 1m 27.345s	**SCHIATTARELLA** (Simtek S951) 1m 27.575s
MONTERMINI (Pacific PR02) 1m 28.094s	**GACHOT** (Pacific PR02) 1m 28.598s
MORENO (Forti FG01) 1m 28.963s	**DINIZ** (Forti FG01) 1m 29.540s

RACE CLASSIFICATION

Pos	Driver	Nat	Car	Laps	Time
1	Michael Schumacher	D	Benetton B195-Renault	65	1h 34m 20.507s
2	Johnny Herbert	GB	Benetton B195-Renault	65	1h 35m 12.495s
3	Gerhard Berger	A	Ferarri 412 T2	65	1h 35m 25.744s
4	Damon Hill	GB	Williams FW17-Renault	65	1h 36m 22.256s
5	Eddie Irvine	GB	Jordan 195-Peugeot		1 lap behind
6	Olivier Panis	F	Ligier JS41-Mugen Honda		1 lap behind
7	Rubens Barrichello	BR	Jordan 195-Peugeot		1 lap behind
8	Heinz-Harald Frentzen	D	Sauber C14 Ford Zetec		1 lap behind
9	Martin Brundle	GB	Ligier JS41-Mugen Honda		1 lap behind
10	Mika Salo	SF	Tyrrell 023-Yamaha		1 lap behind
11	Gianni Morbidelli	I	Footwork FA16-Hart		2 laps behind
12	Jos Verstappen	NL	Simtek S951-Ford		2 laps behind
13	Karl Wendlinger	A	Sauber C14-Ford Zetec		2 laps behind
14	Pier-Luigi Martini	I	Minardi M195-Ford		3 laps behind
15	Domenico Schiattarella	I	Simtek S951-Ford		4 laps behind

Retirements	Nat	Car	Laps	Reason
Ukyo Katayama	J	Tyrrell 023-Yamaha	56	Engine
David Coulthard	GB	Williams FW17-Renault	54	Gearbox
Mika Häkkinen	SF	McLaren MP4/10-Mercedes	53	Fuel pressure
Taki Inoue	J	Footwork FA16-Hart	43	Fire
Bertrand Gachot	B/F	Pacific PR02-Ford	43	Refuelling fire
Roberto Moreno	BR	Forti FG01-Ford	39	Engine
Jean Alesi	F	Ferarri 412 T2	25	Engine
Luca Badoer	I	Minardi M195-Ford	21	Hydraulics
Nigel Mansell	GB	McLaren MP4/10B-Mercedes	18	Handling
Pedro Diniz	BR	Forti FG01-Ford	17	Gearbox
Andrea Montermini	I	Pacific PR02-Ford	0	Hydraulics

Fastest lap

Michael Schumacher	D	Benetton B195-Renault	1m 24.531s (125.096mph)

DRIVERS' CHAMPIONSHIP

Michael Schumacher	24
Damon Hill	23
Jean Alesi	14
Gerhard Berger	13
David Coulthard	9
Johnny Herbert	9
Mika Häkkinen	5
Heinz-Harald Frentzen	3
Eddie Irvine	2
Mark Blundell	1
Olivier Panis	1

CONSTRUCTORS' CUP

Ferrari	27
Williams-Renault	26
Benetton-Renault	23
McLaren-Mercedes	6
Sauber-Ford	3
Jordan-Peugeot	2
Ligier-Mugen Honda	1

ROUND 5

28 May1995
Circuit: Monte Carlo

"I can see my flat from here." New Monaco resident David Coulthard (above) prepares for an aerial view as he is entrapped between the Ferraris at the first start.

High-rise anachronism (left): Monaco remains unlike any other racing facility on the planet, defying all modern safety and logistical criteria.

The Monaco GP has been held on the evocative streets of Monte Carlo since 1929, and the unique circuit has changed remarkably little since. Indeed, the only major addition has been the section around the swimming pool, from Tabac to the Rascasse restaurant, which was first used in 1973. It is the most famous Formula One event of them all, but if it wasn't for its history, ambience and prestige there certainly wouldn't be a race there now. The roads are too narrow for passing, and the paddock and pits are necessarily temporary. Plus, you can barely move for people, which makes it a pressurised misery for the teams. But, having said that, the money-laden atmosphere is terrific. The sun-soaked magic of the harbour, the yachts, the mixture of old and modern buildings, the restaurants and everything else that the punters and sponsors adore is very real. If there is one Grand Prix to win, or even just to see, this is it.

One driver who never had won here, Nigel Mansell, now looked as though he never would. The marriage between *Il Leone* and McLaren, which so many people had said would never work, had ended in divorce after his outspoken criticism of the unsuccessful MP4/10B following his retirement in Spain. The parting was amicable on the surface, with both Nigel and Ron Dennis saying nice things about each other but, sadly, it seemed that the career of Britain's former racing hero had ended on a very dull note. What a shame that he hadn't decided to call it a day after his last triumph with Williams, at Adelaide in 1994. His replacement, for Monaco and Canada at least, was to be the capable Mark Blundell. Sauber too was making a change by dropping the unfortunate Karl Wendlinger, who had never been on the pace after his crash at Monaco in 1994. Williams tester and reigning FIA Formula 3000 champion Jean-Christophe Boullion replaced him.

With its lack of straights, its never-ending succession of corners, its 160mph tunnel and its continuous roadside barriers, Monaco is no place to make a mistake. Precision and patience are the name of the game. If you get stuck behind someone, as you certainly will at some time during the 78 lap race, you just have to bide your time. So getting the car set up perfectly, being at the front of the grid and, nowadays, choosing the right refuelling strategy are all absolutely vital.

Most of the teams had been away testing after Spain and Williams had made major improvements in an effort to get back into contention with Benetton after Barcelona. But it was Ferrari who made the running an Thursday. (Things start a day earlier in Monte Carlo.

Think of all that extra business!). Maranello's steady improvement of the 412 T2 was paying off and Jean Alesi was in sensational form. Fastest in the morning. Fastest in qualifying. With last year's winner Michael Schumacher, who loves street circuits, second and Hill only fourth, Damon needed to get his skates on come Saturday, which is exactly what he did. The luckless Alesi lost virtually the whole session with a car problem and slipped down to fifth, but the battle for pole was riveting as Schumacher and Hill fought for the grid slot which matters more at Monaco than anywhere else. In the end it was a great lap by Damon, an incredible 0.8s faster than Michael, which gave him pole. Just as impressive was David Coulthard's third place, for it was his first racing appearance at Monaco and there was limited time to learn a demanding circuit. So, Hill and Schumacher on the front row; Coulthard and Berger on the second; two meteoric chargers in Jean Alesi and Mika Häkkinen on the third. The run up to the first corner, Ste Devote, is always hazardous at Monaco. Would they all get round it after the green light? Most certainly not!

As Hill made a faultless start and Schumacher tucked in behind him, there was a gigantic coming-together between Alesi, Coulthard and Berger. With wreckage everywhere the race was stopped. Knowing

Back off the substitutes' bench (again), Mark Blundell (top) was getting used to his role as a surrogate Mansell.

Contrary to popular opinion, there are actually two top-line drivers in Germany. Frentzen and Schumacher compare notes (above).

Against a backdrop far removed from his native Romford, Johnny Herbert threads his way to fourth place (left).

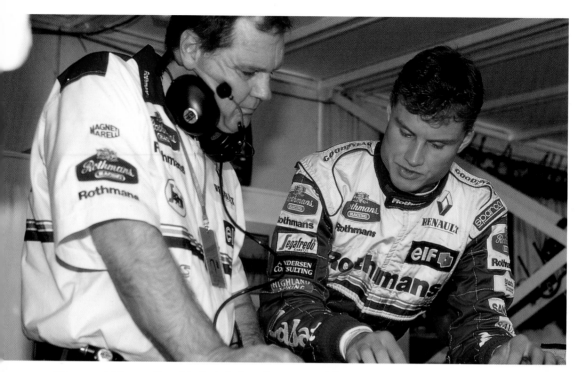

the score at Monaco, Ferrari had wisely brought spare cars for both their drivers, but neither was set up to perfection. Coulthard had to restart in Hill's spare, hastily adjusted. Others were affected too, so already the race had lost some of its competitiveness.

There was no chaos second time round. Another crackerjack start from Damon took him up the hill to Casino Square in the lead with Schumacher's Benetton under his rear wing. By lap five they were nearly six seconds ahead of the battle for third between Coulthard, Alesi and Berger. Two Williams, two Ferraris and two Benettons in the top six because Johnny Herbert, starting seventh, had passed Häkkinen's McLaren to take sixth. By lap nine Mika was out with a broken hydraulic pump shaft and Hill was two seconds ahead of Schumacher. Starting to look good for Damon? It depended on refuelling strategy. We'd just have to wait and see. On lap 14 Damon had pulled another 0.3s out of the bag. On lap 16 Coulthard retired, stuck in second gear. His time would come.

When Hill fuel-stopped for 8.5s on lap 23, delayed by traffic and only 0.6s ahead of Schumacher, he dropped to fourth place. But no matter, the top three – Schumacher, Alesi and Berger – would be making their stops soon. Gerhard did, one lap later, but to Damon's horror Schumacher and Alesi didn't. On they sped, now first and second, separated by some eight seconds as Damon grimly realised that not only had he and his team once again made the wrong plan but that Schumacher, on a one-stop strategy with a heavier fuel load, had been keeping up with his lighter Williams.

"Let's see. If Schumacher gets ahead of Damon at the start, I shove Alesi into the barrier on the right. That should be enough to block the track." David Coulthard (top) plans his race strategy.

It costs almost as much to park your yacht here (above) as it does your car at Heathrow...

He may have dominated qualifying, but Damon Hill knew from the opening moments of the race that containing Michael Schumacher was going to be a problem. An insurmountable one, as it transpired (right).

Unless something happened to Michael, it was already clear that Hill, on two stops, was effectively out it. If Schumacher was going to be denied a second successive win it was now up to Jean Alesi, who would also only be stopping once. How he tried! Despite the fact that he was slower than he would have been in his nominated race car, Jean briefly took the lead when Schumacher stopped and set the fastest lap of the race as he strove to gain time. The gap was eight seconds when he stopped. It was 10.8s when he rejoined and it grew to 14.2s by lap 41. "I was pushing very hard and I think I could have fought for the lead," said Jean. But then Martin Brundle, pushing equally hard in an effort to overcome a 10s jump-start penalty, lost control of his Ligier at the Tabac and spun right in front of Jean. With nowhere to go Alesi hit the Armco hard and was out of the race, furious with Brundle. "My fault," said the honest Martin. "Jean was an innocent bystander." A noble admission, but it was no consolation to poor Alesi, I doubt that he would have caught, let alone passed, Schumacher. But who knows?

For several laps, as Jean fought to catch Schumacher, he had been fighting just as hard to stay ahead of Hill. When Alesi hit the barrier Damon was under two seconds behind the Ferrari, more than close enough to see it all happen. Racing past he moved up to second, now 16s behind Schumacher but with the unhappy knowledge that Michael had made his one stop whereas he still had one to go. The race for victory was over if Schumacher just kept going. Try as he might, Damon could make no impression on the Benetton and when he rejoined after his second stop (lap 51) the gap had increased to a depressing 38s with 26 laps to go. Bitter disappointment for Hill, who had been so strong in qualifying the day before and who had hoped so much to repeat his father Graham's Monaco winning habit.

The last 28 laps were, I have to say, a drag even for the most rabid of enthusiasts: no sign of a change to the top six places. It was another immaculate victory for Michael Schumacher and for Benetton who, in the process, gave Renault its first victory at Monaco. Hill was a demoralising 35s behind, and third – for the fourth time in five races – was Gerhard Berger, who was the last to go the full distance. After a satisfying drive, albeit a lap behind his team mate, Johnny Herbert was fourth and his three points helped Benetton to leap-frog over Ferrari and Williams to lead the constructors' championship.

Just as pleased as any of the first four must have been Mark Blundell who, with only five days notice, had driven to an excellent fifth in the McLaren that Mansell had rejected and Heinz-Harald Frentzen, who had finished sixth in a brand new Sauber, built up overnight after he had destroyed his race car on Saturday morning.

Monaco had been its usual car-breaking self. Only 10 cars were classified out of the 24 that had started. Neither of the Simteks had been able to take the second start and neither of the Tyrrells, Footworks, Jordans, Pacifics or Ligiers had finished. The tables had been well and truly turned. Benetton, who had seemed to be struggling to match a confident and superior Williams team in the opening races of the season, had convincingly won the last two races. Williams now had it all to do. "I'm still within striking distance of Michael for the championship, and we have more things to do with the car," said Hill. If the racing at the front was to perk up, we could only hope that the optimism of Williams – and Ferrari – would turn out to be well-placed.

We could only hope too that Nick Wirth, the gallant young boss of the excellent little Simtek team, would get the substantial extra sponsorship needed within the next week if he was to be at Montreal for the Canadian Grand Prix.

Benetton-Renault

Another great result against expectations. Schumacher hit by Frentzen's Sauber in Saturday free session but, with new track rods for qualifying, takes second on grid to Damon Hill. Expresses great confidence for race. Despite heavier fuel load (one-stop strategy) runs close second to two-stop Hill until Damon makes first stop, lap 23. Then stays comfortably ahead of Alesi (14s) after Jean tangles with Brundle, lap 42. Is over 35s ahead of Hill after Damon's second stop and wins second successive Monaco GP by crushing 34.8s to extend lead in World Championship. Herbert drives strong race too. Passes Häkkinen to take sixth at start. Also on superior one-stop strategy, is third at lap 38 stop. Drops to fourth behind Berger and finishes there, albeit lapped. Team's 13 points vault it from third to first in constructors' championship. Benetton also gives Renault its first-ever win at Monaco.

Tyrrell-Yamaha

Team uses Hydralink front and rear suspension for first time but both drivers complain about nervousness over bumps. Katayama, 15th, out-qualifies circuit debutant Salo, 17th, but nearly four seconds off pole. Salo stops at first corner accidents and engine overheats. Takes second start from pit lane in spare car set up for Katayama. Drives it with great difficulty until retiring from 11th, lap 64. Katayama upsets car by hitting Morbidelli at second start, but up to sixth during first pit stops. Spins out, lap 27, prior to his own planned first stop.

Williams-Renault

Confident team drops ball after making great improvements at post-Spain tests. With "almost perfect lap" Hill takes pole position and, like Schumacher, is very confident for race. David Coulthard equally impressive with outstanding third on grid for first Monaco GP. Then it all comes apart. Coulthard collides with Alesi and Berger at first start and has to restart in Hill's hastily reset spare car. At first stop, lap 23, two-stop Hill leads heavier one-stop Schumacher by only 0.6s. Then runs third to Alesi, inheriting second after Jean crashes. After second stop, lap 51, gap to Schumacher up to 43s. Despite understeer Damon gets closer, but finishes second, 35s down, bitterly disappointed with wrong strategy and now five points behind Michael. Coulthard does well to run third, holding off both Ferraris until gearbox jams, lap 17. Team now four points behind Benetton in constructors' championship.

McLaren-Mercedes

Dramatic pre-Monaco goings-on when Nigel Mansell and McLaren announce immediate end to their association following Mansell's condemnation of car in Spain. Test driver Mark Blundell takes Nigel's place for at least two races. Does well to qualify 10th, four places behind Mika Häkkinen – who is reprimanded and given suspended $10,000 fine for ignoring yellow flag during Thursday qualifying. Mika 1.9s off pole time so car still far from right. Häkkinen retires from seventh, lap nine, with first Mercedes failure of season (hydraulic pump drive). Delighted Blundell up to sixth after first of two stops, lap 22. To fifth after Alesi crash and finishes there (one lap down) to score points for second time in three races.

Arrows-Hart

After going off in Thursday rain shower, Morbidelli starts 13th. Hit by Katayama at start. Down to last after lap six tyre change caused by tyre-warmer string caught under wheel nut! Takes 10s jump-start penalty, lap 18. Hits Boullion's Sauber (a lap ahead) at last corner but finishes ninth (four laps down). Inoue 26th on grid after missing Saturday qualifying as result of being rammed by dangerously fast safety car (!) when being towed in during free session interval. Starts after medical clearance and runs at rear of field until lap 28 retirement (gearbox).

Simtek-Ford

Circuit rookie Jos Verstappen does only 16 out of possible 70 laps to qualify 23rd after return of gearbox software problem and crashes on both days. Schiattarella given suspended $20,000 fine for driving towards traffic during unsuccessful spin-turn. Qualifies 19th. Involved with lap one Ste Devote shambles and unable to restart due to damage when car dropped off recovery truck. After engine change following warm-up, JV cannot select gears at start and car pushed away. "This has been the team's worst ever weekend," says Nick Wirth, who also divulges that team will not continue if substantial extra sponsorship cannot be raised.

Jordan-Peugeot

On his first visit, Eddie Irvine does well to start ninth, two places ahead of Rubens Barrichello. Hits Tabac barrier in Saturday qualifying and destroys car. Team builds new car but Eddie uses spare for race. Rubens has worrying wheel rim failure in warm-up. Stops for 10s jump-start penalty when ninth, lap 13. Then again for tyres, lap 22. Back to ninth, lap 42, but out, lap 62, when throttle sticks open. Irvine into sixth, lap 17, only for wheel rim to break, like Barrichello's, for no apparent reason. Two more DNFs for anxious, points-hungry Jordan.

Pacific-Ford

No time for Gachot on Thursday when wheel departs due to sheared disc bolts, but he starts 21st. Montermini 25th with Thursday time as gearbox problem prevents Saturday running. Gachot retires from 13th, lap 43 (gearbox hydraulics). AM given 10s jump-start penalty when 18th on lap 18 but black-flagged (disqualified) on lap 23 for not coming in within three laps. One day something will go right for the hard-trying team.

Forti-Ford

In lighter car with improved aerodynamics, Diniz and Moreno qualify 22nd and 24th – over seven seconds off pole. Roberto out, lap 10, when brakes fail. Pedro finishes 10th, six laps down.

Minardi-Ford

Using engine-cover mid-wing, Minardi beats off the other Ford ED V8-powered cars on grid: Badoer 16th, Martini 18th. Badoer excellent sixth at first stop, lap 23. Sixth again at second stop, lap 49, but hits barrier when seventh, lap 69, and retires shortly afterwards with broken suspension arm. Seventh then inherited by Martini who finishes, two laps down.

Ligier-Mugen Honda

Monaco expert Martin Brundle (second for McLaren in 1994) starts eighth, with Panis 12th. Both receive 10s penalty for jumped starts when running well in eighth (MB) and 10th (OP). In on laps 12 and 13, they drop to 11th and 14th. In again for tyres/fuel laps 20 and 23. Both drive hard to recover. Martin loses control and crashes out at Tabac when lapped seventh, lap 41, taking second-placed Jean Alesi with him. Alesi accuses Brundle of blocking him deliberately. Panis also crashes out at fast Casino Square, lap 66, when eighth after second stop.

Ferrari

Yet again, so near and yet so far. Wisely (as events turned out) takes four cars to Monaco, with new rear wing, revised rear suspension and, for all but one, with new spec V12. In terrific form Alesi, is fastest in both Thursday sessions but drops to fifth (again!) on Saturday when hydraulics fail on out-lap and has to transfer to Berger's car. Gerhard excellent fourth on grid in spite of losing laps due to generously letting Alesi take his car at end of Saturday session. Alesi/Berger fastest and second fastest in warm-up and looking good. But both cars heavily damaged in collision with Coulthard's Williams at approach to first corner. Both transfer to spare cars, but these are not set up so well and Gerhard's has old-spec engine. On one-stop strategy, Alesi drives superbly. To second at Hill's first stop and leads, lap 36, when Schumacher has sole stop. After lap 36 fastest lap (1m 24.621s, 87.98mph) and own stop, lap 37, runs second until crashes out, 14s down, avoiding Brundle's spinning Ligier on lap 42. Two-stop Berger does best he can in 'underpowered' car on wrong strategy. Finishes third (full distance) for fourth time in five races. An unlucky race which drops Ferrari from first to third in constructors' championship. Team confident about Canada, where further revisions will be introduced.

Sauber-Ford

One year after Monaco practice crash, off-form Karl Wendlinger dropped in favour of Jean-Christophe Boullion, Williams test driver and 1994 FIA Formula 3000 champion. Frentzen destroys car in massive crash at Massenet on Saturday morning. Boullion also crashes there in afternoon but both qualify, H-HF 14th with Thursday time and J-CB 19th. Team rushes new tub from Switzerland and builds new Frentzen car overnight. H-H given 10s penalty for jumped start but, with correct one-stop strategy, drives fine race to finish sixth despite being stuck in fourth for last three laps. Also stopping once, Boullion finishes eighth in tough first GP, even though he spins after last-corner nudge from Morbidelli.

Monte Carlo

Ste Devote · Montée de Beau Rivage · Mirabeau · Tabac · Nouvelle Chicane · Virage du Portier · Tunnel · Virage Anthony Noghes · La Rascasse

Circuit length
2.068 miles/3.328 km

STARTING GRID

SCHUMACHER (Benetton B195) 1m 22.742s	**HILL** (Williams FW17) 1m 21.952s
BERGER (Ferrari 412 T2) 1m 23.220s	**COULTHARD** (Williams FW17) 1m 23.109s
HÄKKINEN (McLaren MP4/10)	**ALESI** (Ferrari) 1m 23.754s
BRUNDLE (Ligier JS41) 1m 24.447	**HERBERT** (Benetton B195) 1m 23.885s
BLUNDELL (McLaren MP4/10B) 1m 24.933s	**IRVINE** (Jordan 195) 1m 24.857s
PANIS (Ligier JS41) 1m 25.125s	**BARRICHELLO** (Jordan 195) 1m 25.081s
FRENTZEN (Sauber C14) 1m 25.661s	**MORBIDELLI** (Footwork FA16) 1m 25.447s
BADOER (Minardi M195) 1m 25.969s	**KATAYAMA** (Tyrrell 023) 1m 25.808s
MARTINI (Minardi M195) 1m 26.913s	**SALO** (Tyrrell 023) 1m 26.473s
SCHIATTARELLA (Simtek S951) 1m 28.337s	**BOULLION** (Sauber C14) 1m 27.154s
DINIZ (Forti FGP01) 1m 29.244s	**GACHOT** (Pacific PR02) 1m 29.032s
MORENO (Forti FGP01) 1m 29.608s	**VERSTAPPEN** (Simtek S951) 1m 29.391s
INOUE (Footwork FA16) 1m 31.542s	**MONTERMINI** (Pacific PR02) 1m 30.149s

RACE CLASSIFICATION

Pos	Driver	Nat	Car	Laps	Time
1	Michael Schumacher	D	Benetton B195-Renault	78	1h 53m 11.258s
2	Damon Hill	GB	Williams FW17-Renault	78	1h 53m 46.075s
3	Gerhard Berger	A	Ferrari 412 T2	78	1h 54m 22.705s
4	Johnny Herbert	GB	Benetton B195-Renault		1 lap behind
5	Mark Blundell	GB	McLaren MP4/10B		1 lap behind
6	Heinz-Harald Frentzen	D	Sauber C14-Ford Zetec		2 laps behind
7	Pier-Luigi Martini	I	Minardi M195-Ford		2 laps behind
8	J-Christophe Bouillion	F	Sauber C14-Ford Zetec		2 laps behind
9	Gianni Morbidelli	I	Footwork FA16-Hart		4 laps behind
10	Pedro Diniz	BR	Forti FGP01-Ford		6 laps behind

Retirements	Nat	Car	Laps	Reason
Luca Badoer	I	Minardi M195-Ford	68	Suspension
Olivier Panis	F	Ligier JS41-Mugen Honda	65	Accident
Mika Salo	SF	Tyrrell 023-Yamaha	63	Engine
Rubens Barrichello	BR	Jordan 195-Peugeot	60	Throttle
Bertrand Gachot	F/B	Pacific PR02-Ford	42	Gearbox
Jean Alesi	F	Ferrari 412 T2	41	Accident
Martin Brundle	GB	Ligier JS41-Mugen Honda	40	Accident
Taki Inoue	J	Footwork FA16-Hart	27	Gearbox
Ukyo Katayama	J	Tyrrell 023-Yamaha	26	Spin
Andrea Montermini	I	Pacific PR02-Ford	23	Black flagged
Eddie Irvine	GB	Jordan 195-Peugeot	22	Wheel failure
David Coulthard	GB	Williams FW17-Renault	16	Gearbox
Roberto Moreno	BR	Forti FGP01-Ford	9	Brakes
Mika Häkkinen	SF	McLaren MP4/10	8	Engine
Domenico Schiattarella	I	Simtek S951-Ford	0	Gearbox
Jos Verstappen	NL	Simtek S951-Ford	0	Gearbox

Fastest lap				
Jean Alesi	Ferrari 412 T2	lap 36	1m 24.621s (87.978mph)	

Results and Data © FIA 1995

DRIVERS' CHAMPIONSHIP		CONSTRUCTORS' CUP	
Michael Schumacher	34	Benetton-Renault	36
Damon Hill	29	Williams-Renault	32
Gerhard Berger	17	Ferrari	31
Jean Alesi	14	McLaren-Mercedes	8
Johnny Herbert	12	Sauber-Ford	4
David Coulthard	9	Jordan-Peugeot	2
Mika Häkkinen	5	Ligier-Mugen Honda	1
Heinz-Harald Frentzen	4		
Mark Blundell	3		
Eddie Irvine	2		

ROUND 6

11 June1995
Circuit: Montreal

He finished fourth in his very first Grand Prix...and it took him another 90 to score a victory. Jean Alesi's first F1 success (left) is believed to have boosted Kleenex's annual profit margins by around 300 per cent.

Olivier Panis (above) finished a sterling fourth for Ligier, the Frenchman just holding off the recovering Schumacher at the end.

In the many years that I've been watching and talking about motor sport at the highest level, I've seen some I pretty emotional and popular victories: Geoff Duke and Mike Hailwood winning the Senior TT in the Isle of Man; Stirling Moss in the Mercedes-Benz at Aintree in 1955 and, with Tony Brooks, the Vanwall in 1957; James Hunt, John Watson and, most of all, Nigel Mansell at Silverstone; Senna in Brazil; Ferrari at Monza; Gilles Villeneuve in Canada. But they've all been local heroes winning their national race in front of their adoring home fans. Montreal 1995 was something else.

Formula One isn't such big news in Canada as it is in many other parts of the world, but it has a passionately enthusiastic following amongst a minority. For them, two words matter more than any others: 'Ferrari' and 'Villeneuve'. The zenith of Canada's Formula One achievement was when its favourite son, the late, great Gilles Villeneuve, won the first Canadian GP on Montreal's Ile Notre Dame in 1978, driving Ferrari number 27. Things haven't been the same for Canada since his death in 1982, but when Jean Alesi crossed

the line to win for the first time in 91 Grands Prix, the place just erupted. Jean may not have been Canadian but, as a Frenchman in French Canada, in Ferrari number 27, he was the nearest thing to perfection. It was great to see a new winner – the first since Damon Hill in Hungary 1993 – and although the crowd's premature track invasion was inexcusable, it was perhaps understandable. What's more, Alesi's open delight as he stood in his scarlet Ferrari with his arms spread out to the ecstatic crowd was a joy to behold.

Jean's popular victory was a fortuitous, if well deserved, surprise. For the fifth time in six races he had started from the third row of the grid. Once again the dominant Michael Schumacher was well ahead of him – in pole position. Michael had won the previous year, and his Benetton was again the class of the field. Damon Hill and David Coulthard were starting second and third, ahead of the Ferraris of Berger and Alesi, but the twitchy Williams-Renaults had been "almost undriveable" in Sunday's wet warm-up with Coulthard and Hill a very worried 12th and 16th fastest. Everyone expected another victory for Schumacher, and for the majority of the race it looked as though they were going to be right. But, as the old cliche goes, you haven't won until you've seen the chequered flag first – and Schumacher was destined not to do so.

The 2.75-mile Circuit Gilles Villeneuve, which is used just once a year, is on a man-made island in Montreal's mighty St Lawrence River. Although there is nothing particularly demanding about it from the

High riser. Eddie Irvine (top) heads for third place.

They think it's all over...It isn't yet. Mika Salo pulls over as whatever the collective noun is for a mass of rabid French-Canadians invades the track a wee bit too soon (above).

Emerging from the shadows (right): there could have been no more apposite a place for Alesi to have scored a maiden win in car number 27, which will forever be associated with the man whose name adorns the Montreal track, formally known as the Circuit Gilles Villeneuve.

driver's point of view, it is – with two 35mph hairpin bends which are approached at over 170mph – very hard indeed on brakes, gearboxes and fuel consumption. Canada's winter/summer temperature extremes make the surface very bumpy, so traction is a problem and the race is invariably one of attrition where few cars finish. Do so, and you are likely to be in the points. As ever the question was one stop or two? Schumacher had made two in 1994, but the general view was that most people would be making one in 1995. Williams, who had been much-criticised for Hill's refuelling strategy in Monaco, had since established that Damon's comparative lack of pace had, in fact, been due to a faulty differential, but future pit stop tactics would capture their earnest attention.

To the undisguised relief of Williams, the track was dry for the start. Their Saturday qualifying set-ups, which had seen them some 0.4s slower than Schumacher, would be tolerable…But, once again, Michael's getaway was perfect and, at the end of the first lap, he led Hill by an incredible 2.5s. It was already looking like another Schumacher/Benetton walkover. And his was the only B195 still in the running. Johnny Herbert had started sixth, only 0.7s slower than his team leader and much happier with his car, but at the

ultra-tight East Hairpin he had been rammed and taken out by the over-enthusiastic Mika Häkkinen's McLaren-Mercedes. It was the end of the race for both of them, and Herbert was furious. On lap two David Coulthard's race was over, too. With both the Ferraris virtually attached to his rear wing he lost the Williams on a bump, spun out and ended his day's work early. Three of the top men were out in less than five miles.

Forget about the leader. By lap 10 Schumacher was seven seconds ahead of the rest. The man is a phenomenon and he was emphasising it. Clearly no one could live with him but you had to wonder how Benetton would live without him…which was doubtless why Ferrari was rumoured to be offering him some $20 million to join them in 1995. Whilst Michael raced away, the fight for second was well worth watching. Alesi had scrambled past Berger when Coulthard did his disappearing act, and now the Frenchman was right behind Hill with Gerhard a few tenths further back. Was Damon in trouble again? He was certainly making a meal out of staying ahead of the Ferrari duo, who were giving him a very hard time. Trouble or not, he was down to third on lap 17 as Alesi outbraked him and shot up the inside of the Williams at the East Hairpin. In another 10 laps, Berger would do the same thing.

Schumacher led, 12s ahead of Alesi. Berger ran third, Hill fourth and the two Jordans of Barrichello and Irvine were fifth and sixth. Rubens and Eddie had profited from the exits of Herbert, Häkkinen and Coulthard and were separated by only a few seconds – as they were to be for the whole race. Jordan was in desperate need of some points after only one top six finish from the first five races; now it looked as though some were within reach.

The prophets had been right about the refuelling strategies. Nearly everyone stopped once. Eddie Irvine was the first to do so on lap 32. Then Alesi, Hill, Barrichello and Panis (up to an excellent sixth in his Ligier after Irvine's stop) on lap 33 and Berger on lap 34. Smooth stops for the first five mentioned, but certainly not for Berger. Almost within sight of the pits he ran out of fuel and had just enough momentum to carry him to his pit crew. A very lucky man, but he lost nearly one and a half minutes and was down to eighth. That promoted Barrichello and Irvine to fourth and fifth behind Schumacher, Alesi and Hill. The incredible Schumacher was still out there though, demonstrating that he was not only quicker than the rest, but driving more economically too. In fact it was lap 37 before Michael came in; when he rejoined he was still 26s ahead of Alesi. In the commentary box my heart sank at the thought of trying to make an increasingly processional race sound exciting, but I needn't have worried!

Suddenly, Damon Hill was out! Slowly he drove up to the pit wall in front of the Williams garage, levered himself out of the car, climbed over the wall, shouted furiously at Frank Williams and flung himself into the

Thanks to the efforts of those who mated a portable TV with a warehouse full of fertiliser, spectators get a Big Brother's eye view of the start as Schumacher gets the jump on Hill (top).

Gianni Morbidelli (above) scored a point for Arrows, but that was hardly going to be enough to prevent speculation that his seat was under threat from several better-heeled suitors.

Subtle reminder: well-known Frenchman Tom Walkinshaw, flanked by Olivier Panis and Frank Dernie reminds Eddie Jordan of the Rugby Union World Cup result (right). The Irishman had the final word come the race.

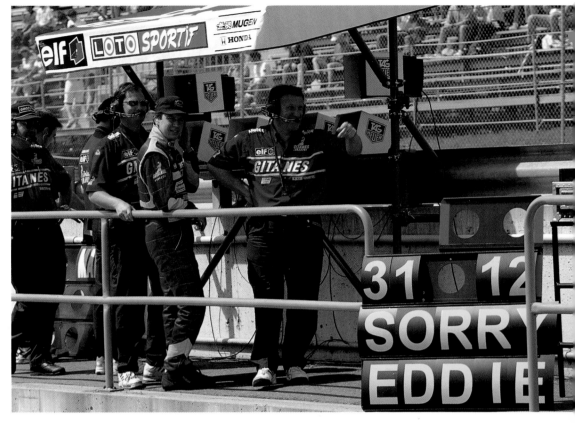

motorhome. All was very clearly not well. "The car was dreadful to drive. It was handling badly and then I got a repeat of the hydraulic problem I had in Spain. I was stuck in fifth gear and then I lost the throttle. We've been struggling all weekend and we've certainly got a lot of work to do." With Damon out, the Jordans were third and fourth, better by far than they'd been all season but would they finish?

Well, on lap 58, with only 12 to go, they were second and third. The hitherto apparently invincible Schumacher was touring. The race which had been exciting at the beginning and, frankly, dull in the middle was now red hot. Alesi was in the lead! But that had been the case several times in the past, before terrible luck had intervened.

Not this time, though. As he literally struggled to see through the tears of emotion that were blurring his visor, Jean was over 20s ahead of the Jordan twins who, with reduced revs to conserve fuel, were no threat to his Ferrari. Panis was an excellent fourth ahead of his Ligier team-mate Martin Brundle, whilst Martin was engaged in a nose-to-tail battle with the charging Gerhard Berger for fifth place.

But it was Schumacher who was providing the excitement. His sudden loss of pace had been caused by an electrical problem which had jammed his Benetton

in third gear. Into the pits he came to swap his steering wheel (where the electrical junctions are housed) whilst his engineer Pat Symonds re-programmed the software. Then off he shot, good as new, to start an absolutely riveting charge. Seven of his last nine laps were under 1m 30s, including the fastest of the race (1m 29.174s, 111.13mph). No one else got under 1m 30s even once. His efforts were rewarded, for he not only did he finish just 37s behind Alesi but it took him to fifth place…after Berger had tried a bit too hard on lap 62, clobbering poor Martin Brundle in Turn One and removing both from the race. It was the first tine that Gerhard hadn't finished in the points in 1995 and it denied Ligier a double finish in the top six. Martin was astonishingly phlegmatic about it.

When the time came to spray the champagne the three overjoyed men on the podium were all celebrating their highest-ever Grand Prix finishes: Alesi the emotional winner; Barrichello second, feeling that at last his luck had changed; the usually laconic Irvine, looking as though Formula One wasn't so bad after all. But the happiest man was Eddie Jordan. Not only was Canada 1995 the best race in the team's five-year history, but it was Eddie who had introduced both Jean Alesi (via a deal at Tyrrell, in 1989) and Michael Schumacher (1991 Belgian GP) to Formula One!

CANADIAN GRAND PRIX – TEAM ANALYSIS

Benetton-Renault

Schumacher supreme again but defeated by electronic gremlin. Takes ninth career pole, 0.4s faster than Alesi. Team promptly revises livery strongly to feature 'Renault' in celebration of the marque's 100th pole position (one in the eye for Williams!). On one-stop strategy, Michael is devastating 53s ahead of Jean at lap 38 stop. Rejoins in lead but, with 11 laps to go, gearbox sticks in third. After calm 1m 57s stop for new steering wheel (where the electrical junctions are) and reprogramming of software, rejoins seventh – 1m 17s behind leader Alesi. Becomes only man to crack 1m 30s in final stages of the race, doing so seven times in last nine laps. Finishes fifth, 37s behind Alesi and only 5.2s behind second-placed Barrichello. Now seven points ahead of Hill in championship. Herbert qualifies sixth, 0.7s slower than Schumacher, but is taken out by Häkkinen on first lap. Johnny's anger compounded by $10,000 suspended fine for jump start. Benetton down to second in constructors' championship, three points behind Ferrari.

Tyrrell-Yamaha

Katayama and Salo qualify 16th and 15th, complaining of lack of grip. Both given 10s stop/go penalty for jumping start; Katayama also given second penalty for speeding in pit lane when he complies! Ukyo retires from lapped last place, lap 43, when engine air pressure fails. Salo drives praiseworthy race with two tyre/fuel stops, laps 26/48. Running seventh on last lap but stops short of line, on instructions from pit, due to crowd invasion. Luca Badoer irresponsibly charges on and takes place from Mika, who therefore finishes eighth, one lap down. Ken Tyrrell submits protest to stewards but no immediate action taken. The results are later modified in Salo's favour.

Williams-Renault

A thoroughly miserable meeting. Both Hill and Coulthard unhappy with FW17, even if they qualify second and third. In wet Sunday warm-up, DC is 12th and DH 16th as both spin "virtually undriveable" cars. Fortunately (for them), race is dry. Under pressure from Alesi and Berger, Coulthard spins out on second lap. As Schumacher disappears, Hill fights the Ferraris but loses second to Alesi, lap 11, and third to Berger at lap 33 tyre/fuel stop. Regains third when Gerhard bodges his stop but retires, stuck in fifth, lap 51, with repeat of Spanish GP hydraulic failure. Furiously condemns inadequacy of car. With no points, team drops to third in constructors' championship.

McLaren-Mercedes

Both drivers use wider-tub MP4/10B, now without high mid-wing as Canada is a low downforce track – but its return is promised for Hungary. Using more flexible Mercedes V10, Häkkinen qualifies seventh but previously received $10,000 fine is implemented after he ignores yellow flags again. Collides with Herbert on first lap and retires. Mark Blundell still on race-by-race deal, and pressured by rumours that Heinz-Harald Frentzen being considered for his place. Qualifies 10th but spins and stalls on way to grid for start. Takes spare car set up for Häkkinen. Detached headrest causes major problem with neck muscles until engine fails when ninth, lap 48. Team's third blank race of season.

Arrows-Hart

Best 1995 race yet. Brings only two cars after Inoue's Monaco debacle. Despite Saturday morning gearbox failure, Gianni Morbidelli starts 13th amidst rumours that he is to be replaced by better-funded Pedro Lamy. Delayed by wheel nut problem but finishes lapped sixth to give team first point since Belgium 1994, 11 races ago. Inoue misses Saturday qualifying (gearbox), but starts 22nd with Friday time. Races at rear to first GP finish, in 10th place, two laps down.

Simtek-Ford

To everyone's regret, the gallant little Simtek team fails to appear due to financial pressures and later announces that it has been put into receivership with, seemingly, little chance of a return. A very sad loss. What will happen to the excellent Jos Verstappen?

Jordan-Peugeot

Jordan's finest race achievement in its five-year F1 history. Barrichello has major off on Saturday morning but car rebuilt for afternoon qualifying. Detuned Rubens takes ninth on grid, one place behind team-mate Eddie

Irvine. Is then superb second fastest to Alesi in wet Sunday warm-up. Barrichello to sixth past Irvine, lap one, after which they race together, coping with ever-present fuel consumption problems. Fifth/sixth after Coulthard retires, lap two. Fourth/fifth, lap 36, thanks to Berger's long pit stop. Third/fourth, lap 51, when Hill retires. Second/third, lap 58, when Schumacher pits. Second place for Rubens and third for Eddie, 1.6s apart. The 10 points lift Jordan to fourth in the constructors' championship – ahead of McLaren.

Pacific-Ford

After a host of handling, vibration, clutch and oil cooler problems, Gachot and Montermini start 20th/21st, five seconds off the pace. Neither finishes: Montermini out lap five (hydraulic pump drive); Gachot stops three times for steering column check and tyres/fuel before retiring, lap 37, with faulty battery. "We are beginning to see the light," says team boss Keith Wiggins.

Forti-Ford

Still struggling with an overweight, oversize car, Moreno and Diniz start from the back row, 23rd and 24th, some seven seconds off pole time. Both retire, Diniz on lap 27 (gearbox) and Moreno on lap 55 (out of fuel, due to rig failure). Much-needed major car changes to be introduced at French GP.

Minardi-Ford

New wings and deflectors but continued outrage over Ligier having acquired Mugen engines...which the Faenza team thought were heading in its direction. After qualifying 17th, Martini penalised 10s for jumping start and then 10 more for blocking Berger's Ferrari. Gian Carlo Minardi furious over this. Martini retires from lapped 12th, lap 61 (broken accelerator cable). After qualifying 19th, Luca Badoer does well to be eighth at start of last lap but recklessly takes seventh (one lap down) by ignoring crowd invasion at finish and racing past stationary Salo. Tyrrell team protests, and race result is eventually taken one lap early, dropping Luca back to eighth.

Ligier-Mugen Honda

Team announces, to no one's surprise, that Cesare Fiorio will stand down as team manager after French GP, in favour of Tom Walkinshaw. Disappointing qualifying. Panis 11th with Friday time after oil leak fire on Saturday. Brundle 14th with lack of grip. But race goes well. Olivier and Martin fourth and fifth on lap 62 when Berger, charging hard after running out of fuel, punts Brundle (and himself) off track. Panis finishes excellent fourth, only 0.5s ahead of fast-recovering Schumacher.

Ferrari

Thanks to slice of luck, Ferrari achieves victory – despite development delays caused by car damage at Monaco. Berger/Alesi qualify third and fourth on Friday, but slip to fourth/fifth on Saturday when Coulthard pips them. JA first and GB third in wet Sunday warm-up in cars that look most impressive. In dry race Alesi passes Berger to third, lap two, as Coulthard spins off in front of them. To second past Hill, lap 17, with Berger following 10 laps later after being consistently baulked by the lapped Martini. Gerhard runs out of fuel, lap 35, as he approaches pits for scheduled stop. Just gets in. Rejoins, eighth and lapped, and charges after 1m 27s delay. Catches Brundle and, after Schumacher's long stop, has fierce battle for fifth place until overdoing it at turn one, lap 62, and takes out both Martin and himself. Alesi looks set for second place, over 30s behind MS, until Michael is forced to pit with electrical problem, lap 58. On his 31st birthday Jean paces himself to take the most popular win for years – his first in 91 Grand Prix starts. Ferrari's 105th victory returns team to the top of the all-time winning constructors' table, and takes it past Williams and Benetton to lead the 1995 constructors' championship.

Sauber-Ford

Not a happy meeting for Sauber. Amidst denied rumours that he is to be transferred to McLaren, Heinz-Harald Frentzen complains of simultaneous understeer and oversteer! He qualifies only 12th. Sixth in wet warm-up and up to fourth, lap two, following Coulthard's retirement. Drives strong race, matching pace of the two Jordans ahead, until lap 27 retirement when engine stops. Unimpressed with track Jean-Christophe Boullion starts 18th for second GP before spinning out, lap 20, in battle for 13th with Luca Badoer.

RACE

CANADA

11 JUNE 1995

Circuit Gilles Villeneuve – Montreal

Pits Hairpin

Island Hairpin

Circuit length
2.752 miles/4.429 km

STARTING GRID

SCHUMACHER
(Benetton B195)
1m 27.661s

HILL
(Williams FW17)
1m 28.039s

COULTHARD
(Williams FW17)
1m 29.091s

BERGER
(Ferrari 412 T2)
1m 28.189s

ALESI
(Ferrari 412 T2)
1m 28.474s

HERBERT
(Benetton B195)
1m 28.498s

HÄKKINEN
(McLaren MP4)
1m 29.910s

IRVINE
(Jordan 195)
1m 29.021s

BARRICHELLO
(Jordan 195)
1m 29.171s

BLUNDELL
(McLaren MP4)
1m 29.641s

PANIS
(Ligier JS41)
1m 29.809s

FRENTZEN
(Sauber C14)
1m 30.017s

MORBIDELLI
(Footwork FA16)
1m 30.159s

BRUNDLE
(Ligier JS41)
1m 30.255s

SALO
(Tyrrell 023)
1m 30.657s

KATAYAMA
(Tyrrell 023)
1m 31.382s

MARTINI
(Minardi M195)
1m 31.445s

BOULLION
(Sauber C14)
1m 31.838s

BADOER
(Minardi M195)
1m 31.853s

GACHOT
(Pacific PR02)
1m 32.841s

MONTERMINI
(Pacific PR02)
1m 32.894s

INOUE
(Footwork FA16)
1m 32.995s

MORENO
Forti FGP 01)
1m 34.000s

DINIZ
(Forti FGP 01)
1m 34.982s

RACE CLASSIFICATION

Pos	Driver	Nat	Car	Laps	Time
1	Jean Alesi	F	Ferrari 412 T2-Ferrari	69	1h 46m 31.333s
2	Rubens Barrichello	BR	Jordan 195-Peugeot	69	1h 47m 03.020s
3	Eddie Irvine	GB	Jordan 195-Peugeot	69	1h 47m 04.603s
4	Olivier Panis	F	Ligier JS41-Jugen Honda	69	1h 47m 07.839s
5	Michael Schumacher	D	Benetton B195-Renault	69	1h 47m 08.393s
6	Gianni Morbidelli	I	Footwork FA16-Hart		1 lap behind
7	Luca Badoer	I	Minardi M195-Ford ED		1 lap behind
8	Mika Salo	SF	Tyrrell 023-Yamaha		1 lap behind
9	Taki Inoue	J	Footwork FA16-Hart		2 laps behind

Retirements	Nat	Car	Laps	Reason
Martin Brundle	J	Ligier JS41-Mugen Honda	61	Collision
Gerhard Berger	A	Ferrari 412 T2-Ferrari	61	Collison
Pier-Luigi Martini	I	Minardi M195-Ford	60	Throttle
Roberto Moreno	BR	Forti FGP 01-Ford	54	Out of fuel
Damon Hill	GB	Williams FW17-Renault	50	Hydraulics
Mark Blundell	GB	McLaren MP4/10B-Mercedes	47	Engine cut out
Ukyo Katayama	J	Tyrrell 023-Yamaha	42	Engine
Bertrand Gachot	F/B	Pacific PR02-Ford	36	Battery
Heinz-Harald Frentzen	D	Sauber C14-Ford	26	Engine
Pedro Diniz	BR	Forti FGP 01-Ford	26	Gearbox
Jean-Christophe Boullion	F	Sauber C14-Ford	19	Spin
Andrea Montermini	I	Pacific PR02-Ford	5	Hydraulics
David Coulthard	GB	Williams FW17-Renault	1	Spin
Johnny Herbert	GP	Benetton B195-Renault	0	Collision
Mika Häkkinen	SF	McLaren MP4/10B-Mercedes	0	Collision

Fastest lap

Michael Schumacher   Benetton B195-Renault   lap 67   1m 29.174s (111.129mph)

DRIVERS' CHAMPIONSHIP		CONSTRUCTORS' CUP	
Michael Schumacher	36	Ferrari	41
Damon Hill	29	Benetton Renault	38
Jean Alesi	24	Williams Renault	32
Gerhard Berger	17	Jordan Peugeot	12
Johnny Herbert	12	McLaren Mercedes	8
David Coulthard	9	Ligier Mugen-Honda & Sauber Ford	4
R Barrichello & E Irvine	6	Footwork Hart	1
Mika Häkkinen	5		
O Panis & H-H Frentzen	4		
Mark Blundell	3		
Gianni Morbidelli	1		

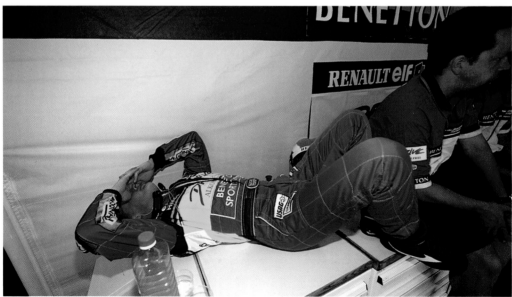

France

2 July 1995
Circuit: Magny-Cours

They've always been keen on motor sport in France. The first major motoring competition was a reliability run from Paris to Rouen in 1894. The first real race was from Paris to Bordeaux in 1896. The great city-to-city races of the early 1900s were held in France. The first Grand Prix was staged at Le Mans in 1906. The 1995 French GP at Magny-Cours was special, too, for it marked the 100th anniversary of the Automobile Club de France, organiser of the French GP. It was particularly noteworthy for Renault. Not only had that first GP been won by Hungarian Ferdinand Szisz in a Renault, but the French giant had 6000 guests at the track, hoping to celebrate another victory in the 81st French Grand Prix. Their money was to be well spent.

Magny-Cours is a motor racing showpiece designed and built to stimulate the local economy. The 2.65-mile track near Nevers, 150 miles south of Paris, is massively backed by the local state and strongly supported by the government. Everything is of the very best, and it is also the headquarters and test track of the Ligier team which was about to compete in its 300th Grand Prix. In spite of all that, the atmosphere was strangely sterile. On the other hand, the weather was fantastic with temperatures of over 30 degrees…and expectations were almost as high as Williams seemed to have regained form in post-Canada testing. Ferrari was optimistic, too.

But not everything was joy and sunshine, for the Minardi team had arrived to find its cars and equipment impounded after action by Ligier owner Flavio Briatore to force payment of an alleged debt. Pier-Luigi Martini and Luca Badoer could only wait in frustration whilst their rivals set up their cars and qualified on Friday.

Sure enough Williams did look good, with both Hill and Coulthard quicker than the dreaded Schumacher. But, as ever, there was always tomorrow and the final session. The conditions at Magny-Cours are unique, with a billiard-table smooth surface which the Ligier team obviously knows to perfection. With boss Tom Walkinshaw so closely allied to owner Flavio Briatore, who is also the top man at Benetton, the assumption was that advice on the best set-up would find its way from one team to the other. Whatever, Saturday's final qualifying session, in cooler weather, was a cracker as Coulthard, Hill and Schumacher fought for starting grid supremacy. David was the first to improve an

From the top of the big wheel, it's easy to discern that Magny-Cours is miles from anywhere. From the lead of the race, Hill is similarly aware that Williams has much to do to shake off the pesky, and omnipresent, Schumacher (above).

Herbert finds out, too late, that his nutritious drinks bottle was brimful of Theakston's Old Peculier (left).

Hill's Friday time – a superb effort aided by the fact that he had had his tonsils taken out since Canada and was feeling much sharper. Then Michael went two-tenths quicker, only to have Damon go three-tenths quicker still. Out went the Benetton and off came another three-tenths. This was terrific! But the last word was Damon's with a superb lap in 1m 17.225s, yet another three-tenths quicker than Schumacher and 1.2s faster than his own provisional pole time the previous day. It was Damon's third successive pole position at Magny-Cours, a proud record indeed. With Coulthard third, Schumacher was the Benetton meat in a Williams sandwich…but only 0.3s covered the three of them. But Ferrari's hopes had been dashed: only fourth and seventh on the grid for Jean Alesi and Gerhard Berger after hydraulic problems and an inability to set their cars up properly. Good news for Jordan and Ligier though, with Rubens Barrichello an excellent fifth on the grid ahead of Olivier Panis.

In 1994 Schumacher's start had been incredible. From the second row of the grid he had catapulted straight between Hill and Mansell to take the lead amidst suspicions that "he must have traction control". Not this year. Hill's getaway was perfect and he was first into the long, looping 120mph Estoril right-hander ahead of Schumacher, with Rubens Barrichello up to an excellent third past Coulthard and Alesi. The latter was down to seventh after an awful start, while Johnny Herbert had gained four places, moving from 10th to sixth in one lap. Herbert's efforts were to be in vain, as he was to be punted out by the over-optimistic Alesi on lap three. After having had exactly the same thing happen in Canada, when Hakkinen took him out, Herbert was not a happy man. "Alesi always criticises everyone else, but maybe he should have a think about what he does himself."

But while Johnny was fed up, Martin Brundle was delighted. As Herbert spun Martin whipped past the Benetton and both the Ferraris in one glorious swoop to take sixth. As the only one on a three-stop strategy he needed an early break, and this was it. "There is some justice!" he thought, recalling his confrontations with

"But the car was better when those legal guys made us keep it in the truck." Luca Badoer (left) tells all to engineer Andy Tilley.

Familiar sight (below): Michael Schumacher gets another faceful of chess board.

Alesi and Berger at Monaco and Montreal.

With Schumacher's Benetton virtually under his rear wing, Hill drew away from a battle for third between Barrichello and Coulthard, who were followed by the Ligiers of Panis and Brundle. It all came apart for Rubens and Olivier on lap 11 when they had to shoot in to the pit lane to take 10s penalties for jumped starts. After the race they both vehemently denied that they bad left the grid early, but the FIA's new electronic sensors under the cars are impossible to argue against. Even the momentary lurch as the car is put into first gear can activate then. So down to ninth and 10th went the Jordan and the Ligier; up to third, fourth and fifth went Coulthard, Brundle and Alesi, with Berger sixth.

At the front Hill and the ever-present Schumacher were now 8.5s ahead of Coulthard, but when were they coming in? Schumacher had won in 1994 by adopting a unique three-stop strategy. Was he going to do so again?

On laps 18 and 19 of 72, Michael was swarming all over the rear of Hill's Williams, and he would later complain about Damon having backed off excessively as they lapped Moreno's Forti. At the end of lap 19, Schumacher came in for the first of what were to be two stops. Yet again, perfect timing would help him to win the race. He dropped to third initially, behind Hill and Coulthard, but Damon was in traffic – and losing time. His stop on lap 21 took a second longer than Schumacher's. When he rejoined he had not only lost the lead but was eight seconds adrift of Michael. From then on he was history. Try as he may – and he certainly did – he could do nothing about the superior

"I'm sorry, Pier-Luigi and Luca can't come out to play today." French lawyers did their stuff on Friday (above).

Coming through, sucker (right). Jean Alesi employs fairground tactics to eliminate Johnny Herbert from the contest.

As celebrated Clash and Van Morrison fan Damon Hill unclips the earphones from his Walkman, a horrified Michael Schumacher suddenly remembers that he's forgotten his mum's birthday (below).

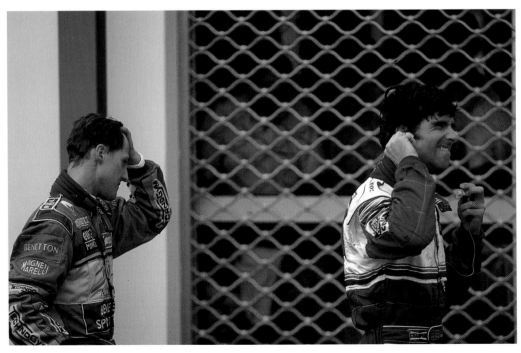

combination of Schumacher, Benetton and Renault. Schumacher only had to keep going to make it two French GP wins in a row and three successive second places for Damon. He did just that. The Williams may have been faster in qualifying but, as a confident Schumacher said after having qualified second, "We always go better in the race and that's what matters."

With Michael increasingly out an his own we had to look elsewhere for interest in what was turning out to be another less than gripping contest. With the first and second positions fixed unless something dramatic happened (which it didn't), the other top six places absorbed us.

Gerhard Berger had been relegated by a grotesque pit stop. When he came in on lap 22 he was fifth but as his refueller frantically tried, time after time, to get the rig nozzle to latch onto the Ferrari's tank valve the seconds and the places slipped away. Gerhard was stationary for 53s before the fuel was delivered and that dropped him to a lapped 17th when he rejoined.

Martin Brundle was doing rather better. His car continually running light on account of its three-stop strategy, he was flying in a fierce tussle for third place with Coulthard. From laps 22-34 he had been in the podium position and on lap 47 he took it again as David made his second and final stop. Martin would have to come in again, though, so it was going to be close at the end.

For a while the threat of rain spiced up the proceedings a bit. Some heavy spots fell but they weren't enough to make Hill and Schumacher switch to grooved tyres when they made their second stops on laps 43 and 47, after which Michael was a demoralising 15s ahead of the Williams. This gap had doubled by the end,

Michael also having set the fastest lap of the race on lap 51 (1 20.218s, 118.52mph). Victory for the world champion increased his championship lead over Hill to 11 points and returned Benetton to the lead of the constructors' championship.

But who was going to be third? It was really close between Coulthard and Brundle. When Martin came in for his third stop he was 12s ahead of Coulthard. He rejoined seven seconds in arrears with 17 laps to go. Time for a charge! On lap 60 the gap was down to 4.5s and Coulthard, in a car with fast-corner handling problems, was struggling. On lap 69, with four to go, the two Britons were virtually together. "I homed in on David," said Martin, "but I was getting too much turbulence to get any closer. Then I tried to pressure him into a mistake but he wasn't to be had that way either. On the last turn I made a last-gasp attempt – I mean, you never know – but it didn't work." So a very relieved Coulthard finished his first French Grand Prix in third place, just 0.4s ahead of a delighted Brundle, very happy to have put up such a fine performance which might help him secure a few extra races at Ligier.

With Alesi a lacklustre fifth, due to handling and engine problems, and Rubens Barrichello a lapped sixth, to score another point for Jordan and consolidate their superiority over McLaren in the constructors' championship, the French Grand Prix came to an end. A great win for Schumacher and a brilliant day for Renault, with a one-two-three in front of the home crowd. For the rest, humiliated and crushed again, a thoroughly depressing occasion – especially for Williams, with the British Grand Prix looming on the horizon.

Benetton-Renault

New, aerodynamically improved airbox, roll-hoop and engine cover plus further evolution Renault engine. Schumacher qualifies second, 0.3s slower than Hill. Understandably concerned over loss of five tyres (out of 28 allowed for whole meeting), which are inadvertently punctured by temperature-testing Goodyear technician. This problem later overcome. In "perfect handling" car, the German shadows Hill until stopping for fuel/tyres, lap 19. Rejoins third but takes lead, lap 22, when Damon pits. Dominates thereafter to take fourth win from seven races. Herbert starts unimpressive 10th, but has superb first lap, passing Brundle, Häkkinen, Berger and Alesi to move up to sixth – only to be pushed off for second race in succession. In Canada it was Häkkinen, in France it was Alesi. Johnny's misery compounded by FIA implementation of suspended $10,000 after he jumps the start for the second race in succession, and is again unable to pay his dues with a stop/go penalty. Schumacher's 10 points lift Benetton back to top of constructors' championship.

Tyrrell-Yamaha

Despite successful post-Canada testing and revised front and rear suspension, Salo and Katayama only qualify 15th and 19th. Katayama tangles with Taki Inoue and is out at first corner. Salo, suffering from lack of grip and speed, finishes 15th, three laps down.

Williams-Renault

A worrying and disappointing race. With aerodynamic changes and new Renault RS7B engine evolution, Damon Hill takes third successive French GP pole position by 0.3s in terrific Saturday battle with Schumacher and Coulthard, who takes third on the grid and is much happier after removal of tonsils. Things look good when Hill leads, with Schumacher attached to rear wing for 21 laps. Drops to second after tyre/fuel stop and being delayed by traffic. Can then do nothing about Schumacher and finishes second again, a demoralising 31s behind the Benetton. Despite handling problem in quick corners, Coulthard finishes third, a tad ahead of Martin Brundle after a terrific scrap. Renault delighted with 1-2-3, but can Williams regain early season superiority over Benetton by British GP?

McLaren-Mercedes

Both Häkkinen and Blundell use new-evolution engine but both have problems. Neither can get car balanced and Mika has hydraulic defect which necessitates post-qualifying testing at nearby Danielson track. Häkkinen qualifies eighth on grid, Blundell 13th. Mika loses two places on first lap after crossing gravel trap in battle with Alesi. Spends 50 laps resisting attacks from Olivier Panis's Ligier and finishes seventh, one lap down. Mark Blundell fends off Gerhard Berger, charging after long fuel stop, to finish 11th, two laps down. Team makes confident post-race noises but does not appear to be making much progress.

Arrows-Hart

Still afflicted by understeer and gearbox problems, Morbidelli starts lowest-yet 16th only two places ahead of Inoue. Taki collides with Katayama (and accepts blame) at first corner and retires. Gianni soldiers on to take 14th place, three laps down.

Simtek-Ford

With no white knight in sight, team assets up for auction. Simtek has run its last race.

Jordan-Peugeot

In high spirits after Canada one-two, Peugeot produces new evolution V10 with more power. Rubens Barrichello, rejuvenated after Canadian second place, takes third on grid and charges to third past Alesi and Coulthard at start. Retains third until 10s penalty for jumping the start (served on lap 19), which he strenuously denies. Down to ninth but, including two fuel/tyre stops, recovers to finish sixth, one lap down. Eddie Irvine, out-qualified by Rubens for first time in 1995,

starts 11th. Up to fifth by lap 23 stop but then, struggling with heavy steering, passed by Rubens. Finishes seventh, one lap down. Team pleased with improved reliability.

Pacific-Ford

New front suspension and new differential but, sadly, not much progress. With balance problems, Andrea Montermini and Bertrand Gachot are 21st and 22nd on grid, both over six seconds off pace. Montermini collides with Martini on first lap and heads to pits for rear suspension repairs. Rejoins six laps down; finishes 17th, but unclassified, 10 laps down. Gachot retires, lap 25, with gearbox failure.

Forti-Ford

Much changed car for Pedro Diniz, featuring less weight, high nose, shorter sidepods, higher airbox for revised Ford ED engine and new exhaust system. Not much use for Pedro who has flu and qualifies 23rd, 7.0s off pace. Roberto Moreno, even slower in old car with new nose, starts 24th and last. Diniz collides with Martini at first corner and is out. Moreno brings up rear to finish 16th, six laps down. Enthusiastic and persistent team expects to have two new cars at Silverstone.

Minardi-Ford

Team's aggravation over losing Mugen engine to Ligier exacerbated. Its cars and equipment are impounded and sealed in the paddock following action by Ligier boss Flavio Briatore, who wants to force payment of alleged debt for supply of Ford HB engines in 1993. After appeal, authorities allow team to join in on Saturday. Luca Badoer 17th on grid, Pier-Luigi Martini. Martini spins avoiding Katayama/Inoue collision on first lap and is then hit by Montermini. Carries an and gains places but retires, lapped, with gear selection problem immediately after pit stop, lap 24. One-stop Badoer drives hard and reliably to finish 13th, three laps down.

Ligier-Mugen Honda

At its home track, Ligier enjoys an excellent 300th GP. Martin Brundle goes off on Saturday but starts ninth with Friday time; Olivier Panis qualifies excellent sixth despite hurried Saturday session to release car to Brundle. Panis runs fifth until stop/go penalty for jumped start, which he vehemently denies having made. Rejoins 10th. Catches Häkkinen after lap 18 stop but cannot pass and spends 50 laps behind Mika before finishing eighth. Brundle drives superb race, uniquely stopping three times. Passes Berger, Alesi and Herbert to sixth in one go when Alesi nerfs Johnny, lap one. Up to fourth after Barrichello and Panis penalties. Third, laps 22-34, until second stop. Loses third to Coulthard after third stop, lap 55, but reduces seven second gap to one second by lap 67 and harries David ceaselessly for last six laps. Finishes fourth for first points of season, 0.4s behind Coulthard, having set third fastest lap of race.

Ferrari

Disappointing. Alesi loses whole of Friday free session with broken hydraulic pump. Berger has similar problem an Saturday and neither driver is able to get car balanced properly. Result: Alesi starts fourth and Berger seventh. Jean loses three places after bad start and drops to seventh ahead of Berger. Both then passed by Brundle after Alesi brakes too late and hits Herbert. Struggling with poor handling and a down-on-power engine Jean finishes fifth. Berger fifth at first stop, lap 22, but is at rest for 53s due to faulty fuel rig nozzle. Drops to lapped 17th. Catches Mark Blundell's McLaren, lap 33, spends rest of race vainly trying to pass. Finishes 12th. Team down to second in constructors' championship.

Sauber-Ford

Nothing to write home to Hinwil about. Frentzen, baulked by slow cars exiting the pit lane on his start lap, qualifies 12th. Drives consistently but can do no better than 10h, one lap down. The improving Jean-Christophe Boullion qualifies 15th. Makes bad start and finds car will not turn in properly. Retires from 13th, lap 49, when transmission breaks.

FRANCE

2 JULY 1995

Magny-Cours

Nürburgring Golf

Estoril

Adelaide

Imola

Repsol

Chateau D'Eau

Chicane

Lycée

**Circuit length
2.64 miles/4.248 km**

STARTING GRID

SCHUMACHER (Benetton B195) 1m 17.512s	**HILL** (Williams FW17) 1m 17.225s
ALESI (Ferrari 412 T2) 1m 18.761s	**COULTHARD** (Williams FW17) 1m 17.925s
PANIS (Ligier JS41) 1m 19.047s	**BARRICHELLO** (Jordan 195) 1m 18.810s
HÄKKINEN (McLaren MP4) 1m 19.238s	**BERGER** (Ferrari 412 T2) 1m 19.051s
HERBERT (Benetton B195) 1m 19.555s	**BRUNDLE** (Ligier JS41) 1m 19.384s
FRENTZEN (Sauber C14) 1m 20.309s	**IRVINE** (Jordan 195) 1m 19.845s
SALO (Tyrell 023) 1m 20.796s	**BLUNDELL** (McLaren MP4) 1m 20.527s
MORBIDELLI (Footwork FA16) 1m 21.076s	**BOULLION** (Sauber C14) 1m 20.943s
INOUE (Footwork FA16) 1m 21.894s	**BADOER** (Minardi M195) 1m 21.323s
MARTINI (Minardi M195) 1m 22.104s	**KATAYAMA** (Tyrell 023) 1m 21.930s
GACHOT (Pacific PR02) 1m 23.647s	**MONTERMINI** (Pacific PR02) 1m 23.466s
MORENO (Forti FGP 01) 1m 24.865s	**DINIZ** (Forti FGP 01) 1m 24.184s

RACE CLASSIFICATION

Pos	Driver	Nat	Car	Laps	Time
1	Michael Schumacher	D	Benetton B195-Renault	72	1h 38m 28.429s
2	Damon Hill	GB	Williams FW17-Renault	72	1h 38m 59.738s
3	David Coulthard	GB	Williams FW17-Renault	72	1h 39m 31.255s
4	Martin Brundle	GB	Ligier JS41-Mugen Honda	72	1h 39m 31.722s
5	Jean Alesi	F	Ferrari 412 Ts-Ferrari	72	1h 39m 46.298s
6	Rubens Barrichello	BR	Jordan 195-Peugeot		1 lap behind
7	Mika Häkkinen	SF	McLaren MP4/10B-Mercedes		1 lap behind
8	Olivier Panis	F	Ligier JS41-Mugen Honda		1 lap behind
9	Eddie Irvine	GB	Jordan 195-Peugeot		1 lap behind
10	Heinz-Harald Frentzen	D	Sauber C14-Ford Zetec		1 lap behind
11	Mark Blundell	GB	McLaren MP4/10B-Mercedes		2 laps behind
12	Gerhard Berger	A	Ferrari 412 T2-Ferrari		2 laps behind
13	Luca Badoer	I	Minardi M195-Ford		3 laps behind
14	Gianni Morbidelli	I	Footwork FA16-Hart		3 laps behind
15	Mika Salo	SF	Tyrrell 023-Yamaha		3 laps behind
16	Roberto Moreno	BR	Forti FGP 01-Ford		9 laps behind
NC	Andrea Montermini	I	Pacific PR02-Ford		10 laps behind

Retirements	Nat	Car	Laps	Reason
J-C Boullion	F	Sauber C14-Ford Zetec	63	Transmission
Bertrand Gachot	F/B	Pacific PR02-Ford	62	Gearbox
Pier-Luigi Martini	I	Minardi M195-Ford	23	Gearbox
Johnny Herbert	GB	Benetton B195-Renault	2	Accident
Ukyo Katayama	J	Tyrrell 023-Yamaha	0	Accident
Taki Inoue	J	Footwork FA16-Hart	0	Accident
Pedro Diniz	BR	Forti FGP 01-Ford	0	Accident

Fastest lap

Michael Schumacher   Benetton B195-Renault   lap 51   1m 20.218s (118.520mph)

DRIVERS' CHAMPIONSHIP

Michael Schumacher	46
Damon Hill	35
Jean Alesi	26
Gerhard Berger	17
David Coulthard	13
Johnny Herbert	12
Rubens Barrichello	7
Eddie Irvine	6
Mika Häkkinen	5
H-H Frentzen & Olivier Panis	4
Martin Brundle & Mark Blundell	3
Gianni Morbidelli	1

CONSTRUCTORS' CUP

Benetton Renault	48
Ferrari	43
Williams Renault	42
Jordan Peugeot	13
McLaren Mercedes	8
Ligier Mugen-Honda	7
Sauber Ford	4
Footwork Hart	1

Britain

16 July 1995
Circuit: Silverstone

Home blown (above): Blundell limps in on three Goodyears, having been speared by Barrichello's Jordan in the closing stages.

The last waltz (above left). Schumacher and Hill head for the gravel after becoming a mite too well-acquainted at Priory.

Eddie Jordan cultivated Johnny Herbert in F3 and F3000, and the blighter goes on to score an F1 win before he does. Time to beat him to a pulp with a drumstick (below left).

During the closing stages of the British Grand Prix, Silverstone's 3.14-mile lap was a cheering mass of joyous enthusiasm as 90,000 spectators showed their delight. In the past their Union Jacks bad frenziedly waved for Nigel Mansell; this time they'd mainly been used to encourage Damon Hill. But now, joy of joys, with just a few laps to go it was Johnny Herbert in the lead. Johnny Herbert, in his 71st Grand Prix, who had endured so much: dreadful leg injuries; four fruitless years with Lotus; a failure to realise his potential at Benetton; even rumours that he was about to be dropped in favour of Jos Verstappen. Now it was all coming good though. When he crossed the line to win, the emotional floodgates opened.

After a run of dull, processional races, relieved only by Jean Alesi's windfall win in Canada, Formula One needed something special. That's exactly what it got at the revised Silverstone, with its state-of-the-art garages, new medical centre and a fine new restaurant. A shame about the loss of the old 'garden party' motorhome area, but I suppose you can't have everything.

I have to confess that, in common with most other

people, I wasn't too optimistic about a closely-fought race: Benetton seemed to have got on top of Williams; Ferrari had been a great disappointment in France; McLaren was still well off the pace and, understandably, Jordan wasn't yet up with the big three. Friday's qualifying session made us all revise our opinions.

Almost to the end, Schumacher had again seemed to be unapproachable. When he improved his own fastest time by an astonishing eight-tenths of a second, a challenge to his supremacy seemed more than unlikely. It was at that point that Damon Hill reached deep inside to produce an even more remarkable lap, 0.2s faster than Michael's. "I'm not too bothered," said Schumacher. Bothered or not, pole position is the place to be for the start of any race and, like everyone else, he must have been expecting to go faster in Saturday's final session. No one did, however, for it was very wet. No help to Mika Salo, who had his Friday times disallowed for missing the pit lane red light, but for Damon it meant his second successive British Grand Prix pole position, and a chance to close the championship gap between himself and Schumacher.

Under grey, threatening skies the approach roads to Silverstone were full at five o'clock on Sunday morning. Then the helicopters began to flood in as Silverstone temporarily became the busiest airport in Britain. At 10 o'clock, when the warm-up session finished, the crowd was already immense, and there was good news for Mika Häkkinen's fans. With a demon new Mercedes-Benz engine, he was fastest. Maybe McLaren's fortunes were on the upturn?

The Finn made a good start to move up two places from eighth to sixth, but Jean Alesi's getaway was well-

Damon Hill (top) draws a diagram for fan, explaining in precise detail the braking point at Priory.

An experienced F1 observer seeks the sun (above).

The body language says it all. Damon Hill (right) returns to base camp.

70

nigh unbelievable. From sixth place he rocketed up to second past Herbert, Berger, Coulthard and Schumacher to slot in behind Damon Hill. It was sensational for Jean, but even better for Damon. Silverstone is far wider than most tracks, but even so it is almost impossible to pass when the performance of the car ahead is virtually the same as yours. As Michael Schumacher discovered. For lap after lap, with David Coulthard tight up behind him, he had to sit behind Alesi's Ferrari as Hill pulled away at around one second per lap. Fantastic! But what about the pit stops? Were they going to change everything?

David Coulthard was stuck behind Alesi, so Williams brought him in early, on lap 15. Then Alesi pitted on lap 18. Johnny Herbert, now third, stopped on lap 21 followed by Damon Hill on lap 22. Hill was 18.5s ahead of Schumacher and rejoined 9.7s adrift. He was clearly on a two-stop strategy. What about Schumacher? He had stopped twice in 1994, but now he stayed out. The gap between Damon and himself increased as his fuel load lightened. Benetton had done it again; Schumacher was only stopping once! On lap 31, at half-distance, he came in as Hill retook the lead.

Behind the two leaders Herbert was third, for his pit

crew had done a superb job to put him ahead of a terrific battle for fourth between Alesi and Coulthard. With
Mark Blundell sixth in his McLaren (Häkkinen had
retired from fourth place on lap 21 with a hydraulic failure), the crowd was revelling in the sight of four
Britons in the top six. Even so it was Damon who was
getting the mostpart of their attention. With
Schumacher now going through non-stop, and with his
fuel load getting lighter all the time, Hill needed to
build a lead of at least 28s to be in contention after his
second stop. Could he do it? On lap 32 it was 20.6s. On
lap 37 he set the fastest lap of the race (1m 29.752s,
126.043mph) to put himself 25s ahead, but an lap 41, as
he slowed in the long approach to the pit lane, the gap
was down to 20.3s. It was going to be a mighty close
thing. Sure enough, as Hill left the pit lane Schumacher
raced past him. There was now a mere 1.6s between the
leaders with 20 laps to go. Damon was on new tyres
which would give him better grip for about three laps; if
he couldn't get past Schumacher by lap 45, there'd be
no way – as Michael himself had found earlier in the
race when he had been stuck behind Alesi.

So eyes down – this was going to be good! On lap 43
the gap was 0.7s; Damon had halved Schumacher's
lead. On lap 44 it was 0.5s – closer still. On lap 45 it
was back to 0.7s, Michael was looking good. Then, as
they exited the 150mph right-hander at Bridge on lap
46, Damon braked incredibly late for the 70 mph left-
hander at Priory, and shot up the inside of Schumacher
as Michael turned in. They touched, and speared off
into the gravel trap. It was like Senna and Prost at
Suzuka 1989 in 1990, or Senna and Mansell at Adelaide
in all over again. "I thought I saw an opportunity that I
could take advantage of, but I'm afraid Michael is a
harder man to pass than that," said a defensive Damon

"Psst. If you play your cards right
you can probably get out of washing the dishes
for a couple of days. I did." Alesi passes a few
vital tips on to the winner (above).

"Good evening Silverstone (right). On lead
guitar, all the way from, erm, Dublin,
please welcome Mr Damon Hill. And on his
left, Twynholm's finest maracas player
Mr David Coulthard."

New kid on the block (below): Massmiliano
Papis brought invaluable backing to Arrows,
and took over from Gianni Morbidelli. The
Italian's debut concluded in embarrassing
fashion when he clipped the guardrail on
his way out of the pit lane

afterwards. "We had an accident which I would describe as a racing accident." To no one's great surprise, this wasn't quite how Schumacher saw it. "What Damon did was totally unnecessary. In fact it was really stupid. There was no room for two cars and there is no room to overtake there. It was such a nice race until then." Actually, they were both right. It was a case of now or never as far as Hill was concerned; if he hadn't tried he would have been criticised for lack of effort. But it obviously didn't do anything for their already strained personal relations.

As the hubbub died down, there was now an equally exciting battle for the lead – and it was still between a Benetton and a Williams. Herbert versus Coulthard. With Alesi now 8s behind them, Johnny and David were as close to each other as Schumacher and Hill had been. This race certainly wasn't going to end in an anticlimax, for neither of them had won a Grand Prix, both of them were British and both of them were hugely popular. But there was more…

Behind Alesi, Mark Blundell and Rubens Barrichello were fighting just as hard for fourth place, despite the Brazilian having sustained yet another 10s penalty on lap 15 for again jumping the start.

On lap 49 Coulthard fought his way past Herbert, but Johnny wasn't worried. He'd already been told by his pit people that David had been penalised for speeding in the pit lane (due to a speed limiter malfunction). On lap 51 Coulthard came in to take his punishment. Up to second went Alesi, but with his Ferrari oil pressure failing he was unable to challenge Herbert, who anxiously drove the final laps with the crowd willing him on.

The question now was who would be fourth, Blundell or Barrichello? The answer was neither. In his efforts to pass the defensive Blundell, Rubens drove into the McLaren, took himself out of the race and enabled Ligier's Olivier Panis to snatch the place from Blundell as Mark nursed the McLaren home to fifth place with its left rear tyre in ribbons. But at last, and not before time, it was Johnny's race and everyone, but everyone, was overjoyed. Damon Hill carried him up the stairs to the podium on his shoulders and, when he got there, Coulthard and Alesi hoisted him on to their shoulders – something I've never seen before in all the years that I've been watching Grands Prix. It was a truly joyous scene, and it couldn't have happened to a nicer bloke.

That evening, at the traditional Eddie Jordan rock and roll concert in the paddock, Damon Hill, whose wife 'Georgie' had unexpectedly joined him for the race despite the fact that their third child was literally due that very day, played the guitar with verve and skill. David Coulthard 'played' the maracas and Johnny Herbert sang "Go Johnny Go!" A great way to end a great day. Sadly, I have to end on a dull note. As we chewed over Silverstone 1995, the next day we learned that Juan Manuel Fangio, who had won there for Ferrari in 1951 had died in his home at Balcarce, Argentina, at the age of 84. Although it is impossible directly to compare drivers of one generation with those of another, few would deny that he was the greatest of all time. A five times world champion, a true gentleman with enormous charisma and a genius at the wheel. May he rest in peace.

Benetton-Renault

Universal affectionate joy for Johnny Herbert's richly deserved first win, but team anger over Schumacher's loss of potential fifth 1995 victory. Michael second on grid to Hill after exciting battle in Friday dry session. Passed by demonic Alesi at start and races third until Jean's lap 8 pit stop. On one-stop strategy, takes lead from two-stop Hill when Damon pits, lap 22. Builds 12s lead but down to second after own stop, lap 31. Leads Hill by 1.5s after Damon's second stop, lap 41. Hill closes gap to zero but then rams Benetton during controversial passing move, lap 46. Stewards severely reprimand both drivers. Herbert starts fifth with Friday time but goes off heavily during wet Saturday qualifying. With two-stop strategy is up to third, lap 18, profiting from earlier Alesi and Coulthard stops. Stays ahead of Jean and David after his first stop, lap 21. Has exciting battle for lead with Coulthard after Schumacher/Hill retirements which terminates when David takes pit lane speeding penalty. Johnny wins first GP at 71st attempt to become 1995's second new victor – to euphoric delight of teams, crowd and everyone else. Benetton further extends constructors' championship lead to nine points over Ferrari.

Tyrrell-Yamaha

Team reverts to non-Hydrolink rear suspension. Salo 15th in dry Friday qualifying but all times disallowed due to missing pit lane red light for weight check. Is superb fourth fastest on wet Saturday but time only qualifies him 23rd. With Martini for much of race and finishes eighth, 0.7s behind Pier-Luigi (one lap down). "I would have been seventh but Martini pushed me on to the grass and I did a 360 at 180mph!" Katayama starts 14th, unhappy with balance. Races well, up to eighth before retiring with fuel starvation. Team still has no points after eight races.

Williams-Renault

Damon Hill digs very deep indeed in dry Friday qualifying to take superb second successive British GP pole position, 0.2 faster than Schumacher. On two-stop strategy, takes lead at start and heads Schumacher by 18.5s at first stop, lap 22. Rejoins second but takes lead again when one-stop Michael comes in, lap 31. Sets fastest lap on lap 37 (1m 29.752s, 126.043nph). After second stop, lap 41, rejoins 1.5s behind Schumacher and literally closes gap to zero by braking too late at Priory on lap 46 and colliding with the Benetton. Both are eliminated; each blames the other. The stewards apportion blame equally. David Coulthard, free of medication for the first time in 1995 after his tonsils operation, starts disappointed third. Races fourth with Alesi and Schumacher until first of two stops, lap 15. After second stop, lap 43, has fierce battle for lead with Herbert following Hill/Schumacher collision. Fights past Johnny to take lead, lap 51, but has to stop for 10s pit lane speeding penalty. Finishes third, disappointed for himself but genuinely delighted for Herbert.

McLaren-Mercedes

Revised front suspension but Häkkinen and Blundell only eighth and 10th on grid, still two seconds off pace. However, with new Mercedes V10 Mika is fastest in Sunday warm-up. Gains two places at start and up to fourth, lap 19, benefiting from pit stops. Then electronic and hydraulic failures affect gearbox and clutch, causing lap 21 retirement. Mark Blundell stops twice and battles with Barrichello for sixth from lap 52. Controversially defending his line when he is hit by Rubens, lap 60. Finishes fifth, on three wheels, and receives stewardly reprimand into the bargain.

Arrows-Hart

Team now has no experienced driver as Italian F3000 graduate Massimiliano Papis replaces Gianni Morbidelli for financial reasons. Qualifies 17th. Hits pit lane barrier after lap 29 stop and retires with collapsed suspension. Inoue starts 19th. Spins, stalls and retires from 18th, lap 17.

Jordan-Peugeot

Eddie Irvine denied benefit of special Peugeot qualifying engine during wet Saturday, but starts seventh with Friday time, two places ahead of Barrichello. After a slow start, spins trying to pass Panis. Race ends when sensor problem stops engine, lap two. Rubens advances to seventh only

to take another 10s penalty for jump start. Back to seventh by first of two stops, lap 21, during which he hits mechanic Phil Howell (not hurt). Stalls at second stop, lap 40, when again seventh. Charging hard, steadily gains on Blundell and battles for fourth from lap 52. Hits the McLaren, lap 60, and retires (classified 11th two laps down). Accuses Blundell of brake-testing (which Mark denies, of course). Both drivers severely reprimanded by stewards.

Pacific-Ford

Montermini fails to set Friday time due to brake master cylinder failure and therefore qualifies 24th and last on wet Saturday. Runs behind Gachot at tail of field until spinning out on lap 22. Bertrand Gachot (who is to yield seat to renta-driver Giovanni Lavaggi from Hockenheim onwards) qualifies 22nd with gear selection problem. Races reliably to 12th, three laps down, for first (and last?) finish of year.

Forti-Ford

Diniz, with new-spec car and latest Ford ED engine, starts 20th, two places ahead of Moreno in old car. Both retire from last place, Diniz on lap 14 (gear selection), Moreno on lap 49 (pneumatic valve pressure).

Minardi-Ford

Gian Carlo Minardi resolves French GP litigation problem with Benetton's Flavio Briatore, but team can not return to Faenza and travel directly to Silverstone to do its servicing. From 15th and 18th on grid, Pier-Luigi Martini and Luca Badoer race with the works-engined Sauber-Fords of Frentzen and Boullion and Salo's Tyrrell to finish seventh (P-LM) and 10th (LB), both one lap down. A very happy Minardi proclaims that his team is the best of the Ford ED entrants.

Ligier-Mugen Honda

Team making steady progress, now with power steering and further aerodynamic changes. Despite alleged collaboration over settings with sister Benetton team, Martin Brundle and Olivier Panis can only qualify 11th and 13th in Friday's dry conditions and are unable to improve on wet Saturday. Martin spins in warm-up and is rammed by Diniz's Forti but starts in repaired car. Up to eighth after great start but then handling deteriorates. Spins out when seventh on lap 17. Panis also unhappy with handling but stays on the island, taking second successive jump-start penalty on lap 12. Resumes 14th, but up to seventh by second tyre/fuel stop, lap 42. Finishes excellent full-distance fourth after retirements of Schumacher, Hill and Barrichello. Team has now scored points in four of last five races and lies fifth-equal in constructors' championship with once-mighty McLaren. New engine evolution due in Belgium.

Ferrari

Despite poor performance in France, no testing at Silverstone and concern over new Renault RS7B engine for Benetton and Williams, team is confident at Silverstone. But, with lack of mileage at track, Berger only fourth on grid after fuel pressure and gearbox hydraulics problems and Alesi sixth, with both having no chance to improve in wet Saturday session. Alesi makes absolutely sensational start to rocket from sixth to second at first corner. Stays ahead of Schumacher and Coulthard until lap 18 tyre/fuel stop, now 18s behind Hill. Down to fourth behind Herbert after first round of stops and then to fifth after second stop, lap 39, due to time lost adding extra fuel needed for thirsty V12. Charges hard and finishes contented second (for third time in 1995), despite failing oil pressure, after Schumacher and Hill retire and Coulthard stops for penalty. A miserable race for Gerhard Berger though. Down five places to ninth with clutch problem at start. Fifth at lap 20 tyre/fuel stop but furiously out on lap 21 with badly fitted loose front left wheel.

Sauber-Ford

No Silverstone testing and a wet Saturday limit Frentzen and Boullion to 12 laps on Friday to set their grid times. Heinz-Harald starts "usual" 12th with Jean-Christophe 16th. With a car that handles better on a heavy fuel load, Frentzen stops only once, from an excellent seventh on lap 29. Loses brake duct at pit stop and handling deteriorates. Nevertheless finishes in points – sixth, one lap down. Boullion makes bad start and grapples with understeer throughout race but finishes ninth.

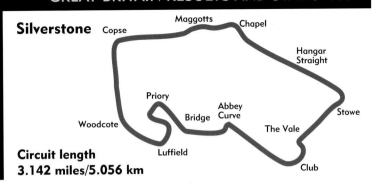

Silverstone

Copse · Maggotts · Chapel · Hangar Straight · Priory · Abbey Curve · Bridge · Stowe · Woodcote · The Vale · Luffield · Club

**Circuit length
3.142 miles/5.056 km**

STARTING GRID

HILL
(Williams FW17)
1m 29.124s

SCHUMACHER
(Benetton B195)
1m 28.397s

COULTHARD
(Williams FW17)
1m 29.947s

BERGER
(Ferrari 412 T2)
1m 29.657s

HERBERT
(Benetton B195)
1m 29.867s

ALESI
(Ferrari 412 T2)
1m 29.874s

IRVINE
(Jordan 195)
1m 30.354s

HÄKKINEN
(McLaren MP4/10B)
1m 30.140s

BARRICHELLO
(Jordan 195)
1m 30.354s

BLUNDELL
(McLaren MP4/10B)
1m 30.453s

BRUNDLE
(Ligier JS41)
1m 30.946s

FRENTZEN
(Sauber C14)
1m 31.602s

PANIS
(Ligier JS41)
1m 31.842s

KATAYAMA
(Tyrrell 023)
1m 32.087s

MARTINI
(Minardi M195)
1m 32.259s

BOULLION
(Sauber C14)
1m 33.166s

PAPIS
(Footwork FA16)
1m 34.154s

BADOER
(Minardi M195)
1m 34.556s

INOUE
(Footwork FA16)
1m 35.323s

DINIZ
(Forti FGP 01)
1m 36.023s

GACHOT
(Pacific PR02)
1m 36.076s

MORENO
(Forti FGP 01)
1m 36.651s

SALO
(Tyrrell 023)
1m 48.639s

MONTERMINI
(Pacific PR02)
1m 52.398s

RACE CLASSIFICATION

Pos	Driver	Nat	Car	Laps	Time
1	Johnny Herbert	GB	Benetton B195-Renault	61	1h 34m 35.093s
2	Jean Alesi	F	Ferrari 412 T2-Ferrari	61	1h 34m 51.572s
3	David Coulthard	GB	Williams FW17-Renault	61	1h 34m 58.981s
4	Olivier Panis	F	Ligier JS41-Mugen Honda	61	1h 36m 08261s
5	Mark Blundell	GB	McLaren MP4/10B-Mercedes	61	1h 36m 23.265s
6	Heinz-Harald Frentzen	D	Sauber C14-Ford Zetec-R		1 lap behind
7	Pier-Luigi Martini	I	Minardi M195-Ford ED		1 lap behind
8	Mika Salo	SF	Tyrrell 023-Yamaha		1 lap behind
9	J-C Boullion	F	Sauber C14-Ford Zetec		1 lap behind
10	Luca Badoer	I	Minardi M195-Ford ED		1 lap behind
11	Rubens Barrichello	BR	Jordan 195-Peugeot		2 laps behind
12	Bertrand Gachot	F/B	Pacific PR02-Ford ED		3 laps behind

Retirements	Nat	Car	Laps	Reason
Roberto Moreno	BR	Forti FGP 01-Ford ED	48	Engine
Michael Schumacher	D	Benetton B195-Renault	45	Accident
Damon Hill	GB	Williams FW17-Renault	45	Accident
Massimiliano Papis	I	Footwork FA16-Hart	28	Suspension
Ukyo Katayama	J	Tyrrell 023-Yamaha	22	Fuel starvation
Andrea Montermini	I	Pacific PR02-Ford ED	21	Spin
Mika Häkkinen	SF	McLaren MP4/10B-Mercedes	20	Gearbox ECU
Gerhard Berger	A	Ferrari 412 T2-Ferrari	20	Loose wheel
Martin Brundle	GB	Ligier JS41-Mugen Honda	16	Spin
Taki Inoue	J	Footwork FA16-Hart	16	Spin
Pedro Diniz	BR	Forti FGP 01-Ford ED	4	Gear selection
Eddie Irvine	GB	Jordan 195-Peugeot	2	Crank sensor

Fastest lap

Damon Hill — Williams FW17-Renault — lap 37 — 1m 29.752s (126.044mph)

DRIVERS' CHAMPIONSHIP

Michael Schumacher	46
Damon Hill	35
Jean Alesi	32
Johnny Herbert	22
G Berger & D Coulthard	17
R Barrichello & O Panis	7
Eddie Irvine	6
Häkkinen, Frentzen & Blundell	5
Martin Brundle	3
Gianni Morbidelli	1

CONSTRUCTORS' CUP

Benetton-Renault	58
Ferrari	49
Williams-Renault	46
Jordan-Peugeot	13
McLaren-Mercedes	10
Ligier-Mugen Honda	10
Sauber-Ford	5
Footwork-Hart	1

Germany

30 July 1995
Circuit: Hockenheim

"Alright, we'll only lap you six times then." Schumacher and Herbert strike a deal with the Forti boys, after they suffered a breakdown on the drivers' parade lap and had to rely on a lift from the nether regions of the grid (above).

Damon Hill (left) did his best to quieten the locals with a storming opening lap, but for some reason they all burst out laughing at the start of lap two.

The atmosphere at Silverstone for Damon Hill's home Grand Prix may have been lively, but it was almost funereal compared with that at Hockenheim. With names like Mercedes-Benz, Audi, BMW, Porsche and Volkswagen, Germany possesses a vibrant motor industry but, surprisingly, it has produced remarkably few Grand Prix stars. In fact the last time a German had won his home Grand Prix was 1939, when Rudolf Caracciola had taken his Mercedes-Benz W163 to victory at the fabled Nürburgring. Ever since, the patriotic and enthusiastic German fans had yearned for one of their countrymen to repeat Rudi's success. Michael Schumacher was the man on whom all their hopes rested.

Clean-cut, cheerful, likeable and enormously talented, 'Schumi' had burst into Formula One in 1991, won his first Grand Prix a year later and was now reigning world champion. On home soil, he had been third behind Nigel Mansell and Ayrton Senna in 1992, second to Alain Prost in '93 and a retirement in '94 after fruitlessly chasing the Ferrari of eventual winner Gerhard Berger. But now Michael was on a roll, first in

Brazil, Spain, Monaco and France and, in the eyes of his fans, the moral winner in Canada and deprived of victory in Britain. Surely he would satisfy Germany's dearest wish in 1995?

He would, but not in the way that people had expected.

Germany 1995 wasn't only about Michael Schumacher. It was just as much about Damon Hill. Under a cloud of ill-informed and unjustified criticism after his Silverstone collision with Schumacher, Damon was under enormous pressure when he arrived at Hockenheim. He had to do well to close the championship gap to his German rival, but Schumacher and Benetton were mighty formidable opposition. Damon, who had just become a father for the third time, is the last person in the world to cave in, and he seemed to have the right car with which to fight back.

Hockenheim, near Heidelberg, is a four-mile flattened oval with three chicanes. It slashes its way through a tightly-packed pine forest into a much slower, stadium section surrounded by gigantic concrete grandstands that hold over 100,000 roaring, flag-waving, rocket-firing (yes, really!) spectators and it seemed to suit the Williams-Renault. Hill was fastest in Friday qualifying, followed by team-mate David Coulthard. Schumacher was third, unhappy with the set-up and gear ratios of his Benetton. Coulthard was fastest on Saturday morning with Hill second and Michael down in sixth, but no one was underestimating Benetton. In the vital Saturday qualifying session, bursting with people and throbbing with passion,

If only everything in life were as reliable as a Renault...Runner-up Coulthard gives Barrichello a lift home after the latter's retirement (top). As partial encouragement, the Brazilian's Jordan-Peugeot had run as high as third.

Alain Prost to rejoin McLaren rumours were one thing, but Stewart to Tyrrell..? The 1973 World Championship-winning combo discuss Uncle Ken's total failure to score a point thus far (above).

A few of the crowd were alert to the presence of a second talented German in the field. Heinz-Harald Frentzen (right) did not have such a good day as his more famous compatriot, engine failure putting him out.

Schumacher was right there, slugging it out with the Williams men for the pole position that was going to mean so much in terms of a psychological and practical advantage.

Whatever Benetton technical boss Ross Brawn and Schumacher's race engineer Pat Symonds had done had certainly worked, because Michael was right on the pace. Coulthard, now fully fit after his tonsils operation and raring for success after four retirements from eight races, was the first to improve on Hill's Friday time. Only by a razor-thin 0.008s, admittedly, but faster is faster. Then it was Schumacher with a lap 0.1s quicker than David. That's how close it was until Hill did what he had done at Silverstone – reached deep and found a mega-lap over 0.4s faster than Schumacher's. Pole position was his. It was Damon's third successive pole, his fourth from the last five meetings, his ninth in all and he'd never had one sweeter. On Friday morning he had slid off on a damp track right in front of the packed grandstands which erupted with jeers, whistles and rockets. Damon got out of the Williams, waved to the crowd and blew kisses at them. They loved it. The cheers became genuine and respectful and now the last laugh was truly his. The scene was set for a great race, though sadly it was to be a monumental non-event in terms of exciting racing.

Effectively the race for victory was over after the first of its 45 laps. Happily there were no 1994-style multiple collisions at the start. Damon made a superb getaway for what was intended to be a one-stop race. With Schumacher on a two-stop strategy, Hill was carrying a heavier fuel load. In spite of this he led the Benetton by a very impressive 1.3s at the end of the first lap…which was also his last. As he turned in to the 125 mph North Curve, the back of his Williams stepped out and he skated across the wide gravel trap into the tyre wall. What an anti-climax. "I am very shocked because I was comfortable in the car, I went into the corner and the rear suddenly locked up. I don't have an explanation for it, but I've been round that corner enough times to know whether I am on the limit or not. It is pretty devastating." Once again Damon was to be the subject of much wounding criticism. Later, however, his feeling that something had gone wrong with the car was supported by Patrick Head, the technical boss of Williams, who said that a worn driveshaft joint could have contributed to Damon's spin. Whatever, Schumacher was now in the lead to the understandable euphoric delight of his massed countrymen. And he didn't look like losing it.

The challenge was now David Coulthard's. The Scot was second, 1.3s behind Schumacher, followed by Gerhard Berger, Rubens Barrichello, Mika Häkkinen and Eddie Irvine. To nobody's great surprise, Schumacher drew away. His lead over Coulthard was 1.7s on lap three, 2.85s on lap four and 3.16s on lap five, which was when Gerhard Berger stopped to take a 10s penalty for a jump start. Like Olivier Panis and Rubens Barrichello, who had both been given penalties at Magny-Cours and Silverstone, Gerhard was adamant that although his car had lurched when he engaged a gear, he had not benefited from an early departure.

That view got him nowhere, though it did provide the one bright spot in an otherwise dull race as Gerhard got his head down and charged. Despite the improvements that Ferrari had made, he could do nothing about Schumacher and Coulthard with their superior Renault power but he could – and did – do something about everybody else. "I drove every lap as though it was in qualifying." His progress was a joy to watch. At

Hockenheim the track is very tough on engines and brakes, with its long, 200 mph straights and 60 mph chicanes. The result is a stack of retirements and these helped Gerhard, who had rejoined in 14th place.

His team-mate Jean Alesi was the first of the quick men ahead of him to go – from sixth place on lap 11 with a broken engine. Then Mark Blundell pulled out of an excellent fourth on lap 17 with the same complaint. A resigned Rubens Barrichello, who had been a superb third behind Coulthard for 10 laps, was next when his Peugeot V10 gave up on lap 21. By now, amazingly, Berger was third again, albeit 37s behind the leader and

still needing to stop for fuel. It had been and would continue to be a great drive.

As Gerhard had raced forwards through the field, David Coulthard had taken the lead when Schumacher made his first stop on lap 19. Five laps later Michael was back in front when David came in for his one stop. Now Schumacher really went for it, knowing he had to make a second stop and therefore needed to build the maximum cushion between himself and Coulthard. On lap 22 he set the fastest lap of the race (1m 48.824s, 140.256 mph), and when Coulthard rejoined after his stop Schumacher led by 18s. If he could build that lead

to some 28s he would be safe for his second stop. Try as he might, Coulthard was powerless to contain his rival. On lap 34, when Schumacher made his second stop, he was 27s of the Williams. He emerged from the pit lane in front of Coulthard and now just had to keep going for the remaining 11 laps for a very famous victory. In fact Michael did more than that, for he built his lead to over 11s before backing off on the last lap to win by a comfortable six seconds. The scenes of pure joy and unfettered jubilation at Hockenheim had to be seen to be believed. He had done it. Victory for a German in Germany for the first time in 56 years. No wonder they were happy, and deservedly so.

With only eight of the 24 starters running at the end there were plenty of other stories to tell. There was a sad retirement for Mika Häkkinen, who had driven superbly to force his McLaren up to third after Barrichello's exit. His much-improved Mercedes engine gave up with 11 laps to go. Heinz-Harald Frentzen's Ford Zetec motor did the same thing when he was in the points again. It was even worse for Eddie Irvine, who coasted to a standstill from a certain sixth with only four laps to go. But David Coulthard got his wish with six points for finishing second. Berger was third, "and that was the best I could have hoped for anyway". Johnny Herbert took fourth despite a major gearbox problem from lap 20, while Jean-Christophe Boullion gained his first points from only his fifth Grand Prix. A totally unexpected sixth went to Japan's Aguri Suzuki, who had been lucky even to start after crashing heavily on Friday.

It had been a far from exciting race after the first lap but Germany and Schumacher didn't care. Why should they? For them it had been an absolutely magical day.

Me and my shadow. Mark Blundell (top) found that Mercedes had improved the speed of its V10, but not the reliability.

Two or three people being mildly excitable on a quiet Sunday afternoon near Heidelberg (above).

Fed up with officialdom, Gerhard Berger (left) resented his 10s jump-start penalty, although the high rate of attrition still allowed him to finish third. Yet again.

Benetton-Renault

Another totally superior drive by Michael Schumacher makes him the first German to win his home GP since Rudolf Caracciola in 1939. After struggling to find right set-up, Michael battles for pole position on Saturday with Damon Hill and David Coulthard. Starts second, and takes lead when Hill goes off at start of second lap. Only loses it briefly to Coulthard after first of two stops, lap 19. Sets fastest lap and increases championship lead over Hill to 21 points. Johnny Herbert never gets to grips with set-up and qualifies ninth, 1.9s slower than Hill. On one-stop strategy (to help Schumacher) is fifth when he refuels, lap 23. Troubled by inoperative throttle blipper which affects gearchanging and is lucky to finish fourth as all gears go as he crosses line. Team's first and fourth increase Benetton's lead over Ferrari in constructors' championship to 18 points. Renault delighted with three of top four places on notoriously tough track for engines.

Tyrrell-Yamaha

Team abandons Hydrolink suspension after successful testing at Magny-Cours. Ukyo Katayama stops early during Friday qualifying with gearbox problem and finally starts 17th, five seconds off pace, unhappy with balance. Stops twice and benefits from multiple retirements to finish seventh (one lap down) despite downshift trouble for over half the race. Salo starts 13th but retires when driveshaft fails on first lap. Katayama's finish only his second from nine 1995 races and team still yet to score a point.

Williams-Renault

Major disappointment for team in what could be turning point of season. Under great pressure from fanatically pro-Schumacher crowd, following controversial Silverstone collision, unrepentant Damon Hill performs brilliantly to be fastest in both qualifying sessions and takes his fourth pole in five meetings. Makes superb start and leads Schumacher by 1.3s at end of first lap, despite heavier fuel load. Then skates into the tyre wall at first corner. "I am very shocked. Everything was normal and then the back of the car locked up and I went off. It is pretty devastating." Amidst general belief that Damon had got it wrong, technical director Patrick Head later states that Hill's violent departure could have been caused by a worn transmission joint. Powerful support for Damon's view that he was blameless, but either way he is now demoralising 21 points behind Schumacher in championship. David Coulthard qualifies third, only 0.15s slower than Hill. Runs second to Schumacher from lap two, and leads from laps 20-23 following Michael's first stop. Keeps Schumacher under pressure but is unable to close and, mindful of four previous retirements and desire to score points, takes no risks. Finishes second, six seconds down.

McLaren-Mercedes

Neither driver finishes, but team appears to have made genuine and much-needed progress at Hockenheim. Using Silverstone's evolution of Mercedes V10, both Häkkinen and Blundell are consistently quick with minimum downforce, fastest of all through speed traps at 208 mph). Mika fourth fastest in Friday qualifying, but qualifies seventh with older-style engine after V10 failure on Saturday morning. Mark Blundell starts eighth. Both race strongly. Häkkinen up to third by lap 15, seemingly set for podium until he retires, lap 34, when pneumatic valve pressure fails. Blundell up to fourth behind Mika, laps 16/17, but then out with broken engine. "The results will come," says Ron Dennis. We just have to be patient."

Arrows-Hart

Massimiliano Papis qualifies 15th for second GP, four places ahead of Taki Inoue. Both retire with unrelated transmission failures, Papis at start and Inoue on lap 10.

Jordan-Peugeot

Like McLaren, Jordan defeated by engine problems after looking good. New Peugeot evolution V10 so promising that even Renault congratulates them. Barrichello and Irvine start excellent fifth and sixth, 1.4s off Hill's pole time. Rubens to third after Hill's retirement and Berger's penalty. Fourth after lap 15 fuel stop, with all three ahead yet to stop, but pneumatic pressure fails on lap 21. Irvine fifth, laps 6-15, but with throttle response and brake problems is down to seventh at lap 22 fuel stop. In again with misfiring engine, lap 28, for mapping adjustment. Back in points laps 34-41 thanks to retirements, but engine dies lap 42. Classified ninth, four laps down.

Pacific-Ford

Team shareholder Bertrand Gachot yields seat to 37-year-old sports car driver Giovanni Lavaggi for financial reasons. Team so strapped for cash that both Montermini and Lavaggi allowed only limited laps to save on engine rebuilds. Unsurprisingly they qualify 23rd and 24th with Lavaggi 12s off pace. Keeping out of the way, Giovanni lapped 11th time around. Retires lap 28 when gearbox fails. Montermini also has gearbox problem but survives to finish eighth, three laps down, the team's best 1995 result and third successive finish. But Pacific struggling for survival.

Forti-Ford

Cars further improved but so are everyone else's. Diniz 21st on grid, Moreno 22nd. Both still some nine seconds off pole. Neither finishes. In spare car Diniz out from last, lap nine, after stopping twice with brake problems. Roberto retires from last, lap 28, when driveshaft breaks.

Minardi-Ford

Luca Badoer qualifies creditable 16th in 'customer-engine' car with Martini 20th. Luca delights team by racing with Boullion up to ninth, lap 21. After lap 22 fuel stop retires from 12th, lap 29, with gearbox actuator oil leak. Martini retires from 16th, lap 12, with engine failure.

Ligier-Mugen Honda

Rentadriver Suzuki displaces Martin Brundle. Goes off on Friday morning then crashes in afternoon and sent to Mannheim hospital for check. Qualifies 18th on Saturday after missing morning session. Up to seventh, laps 24/25, during fuel stops, but has left rear puncture and loses time getting to pits. In reliable car benefits from attrition and finishes delighted sixth, especially as car catches fire after crossing line! Olivier Panis starts 12th. Running seventh and closing on Blundell prior to lap 13 pit stop, but senses engine problem. He is right. Retires from 10th on out lap with split water pipe. But Suzuki's point moves Ligier ahead of McLaren in constructors' championship.

Ferrari

Three day test at Imola improves car, but Ferrari advances overwhelmed by Renault's RS7B evolution for Benetton and Williams. 1994 pole-starter and winner Gerhard Berger does only five laps on Saturday morning before losing rest of valuable session changing blown engine. Nevertheless qualifies fourth, but over a second slower than Hill, Schumacher and Coulthard. Jean Alesi a sensational 5.4s faster than anyone else on Friday morning thanks to perfect timing of change to slicks on drying track, but loses five grid places on Saturday afternoon due to too much downforce. Starts a despondent 10th. Gerhard to third on lap two, 2.3s behind Schumacher, after Hill's departure. Loses a second a lap until lap five when in for 10s jump-start penalty. Down to lowly 14th, 32s behind Schumacher, but then makes superb fighting recovery to finish third, after one fuel/tyre stop on lap 23. Even worse for Alesi who passes Herbert to eighth on lap four and Blundell to sixth on lap seven before being brought into pits, lap 11, with engine losing power. After check does one more lap before retiring.

Sauber-Ford

Improvements to Ford Zetec V8 give more power that you can actually feel says Heinz-Harald Frentzen, who qualifies 11th. Battles with Herbert from lap six and gets ahead, to fifth, after their pit stops. Repassed by Johnny on lap 27. Retires from sixth, lap 31, when engine gives up. Jean-Christophe Boullion makes poor start from 14th but sensibly concentrates on finishing a race where to do so is to do well. Up to seventh at only stop, lap 23. Races seventh behind Heinz-Harald, laps 26-32. Inherits sixth when H-H retires and then fifth when Häkkinen goes.

FIA FORMULA 1 WORLD CHAMPIONSHIP

RACE 9

GERMANY

30 JULY 1995

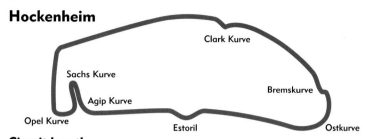

GERMANY RESULTS AND STATISTICS

Hockenheim

Clark Kurve
Sachs Kurve
Bremskurve
Agip Kurve
Opel Kurve
Estoril
Ostkurve

Circuit length
4.235 miles/6.815 km

STARTING GRID

HILL (Williams FW17) 1m 44.385s	**SCHUMACHER** (Benetton B195) 1m 44.465s
COULTHARD (Williams FW17) 1m 44.540s	**BERGER** (Ferrari 412 T2) 1m 45.553s
BARRICHELLO (Jordan 195) 1m 45.765s	**IRVINE** (Jordan 195) 1m 45.846s
HÄKKINEN (McLaren MP4/10B) 1m 45.849s	**BLUNDELL** (McLaren MP4/10B) 1m 46.221s
HERBERT (Benetton B195) 1m 46.315s	**ALESI** (Ferrari 412 T2) 1m 46.356s
FRENTZEN (Sauber C14) 1m 46.801s	**PANIS** (Ligier JS41) 1m 47.372s
SALO (Tyrrell 023) 1m 47.507s	**BOULLION** (Sauber C14) 1m 47.636s
PAPIS (Ligier JS4) 1m 48.093s	**BADOER** (Minardi M195) 1m 49.302s
KATAYAMA (Tyrrell 023) 1m 49.402s	**SUZUKI** (Ligier JS41) 1m 49.716s
INOUE (Footwork FA16) 1m 49.892s	**MARTINI** (Minardi M195) 1m 49.990s
DINIZ (Forti FGP01) 1m 52.961s	**MORENO** (Forti FGP01) 1m 53.405s
MONTERMINI (Pacific PR02) 1m 53.492s	**LAVAGGI** (Pacific PR02) 1m 54.625s

RACE CLASSIFICATION

Pos	Driver	Nat	Car	Laps	Time
1	Michael Schumacher	D	Benetton B195-Renault	45	1h 22m 56.043s
2	David Coulthard	GB	Williams FW17-Renault	45	1h 23m 02.031s
3	Gerhard Berger	A	Ferrari 412 T2-Ferrari	45	1h 24m 04.140s
4	Johnny Herbert	GB	Benetton B195-Renault	45	1h 24m 19.479s
5	J-C Boullion	A	Sauber C14-Ford Zetec	1 lap behind	
6	Aguri Suzuki	J	Ligier JS41-Mugen Honda	1 lap behind	
7	Ukyo Katayama	J	Tyrrell 023-Yamaha	1 lap behind	
8	Andrea Montermini	I	Pacific PR02-Ford ED	3 laps behind	
9	Eddie Irvine	GB	Jordan 195-Peugeot	4 laps behind	

Retirements	Nat	Car	Laps	Reason
Mika Häkkinen	SF	McLaren MP4/10B-Mercedes	33	Engine
Heinz-Harald Frentzen	D	Sauber C14-Ford Zetec-R	32	Engine
Luca Badoer	I	Minardi M195-Ford ED	32	Gearbox
Giovanni Lavaggi	I	Pacific PR02-Ford ED	27	Gearbox
Roberto Moreno	BR	Forti FGP 01-Ford ED	27	Driveshaft
Rubens Barrichello	BR	Jordan 195-Peugeot	20	Engine
Mark Blundell	GB	McLaren MP4/10B-Mercedes	17	Engine
Olivier Panis	F	Ligier JS41-Mugen Honda	13	Engine
Jean Alesi	F	Ferrari 412 T2-Ferrari	12	Engine
Pier-Luigi Martini	I	Minardi M195-Ford ED	11	Engine
Taki Inoue	J	Footwork FA16-Hart	9	Gearbox
Pedro Diniz	BR	Forti FGP 01-Ford ED	8	Brakes
Damon Hill	GB	Williams FW17-Renault	1	Spin
Mika Salo	SF	Tyrrell 023-Yamaha	0	Lost drive
Massimiliano Papis	I	Footwork FA16-Hart	0	Gearbox

Fastest lap

Michael Schumacher   Benetton B195-Renault   lap 22   1m 48.824s (139.815mph)

DRIVERS' CHAMPIONSHIP		CONSTRUCTORS' CUP	
Michael Schumacher	56	Benetton-Renault	71
Damon Hill	35	Ferrari	53
Jean Alesi	32	Williams-Renault	52
Johnny Herbert	25	Jordan-Peugeot	13
David Coulthard	23	Ligier-Mugen Honda	11
Gerhard Berger	21	McLaren-Mercedes	10
R Barrichello & O Panis	7	Sauber-Ford	7
Eddie Irvine	6	Footwork	1
Häkkinen, Frentzen & Blundell	5		
Martin Brundle	3		
J-C Boullion	2		
G Morbidelli & A Suzuki	1		

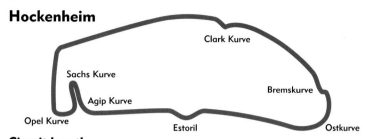

Results and Data © FIA 1995

13 August 1995
Circuit: Hungaroring

The championship was starting to look a foregone conclusion as the Grand Prix world set off for Hungary. Everyone likes Budapest, which is a great city, but the prospects for an exciting race weren't good. The twisty 2.465-mile Hungaroring, with its succession of second and third gear corners and lack of any real straight, makes passing notoriously difficult. It was confidently expected to suit the previous year's winner Michael Schumacher to perfection, with his agile Benetton. With Schumacher 21 points ahead of Damon Hill, who had failed to score at Silverstone and Hockenheim, the general expectation was that Michael would take pole position, clear off as he had done the previous year, prove to have a superior strategy and win his sixth race of the year, virtually to assure himself a second successive World Championship.

Oh ye of little faith! Primarily thanks to Damon, who rose to the occasion magnificently, the 1995 Hungarian Grand Prix meeting was a cracker from Friday's free practice session to the last corner of Sunday's race. When it ended, the championship was alive again. Hill had redeemed himself magnificently, Williams was back in contention for the constructors'

Just Williams (above left): Hill and Coulthard ease out Schumacher at the start, while Berger prepares for an afternoon of holding up every man and his dog.

The most aerodynamically efficient Marlboro-bedecked artefacts in the Hungaroring paddock? Discuss, with reference to the McLaren MP4/10B (left).

Union Flags aren't exactly prolific (below), but the crowd was happy enough to receive Damon Hill.

championship and there was an atmosphere of eager anticipation for the rest of the season.

The Hungaroring is very demanding. It is always baking hot, the track is tight and bumpy and the drivers are on and off the brakes and accelerator the whole time. In a race of nearly two hours' duration, both car and driver need a lot of stamina. Getting pole position is absolutely essential. Do that and you've a more than sporting chance of staying in front if you get your strategy right. Even Ayrton Senna couldn't find his way past an unyielding Thierry Boutsen's Williams in 1990.

Damon Hill had taken the last three poles, but surely he couldn't make it four in a row against the determined Schumacher, who was almost ready to announce that he would be driving for Ferrari in 1996? He did though, and in the most convincing way possible. Damon was

more than aware of his challenge. "I've got to start from pole, win the race and then keep on winning if I'm to be world champion. That's exactly what I'm going to try to do."

On Friday, in 28-degree heat, he took the provisional pole over a second faster than Schumacher and only 0.1s slower than Michael's 1994 pole time, which had been set with a 3.5-litre engine and much more down-force. But if Damon was great on Friday he was sensational on Saturday. As the final qualifying session opened on a track which is always quicker on the second day, his team-mate David Coulthard improved on Hill's time by a mere 0.01s. Damon regained pole only for Coulthard, on his second set of tyres, to improve again by a daunting 0.6s. By this time Hill had slipped down to fourth behind Coulthard, Schumacher and Berger. The chips were down and Damon responded with a magnificent 1m 16.982s, 0.4s faster that Coulthard and an incredible 1.3s faster than Schumacher's 1994 pole. It was the first all-Williams front row since Argentina, with Schumacher third and Gerhard Berger's Ferrari fourth.

The doubters reminded everyone that Damon had been ahead of Schumacher on the grid for four of the last five races, only to lose out in the event itself. Sunday was really hot again. It was going to be the first all-dry meeting of the year and Schumacher, who had suffered major set-up problems with the Benetton for the last two days, was ominously fastest in the warm-up...

Vitally, Damon got into the first corner first. What's more, Coulthard stayed ahead of Schumacher and, at the end of the first lap, Hill was 1.3s clear of Michael's Benetton. It got even better for him as he pulled away by a second a lap. By lap 13 the gap was 15.56s, but maybe Schumacher was up to one his crafty strategy ploys? After all, he had shaken everyone in 1994 by stopping three times to nearly everyone else's twice, and Benetton had got this happy knack of successfully doing the unexpected. Time would tell, but meantime the order was Hill, Coulthard, Schumacher (right behind David's gearbox), Berger, Brundle (after a great start from eighth on the grid) and Alesi. Mika Häkkinen was out again. He started fifth, but his engine lasted just three laps. It was Mika's seventh retirement from 10 races.

On lap 13 Schumacher slipped past Coulthard as the Williams, with its tyres over-pressured, momentarily slid sideways at the chicane. Now the battle was on.

Benetton (above) prepares to welcome Schumacher for the second time in not very many laps, fuel stop one not having passed with the team's habitual methodical efficiency.

Pedro Lamy (left) returned to F1, over a year after his horrific testing accident at Silverstone. The Portuguese acquitted himself at Minardi.

McLaren's mid-wing was back (below), but blistering pace wasn't...

Down came the gap to Damon. On lap 15 it was 14s, and it was down to 12s when Schumacher shot up to his pit lane refuellers on lap 17, Michael arriving at almost the moment Damon departed. Neither lost their place, rejoining first and second with 11.6s between them. Nine laps later, having sprinted to within 6.9s of Hill, Schumacher was in again! What on earth was Benetton up to? This was a really weird strategy…

What we didn't realise was that the reason Schumacher's first stop had been some two seconds quicker than Damon's, and that he had been making such inroads into Hill's lead, was because his fuel rig had only delivered 10 litres instead of the intended 40. Hence his swift return.

Having learned their lesson from last year, nearly everyone was on a three-stop strategy. By the time the first round had been completed Hill, Schumacher and Coulthard were followed by the Ferraris of Alesi and Berger, Johnny Herbert's Benetton (up from ninth an the grid), Brundle's Ligier and Eddie Irvine's Jordan. With only three seconds covering Berger to Irvine, the difficulty of passing at the Hungaroring was again being emphasised. Despite the fact that Gerhard was having major handling problems, Herbert was stuck behind the Ferrari's rear wing.

When Schumacher emerged from his second stop on lap 27 he immediately had David Coulthard right

"How do I look?" Jean Alesi (above) seeks his girlfriend's counsel as he prepares to make a pitch for Schumacher's Benetton seat by wearing his baseball cap backwards, in the preferred manner of Benetton chief Flavio Briatore.

In a Tyrrell which was not performing terribly well, Ukyo Katayama (right) could do little but enjoy the scenery…until he crashed out.

behind him, but any hopes that there would be a battle for second place faded as Michael pulled away from David and strove to close on Hill. But Damon, well aware of the situation, not only stabilised the gap but increased it to over 22s on lap 34, when he posted the fastest lap of the race (1m 20.247s, 110.615 mph). When he came in for his second stop on lap 38, he had further increased his lead to 23.5s – just enough to keep him ahead of the Benetton as he rejoined the track. It was now or never as far as Schumacher was concerned, for if he could get past Hill he might just take the win. Very unlikely at the Hungaroring, but at the time people were remembering that in 1989 Nigel Mansell had started 12th but had still, incredibly, won the race (and that included passing Ayrton Senna!). Laps 39 to 44 were great, with seldom more than a second between the Benetton and the Williams. On lap 44 Michael was right alongside Damon at the chicane where he had passed Coulthard but Hill resolutely held him off. And that, effectively, was the end of Schumacher's challenge. The effect of his botched first stop had been to increase the time he had to spend on his second and third sets of tyres with the result that he lost grip and, therefore, time. His third stop an lap 48 was followed by Damon's on lap 58 and Hill was over 11s ahead – and on fresh rubber – when he set off for his last 19 laps.

Not unnaturally, all eyes had been on the battle for victory, but there had been a lot going on behind. David Coulthard had held an unchallenged third place all the way, even if he had been totally unable to stay with the leaders. Having been fourth for 14 laps, Jean Alesi had retired with, of all things, a broken spark plug whilst, with a potential third place in sight, Mark Blundell had done the same thing when his Mercedes engine gave

up. By lap 60 of 77 the top four places looked settled, with Barrichello trailing Coulthard, one lap adrift.

Fifth was quite a different matter, with the obdurate Berger grimly fighting to keep Martin Brundle, Eddie Irvine and Johnny Herbert behind him. Then the rot set in. Out went Brundle when, most unusually, his Mugen engine let go. Then Eddie Irvine stopped with clutch failure. On lap 74, sensation! Out went Michael Schumacher as he silently rolled to a standstill with fuel pump failure. Instantaneously the championship was transformed. If Damon won he would now be only 11 points behind Schumacher with 70 still to be won from the remaining races.

And win he did for the third time in 1995 in what had been, in his view, "The best drive of my career." I would go further and say the best meeting of his career for, under colossal pressure, Damon had dominated qualifying on both days, won the race, set fastest lap and put himself right back in the championship picture. A great performance.

But the drama still wasn't over. As Rubens Barrichello entered the very last corner, within sight of the chequered flag for a fine third place, his Peugeot engine shut down and a nose-to-tail Berger, Herbert, Frentzen and Panis battle, with 1.2s covering the four of them, swept past. In just a few yards poor Rubens went from third to seventh. The Hungarian Grand Prix had been a race of incident and excitement all the way. You really never know with Formula One!

The next week came confirmation of the news that Schumacher would indeed be leaving Benetton for Ferrari in 1996, and that Damon Hill would still be with Williams. How would this affect Renault's attitude to their two top drivers for the rest of the season? It was going to be interesting to see!

Benetton-Renault

Amidst strong belief that he has signed for Ferrari in 1996, newly-married Schumacher has difficulty setting up car for bumpy Hungaroring. Fourth fastest on Friday and qualifies third behind Hill and Coulthard. Off front row for only second time in 1995, but fastest in warm-up. Runs close third to Coulthard for 12 laps before wriggling past when David runs wide at chicane. Pit stops 12s behind Hill, lap 17, but rig under-delivers fuel. Obliged to stop again only nine laps later and, in three-stop race, therefore has to do extra miles on last two sets of tyres. Has six-lap battle with Hill following Damon's second stop, lap 38, but then drops back due to tyre wear. Retires from second place, 12s behind Hill, when fuel pump fails, lap 74. Championship lead reduced to 11 points. Herbert qualifies disappointing ninth, still lacking confidence in nervous car. Is critical of time lost at pit stops (team has to use same rig for both drivers) but has nose to tail fight with Berger, Frentzen and Panis in closing laps. Finishes fourth, (one lap down), 0.2s behind Gerhard and 0.7s ahead of Heinz-Harald. Benetton now only six points ahead of Williams in constructors' championship.

Tyrrell-Yamaha

Team makes "significant handling, balance and grip progress" in two-day test at Silverstone but this fails to benefit drivers at Hungaroring where Salo and Katayama qualify only 16th and 17th, nearly five seconds off pace. Katayama spins out from lapped 13th, lap 47. Salo retires from lapped 11th, lap 59, with electrical problem.

Williams-Renault

A wonderful meeting at Hungaroring for Frank's team. Damon fastest on Friday, then goes 1.35 faster on Saturday to take fourth successive pole ahead of team-mate David Coulthard and Schumacher. After perfect start, pulls away from Coulthard/Schumacher battle, with all three on three-stop strategy. Retains lead at first stop, lap 17, but rejoins only just ahead of Schumacher after second stop (lap 38) Staves off strong challenge which fades as worn tyres delay Michael Damon brilliantly wins third race of 1995 with fastest lap and closes championship gap to 11 points. "We chose the right strategy this weekend and I got through the traffic well. We knew what we had to do and I think we were pretty much in control." Coulthard cannot keep up with Hill due to over-inflated tyres, but staves off Schumacher for 16 laps. Down to third, lap 17, but inherits second successive second place when Schumacher retires, lap 74, and moves up to distant fourth in championship. Williams passes Ferrari to take second in constructors' championship, six points behind Benetton.

McLaren-Mercedes

Rear suspension and damper changes, remapped Mercedes V10 and experimentation with high mid-wing but Häkkinen, fifth on grid, still 1.4s off Hill's pole time. Mika second fastest in warm-up, only 0.4s slower than Schumacher, but retires from fifth, lap four, when engine fails. Mark Blundell starts 13th after engine failure on third lap of Saturday qualifying when seventh. On two-stop strategy is fourth, laps 23-25, and then again laps 40-48, suffering from inconsistent fuel pressure which causes lap 54 retirement from eighth place.

Arrows-Hart

Another track which is new to both drivers. Taki Inoue improves somewhat to qualify 18th, albeit five seconds off pole. Massi Papis 20th with Friday time. Unable to go out on Saturday afternoon after accident in the morning free session. Neither finishes. Inoue pulls off, lap 14, with loss of oil pressure and is hit by course car as he fetches extinguisher to put out minor fire (heavy bruising but nothing worse). Papis retires from 18th, lap 45, with loss of fluid from brake master cylinder.

Jordan-Peugeot

Another heart-breaking meeting. Barrichello (rumoured to be joining Benetton in 1996) beset with engine problems during both qualifying sessions. Starts 13th. Irvine qualifies strong seventh before having times disallowed when team mechanic helps push car after weight

check. Decision reversed in Eddie's favour. Three-stop Irvine passed by Brundle at start. Eighth at first and second stops, laps 17 and 34. Loses time behind Berger and Frentzen before third stop when sixth, lap 52. Back to sixth, laps 67-69, but retires, lap 70, when clutch fails. Two-stop Barrichello up to fifth at first (late) stop, lap 25. After second stop, is excellent lapped third, laps 60-75, only to have pneumatic pressure fail at last corner and he is passed by Berger, Herbert, Frentzen and Panis within sight of flag. Finishes sad seventh, one lap down.

Pacific-Ford

First time at Hungaroring for both drivers. Shouldn't-really-be-in-Formula One Giovanni Lavaggi nearly 10s off pace to start 24th and last. Gets on marbles and spins out, lap six. But much better race for Montermini who progresses reliably to give team its fourth successive finish (12th) and, astoundingly, sets 11th fastest lap of the race, 2.4s off Hill and only 0.1s slower than Herbert.

Forti-Ford

Roberto Moreno 21st on grid, 7.4s off Hill. Pedro Diniz 23rd. Both utilise standard manual transmissions and old-spec Ford ED V8. Moreno retires from 18th, lap nine, when gearlever comes adrift. Lapped Diniz out from last, lap 33, when engine fails.

Minardi-Ford

Having fully recovered from his very nasty Lotus testing accident at Silverstone in May 1994, Portugal's Pedro Lamy returns to Formula One in place of Pier-Luigi Martini. He impresses by qualifying 15th, despite lack of real testing. Team-mate Luca Badoer starts 12th in spare car and drops to 15th. Using two-stop strategy both race reliably to finish eighth (Badoer) and ninth.

Ligier-Mugen Honda

Martin Brundle returns and does well to qualify eighth, two places ahead of Olivier Panis. Makes excellent start and races to sixth past Alesi and Irvine. Catches fourth-placed Berger on lap nine but can make no further progress. After three stops loses almost certain eventual fourth place when engine fails. Panis spends virtually whole race behind Frentzen. Stops three times, laps 18, 38 and 59, and finishes sixth (one lap down) after Barrichello's engine fails at last corner.

Ferrari

Jean Alesi, under pressure amidst rumours (which prove to be true) that Schumacher will oust him in 1996, goes off heavily into barrier during Friday qualifying. He is stretchered away by helicopter for a medical check. Reappears on Saturday to qualify seventh, two seconds off pace, before going off again and breaking transmission. Third fastest in Sunday warm-up but passed by Brundle at start. Seventh after first stop, lap 20, and then fourth, laps 26-39. Slowed by misfire after second stop, lap 40, caused by broken plug which drops into engine. Retires, lap 43. It soon emerges that Jean will join Benetton in 1996. Gerhard Berger qualifies fourth. "I regard this as a moral pole position because I was absolutely flat out everywhere!" With existing understeer increased by front wing damage, drops to 10th after first stop, lap 18. Climbs to sixth at second and third stops, laps 36 and 48. Then heads lapped four car crocodile (Berger/Herbert/Frentzen/Panis) battling for fifth in closing stages. All four pass unfortunate Barrichello, whose engine fails at last corner, and Gerhard finishes lapped third. Ferrari down to third behind Williams in constructors' championship.

Sauber-Ford

Both drivers detuned by 'flu attacks. Heinz-Harald Frentzen eighth fastest on Friday but angrily drops to 11th on grid after being blocked on fast Saturday lap by Andrea Montermini. Stops twice during race as car handles better on heavier fuel load. Fends off Panis for much of race and finishes fifth (one lap down). Jean-Christophe Boullion finds Hungaroring difficult to learn and, affected by fever, starts 19th in spare car set up for Frentzen after race car develops steering hydraulics problem. Develops leg cramp due to H-H's settings but finishes 10th.

HUNGARY RESULTS AND STATISTICS

Hungaroring

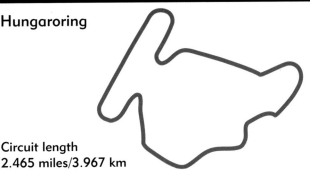

13 AUGUST 1995

**Circuit length
2.465 miles/3.967 km**

STARTING GRID

HILL
(Williams FW17)
1m 16.982s

COULTHARD
(Williams FW17)
1m 17.366s

SCHUMACHER
(Benetton B195)
1m 17.558s

BERGER
(Ferrari 412 T2)
1m 18.059s

HÄKKINEN
(McLaren MP4/10B)
1m 18.363s

ALESI
(Ferrari 412 T2)
1m 18.968s

IRVINE
(Jordan 195)
1m 19.499s

BRUNDLE
(Ligier JS41)
1m 19.748s

HERBERT
(Benetton B195)
1m 20.072s

PANIS
(Ligier JS41)
1m 20.160s

FRENTZEN
(Sauber C14)
1m 20.413s

BADOER
(Minardi M195)
1m 20.543s

BLUNDELL
(McLaren MP4/10B)
1m 20.640s

BARRICHELLO
(Jordan 195)
1m 20.902s

LAMY
(Minardi M195)
1m 21.156s

SALO
(Tyrrell 023)
1m 21.624s

KATAYAMA
(Tyrrell 023)
1m 21.702s

INOUE
(Footwork FA16)
1m 22.081s

BOULLION
(Sauber C14)
1m 22.161s

PAPIS
(Footwork FA16)
1m 23.275s

MORENO
(Forti FGP 01)
1m 24.351s

MONTERMINI
(Pacific PR02)
1m 24.371s

DINIZ
(Forti FBGP 01)
1m 24.695s

LAVAGGI
(Pacific PR02)
1m 26.570s

RACE CLASSIFICATION

Pos	Driver	Nat	Car	Laps	Time
1	Damon Hill	GB	Williams FW17-Renault	77	1h 46m 25.721s
2	David Coulthard	GB	Williams FW17-Renault	77	1h 46m 59.119s
3	Gerhard Berger	A	Ferrari 412 T2-Ferrari		1 lap behind
4	Johnny Herbert	GB	Benetton B195-Renault		1 lap behind
5	Heinz-Harald Frentzen	D	Sauber C14-Ford Zetec-R		1 lap behind
6	Olivier Panis	F	Ligier JS41-Mugen Honda		1 lap behind
7	Rubens Barrichello	BR	Jordan 195-Peugeot		1 lap behind
8	Luca Badoer	I	Minardi M195-Ford ED		2 laps behind
9	Pedro Lamy	P	Minardi M195-Ford ED		3 laps behind
10	J-C Boullion	F	Sauber C14-Ford Zetec-R		3 laps behind
11	Michael Schumacher	D	Benetton B195-Renault		4 laps behind
12	Andrea Montermini	I	Pacific PR02-Ford ED		4 laps behind
13	Eddie Irvine	GB	Jordan 195-Peugeot		7 laps behind

Retirements	Nat	Car	Laps	Reason
Martin Brundle	GB	Ligier JS41-Mugen Honda	67	Engine
Mika Salo	SF	Tyrrell 023-Yamaha	58	Throttle
Mark Blundell	GB	McLaren MP4/10B-Mercedes	54	Engine
Ukyo Katayama	J	Tyrrell 023-Yamaha	46	Accident
Massimiliano Papis	I	Footwork FA16-Hart	45	Brakes
Jean Alesi	F	Ferrari 412 T2-Ferrari	42	Engine
Pedro Diniz	BR	Forti FGP 01-Ford ED	32	Engine
Taki Inoue	J	Footwork FA16-Hart	13	Engine fire
Roberto Moreno	BR	Forti FGP 01-Ford ED	8	Broken gearlever
Giovanni Lavaggi	I	Pacific PR02-Ford ED	5	Spin
Mika Häkkinen	SF	McLaren MP4/10B-Mercedes	3	Engine

Fastest lap

Damon Hill	Williams FW17-Renault	lap 34	1m 20.247s (110.615mph)	

Results and Data © FIA 1995

DRIVERS' CHAMPIONSHIP

Michael Schumacher	56
Damon Hill	45
Jean Alesi	32
David Coulthard	29
Johnny Herbert	28
Gerhard Berger	25
Olivier Panis	8
R Barrichello & H-H Frentzen	7
Eddie Irvine	6
M Häkkinen & M Blundell	5
Martin Brundle	3
J-C Boullion	2
G Morbidelli & A Suzuki	1

CONSTRUCTORS' CUP

Benetton-Renault	74
Williams-Renault	68
Ferrari	57
Jordan-Peugeot	13
Ligier-Mugen Honda	12
McLaren-Mercedes	10
Sauber-Ford	9
Footwork-Hart	1

ROUND 11

27 August 1995
Circuit: Spa-Francorchamps

Jean Alesi and Johnny Herbert contest the lead on lap one, with Berger, Häkkinen and Coulthard tucked in behind (above left).

To finish first, first you have to finish, not just to be Finnish. Häkkinen (below) finds out the hard way, on lap two.

Every so often circumstances create a truly exceptional, hard-fought Grand Prix with drama and excitement all the way. Such an event was Belgium 1995, where championship leader Michael Schumacher drove with outstanding brilliance, even by his standards. He showed courage, consummate skill and tactical acumen. It was a race that will be talked about for a long time, although it was sadly marred by controversy at its conclusion.

The magnificent 4.3-mile Spa-Francorchamps circuit stands out like an oasis when compared to the vast majority of bland, modern circuits with their incessant

PIT ENTRY

second-and third-gear corners. Spa comprises roads which, until recently (when a motorway bypass was completed), were used by the public every day. The track sweeps through glorious, pine-clad, hilly Ardennes countryside to form a unique challenge to the drivers and teams and a magnificent sight for the thousands of spectators who gather from all over Europe.

Apart from its configuration, Spa is famous for two things: its weather, and Eau Rouge. Both were to affect the race. Eau Rouge is a fabulous swooping left/right section at the start of the lap which terminates the flat-out drop after the La Source hairpin and precedes the long, 185 mph climb to Les Combes. In 1994 it had been emasculated by a speed-inhibiting chicane for safety reasons, but some felt this actually made it more dangerous than it had been before. For 1995, to everyone's delight, it was back to its former glory with a greatly increased run-off area.

The other Spa characteristic, the weather, was unchanged – totally unpredictable! One minute it is dry and sunny but the next the skies can darken and rain bucket down, only to dry out – or get worse – immediately afterwards. With such a long lap this can pose major tyre choice problems for the teams. Wets or slicks? It was a question they had to resolve for three whole days.

Not that there was any confusion on Friday. It was really wet in the morning and merely wet in the after-

Incorrect. Schumacher (top) takes the non-approved route at Les Combes during the heat of his battle with Hill. It didn't do him any harm in the long run.

Martin Brundle's superb performance almost gave Ligier second place (above). Third wasn't a bad effort, and knocked a few more dollars from team-mate Olivier Panis's once flourishing market value.

The Placido Domingo to replace Herbert rumours had subsided; now the paddock gossips had a brighter notion (right).

noon qualifying session. Gerhard Berger was fastest, Schumacher second, Alesi third: Ferrari looked good, but only 0.3s covered all three drivers.

Saturday was electrifying. It was dry in the morning with David Coulthard fastest and Mika Häkkinen second, in front of Schumacher. But with only two minutes to go Schumacher had a massive off at the 100 mph Malmédy bend. Miraculously, he was unhurt although his car was heavily bruised. Amazingly his mechanics had it rebuilt for the vital afternoon qualifying session, but by the time Michael got out the rain was back and the track was soaked.

Ferrari got it absolutely right, though. Alesi and Berger shot out of the pit lane when Roland Bruynseraede waved his green flag and, unlike the rest, both got in a quick lap as the rain began to fall. Two Ferraris on the front row of the grid for the first time since Monza 1994. But, even more exciting, with Häkkinen third, Herbert fourth, Coulthard fifth and Mark Blundell sixth (two McLarens in the top six), was the fact that Damon Hill and Michael Schumacher were eighth and 16th! It was Michael's lowest F1 grid position ever, and Damon's lowest for Williams.

There was heavy rain again for the half-hour warm-up, with the spectacular Alesi quickest, but by two o'clock it was dry, although overcast. Anticipating a great race, we wondered whether they'd all get round the hairpin at La Source, only yards after the start. So often in the past the race had been marred by multiple collisions there within seconds of the lights but this

time, heavens be praised, there were no problems as Berger squandered the benefit of his pole position by spinning his wheels to let Alesi and Herbert surge past him. At Les Combes Johnny brilliantly outbraked Alesi to take the lead for the first time since Silverstone, but Jean took it back at the same place a lap later.

By then the wild Mika Häkkinen had blotted his copybook by spinning out at La Source. On lap four the ever-unfortunate Jean Alesi was out with broken suspension, and Herbert was back in the lead. Coulthard and Hill had rocketed up to second and third past Berger; Schumacher was already seventh. Then Johnny lost it. With a grimly determined David Coulthard, his F1 prospects unclear, snapping at his rear wing, Herbert spun the nervous Benetton at Les Combes and then again at the Bus Stop chicane. He dropped down to sixth place behind the two Williamses, Berger, Eddie Irvine's Jordan and the fired-up Schumacher. Herbert would not recover any further lost ground.

Driving brilliantly, Coulthard pulled away from Hill as Schumacher unsuccessfully strove to pass an inspired Irvine's Jordan-Peugeot and catch Berger. It took Michael until lap 11 of 44 to get by Eddie, by which time Coulthard was nearly 23s clear of the Benetton and over five ahead of his team-mate Hill. Calmly extending his lead, David set the fastest lap of the race (lap 11, 1m 53.412s, 137.561 mph), but sadly it wasn't to do him much good. On lap 14 he was out with a broken oil-line which neutered his gearbox. It was bitter luck, for he had felt totally in command.

Now Damon led Berger by a comfortable 18s with Schumacher's Benetton almost welded to the Ferrari's gearbox. Then the tyre-stops began. Damon and Gerhard came in on lap 15 and Schumacher took the lead – 16th to first in 16 laps.

With a new set of slicks Hill rejoined second, now ahead of the Ligiers of Olivier Panis and Martin Brundle (from 13th on the grid), Heinz-Harald Frentzen's Sauber and Mark Blundell's McLaren. On lap 19 Damon retook the lead as Schumacher stopped for slicks and then the rain came. This would destroy Hill's race, and make Schumacher's.

On lap 21, with a 14s lead, Damon stopped again for a set of rain tyres whilst Schumacher, gambling all, stayed out on his slicks. Hill was wrong, Schumacher was right...but it could so easily have been the other way round. "It was a bloody difficult decision to make," said Michael. "It was very difficult to drive, even to keep the car on the straight. A couple of times it snapped a bit, but it was my decision to stay out." A courageous decision which elevated him to the lead again, but it was close.

Damon, on rain tyres, was soon up behind the Benetton and, on lap 22, looking for a way past – here, there and everywhere. At Les Combes Schumacher, vigorously protecting his line, almost had Damon off as they banged wheels. And then again at the left-hander which followed. These tactics were to land him in front of the stewards after the race. On lap 24 the persistent Hill finally got past as Schumacher ran wide at Les

Michael Schumacher (above) celebrates having fathomed out the electric window operation of a Renault Espace.

Just as the race looked like it was going to get interesting again, the FIA intervened and thrilled the crowd by giving Damon Hill a 10s stop/go penalty for infringing the pit lane speed limit (right).

Blundell heads Frentzen and Panis; Salo heads for the model shop, up the road in Francorchamps (below).

Combes, but then it began to dry out. Schumacher's brilliant and Senna-like ability to keep up the pace on slick tyres on a wet track now paid off as he outbraked Hill approaching the Bus Stop, took the lead on lap 25, and pulled away. His decision to stay out compounded his advantage when, on lap 26, Hill had to make a third stop to replace his grossly overheated rain tyres with another set of slicks. With 17 laps to go, Damon emerged 31s behind his rival.

All over? By no means! For some inexplicable reason the safety car came out, despite the fact that the track was not unacceptably wet. It soon was, though, as the rain again poured down and Schumacher and Hill stopped, on lap 30, for rain tyres. It was only Michael's second stop, but Damon's fourth.

The rules require the competitors to line up behind the safety car in race order and to stay there until it goes in. Unused to the procedure they did it in a haphazard sort of way, but the important thing (the cynics said) was that there was only one car, Roberto Moreno's Forti, between Schumacher's Benetton and Hill's Williams when the safety car eventually retreated on lap 32.

With 12 laps to go, it should have been terrific. But...the despondent Hill, only 1.5s behind Schumacher, came into the pits for the fifth time to take a 10s penalty for speeding in the pit lane on his previous stop. Rules are rules, but they destroyed the race. By the time Damon emerged from what was effectively more like a 30s penalty (given the time it takes to get in and out), he was down to third place, 25s behind

Schumacher and 13s behind the superb one-stop Martin Brundle. All he could do was try for second. Martin's rain tyres were virtually destroyed on the drying track, and he could do little to resist. Hill caught and passed him on the last lap, but he had put in one of his best ever drives at an ideal time, with a few top seats for 1996 yet to be settled.

So Michael Schumacher brilliantly won his sixth race of the year by 19.5s, following a magnificent drive. One-stop Frentzen finished fourth, only two seconds behind Brundle, after forcing his way past Mark Blundell's unbalanced McLaren with four laps to go. Rubens Barrichello had another impressive drive in his Jordan-Peugeot to finish sixth, despite having to make an extra stop to tighten a loose safety belt.

Afterwards, controversy raged about Schumacher's blocking tactics in those critical laps. Michael was eloquently unrepentant but unsurprisingly Damon Hill and Williams were considerably put out. Damon had forceful words with a cheerfully dismissive Schumacher immediately after he got out of the car, and Williams lodged a protest against Schumacher's driving, though not about the result. Even Hill was unstinting in his praise of Schumacher's achievement. After some three and a half hours of deliberation, and a long interview, the stewards slapped Schumacher's wrist. A one-race ban suspended for four races, which would take him up to the penultimate race at Aida in Japan. A 15-point disadvantage for Hill was going to be dauntingly tough to overcome but, with 50 points still to be won, not impossible.

Benetton-Renault

Schumacher second fastest on Friday, but goes off heavily on Saturday morning at some 100 mph and is very lucky to be unhurt. In rebuilt car, drops to 16th in wet/dry qualifying, unable to attack due to faulty gearbox electronics. From 16th on grid is superb fifth by lap six. Takes five laps to fight past Irvine to fourth but amazingly leads, laps 16-18, after Hill stops for tyres. Stops for slicks, lap 18, and loses lead to Hill. Regains it on wet track when Hill stops again for wets, lap 21. Stays out on slicks, controversially baulking Hill as Damon tries to pass. Loses lead at Les Combes, lap 24, but back in front as track dries. Stops for rain tyres when safety car is out, lap 30, then benefits from 10s penalty given to Hill for pit lane speeding and wins by 19.5s to extend championship lead. Is unrepentant about driving tactics, but given one-race ban (suspended for four races) after a protest by Williams. Herbert into wall during wet Friday morning but, in rebuilt car, is out at right time in wet/dry Saturday session and qualifies fourth. Makes superb start and passes Häkkinen, Alesi and Berger to lead first lap. Second behind Alesi, laps two/three, and back to lead, laps four/five, when Jean retires. Spins twice, lap six, and down to sixth. Stops three times but, defeated by conditions, finishes seventh. Team now 10 points ahead of Williams in constructors' championship.

Tyrrell-Yamaha

Katayama and Salo qualify 15th and 11th. Katayama up to an excellent fourth on slick tyres in the wet on lap 25, but spins out, lap 28, just as race is slowed by safety car. Salo stops twice, laps 14 and 29, and finishes full-distance eighth. Both drivers mystified by timing of safety car appearance.

Williams-Renault

Hill given suspended one-race ban for illegal pit lane entry on Saturday morning. Qualifies eighth after being caught out by weather. Coulthard fastest on Saturday morning but qualifies fifth. Races second behind Herbert, laps four-five, and takes lead on lap six. Driving confidently and strongly, builds 6.7s lead over Damon Hill by lap 13. Has to retire (for fifth time in '95), lap 14, when gearbox fails after he has set fastest lap of race. Hill inherits lead but loses it to Schumacher at lap 15 stop for slicks. Rejoins second and back into lead, lap 19, when Schumacher pits. Stops for rain tyres, lap 21. Catches Schumacher, lap 22, but is repeatedly baulked as he tries to pass. Leads lap 24 but drops back as track dries and makes third stop, lap 26, for slicks. Im 30s behind Schumacher in wet when safety car comes out, lap 28. Fourth stop for rain tyres, lap 30, and benefits from safety car to close right up to Schumacher as race restarts, lap 32. Prospect of great race is destroyed when Damon given 10s penalty for pit lane speeding. Rejoins lap 34, now third, 13s behind Brundle who is on disintegrating rain tyres. Passes Martin on last lap to finish disgruntled second and has words with dismissive Michael. Schumacher given one-race ban, suspended for four races, but both Hill and team see championship gaps increase by four points.

McLaren-Mercedes

Following announcement that Alain Prost is to help with development and testing programme, cars feature new gearbox to accommodate rear suspension geometry changes. Promising results with Häkkinen and Blundell third and sixth on grid. Mika then blows it by spinning out of fourth on lap two. Mark fourth, laps 33-40 after four stops but, in unbalanced car, is unable to resist Frentzen attack on lap 41 and finishes fifth.

Arrows-Hart

First time in F1 at Spa for both Inoue and Papis who qualify 18th and 20th. Inoue takes second finish of season in 12th place, one lap down. Massi spins out in wet on slick tyres, lap 21.

Jordan-Peugeot

Eddie Irvine, not a fan of Spa, starts seventh but Rubens Barrichello is 12th after being out at wrong time on Saturday. Irvine up to fine fourth, laps 6-10, resisting fierce attack by superb Schumacher. Loses place with brake problem, lap 11. Down to ninth after lap 15 stop for slicks. In again lap 21 for rain tyres but fuel spillage ignites spectacularly and Eddie is out. After lap 13 tyre stop Rubens stops again, lap 18, to tighten seat belt. Recovers from 17th to finish sixth.

Pacific-Ford

After financial disagreement about 1994, team successfully blocks attempt to impound cars by Swiss engine tuner Heini Mader. Andrea Montermini and Giovanni Lavaggi qualify 21st and 23rd. Both retire. Andrea out of fuel, lap 20; Giovanni on lap 31, gearbox failure.

Forti-Ford

Roberto Moreno and Pedro Diniz qualify 22nd and 24th, 9.4s and 15.0s off the pace. Both plan one-stop strategy but Moreno has extra stop for rain tyres after fitting slicks just before rain. Roberto further penalised when safety car comes out between him and Diniz, but both finish, two laps down, with Diniz 14th and Moreno 15th.

Minardi-Ford

After qualifying a strong 13th on Friday, Luca Badoer goes off at La Source on Saturday and drops to 19th on grid. Recent F1 returnee Pedro Lamy starts 17th. Badoer runs with Lamy from first lap and is up to 11th behind Pedro, lap 21, before going off immediately after lap 24 tyre stop. Is then fined $10,000 for pit lane speeding as cannot be time-penalised due to retirement. Lamy drives excellent race to finish 10th, thanks to single-stop strategy and well-balanced car with minimum downforce.

Ligier-Mugen Honda

Oliver Panis has huge engine blow-up after only two laps on Saturday morning, but still qualifies ninth, doing better in the unpredictable weather than Martin Brundle, who starts 13th. Both use new-evolution Mugen V10 engine for race. Martin drives superbly to finish third. Using one-stop strategy, is up to fourth behind Olivier, lap 16, and then to third, lap 21, after Panis pits. When Hill cones in for 10s penalty, Martin up to second, lap 34, 13s ahead of Damon. On disintegrating rain tyres is unable to stay ahead, however, and loses place to Hill on last lap, finishing only 1.9s ahead of Frentzen. Panis suffers from weather variations, stopping three times before finishing full-distance ninth. Brundle's fine drive gives Ligier-Mugen Honda its first podium finish and lifts constantly-improving team to fourth in constructors' championship, ahead of Jordan and McLaren.

Ferrari

In great form and reacting perfectly to constantly-changing weather, Ferraris are first and third (Berger/Alesi) in Friday qualifying and then a superb first and second on Saturday (Gerhard's 36th birthday), to give the team a record 114th pole position and a first front row monopoly since Monza 1994. It all comes apart in the race. Berger makes poor start and drops to third, behind Johnny Herbert and Alesi. Jean passes Herbert to take lead on lap two, only to retire from first place on lap four with broken suspension. Gerhard runs distant third behind Coulthard and Hill, laps 6-13, and then second, 18.4s behind Hill, when David retires lap 14. Tyre stops lap 15 but drops to 10th before second stop, lap 21, with electrical problem. Rejoins last after new control unit fitted but problem persists and Gerhard retires, lap 23. No Ferrari in the points for the first time in 1995.

Sauber-Ford

Another excellent result for Heinz-Harald Frentzen, despite car inadequacies. Second fastest in wet Friday morning session but drops to more normal 10th on Saturday afternoon after gearbox trouble. Stops for slicks when sixth on lap 20 but back to pits for rain tyres a lap later when weather deteriorates. Takes gamble on staying out on wets when weather improves and benefits as others lose time switching to slicks. Back in points at sixth on lap 30, catches and passes Johnny Herbert to fifth on lap 33 and Mark Blundell to fourth on lap 41. Finishes full-distance fourth only 1.9s behind Martin Brundle, further to enhance his prospects of getting a top-team drive in 1996. Jean-Christophe Boullion goes off on Saturday morning and resultant work delays qualifying until weather conditions permit. Starts 14th. Comes in for rain tyres on lap 21 only to find unscheduled Frentzen already there so has to wait. Stops again for slicks, lap 25, loses more time behind safety car and finishes 10th, one lap down. Frentzen's one point ties team with McLaren in constructors' championship.

27 AUGUST 1995

Spa-Francorchamps

Les Combes · Kemmel · Malmédy · Eau Rouge · Pouhon · Rivage · La Source · Bus Stop · Blanchimont · Fagnes · Stavelot

Circuit length
4.334 miles/6.975 km

STARTING GRID

ALESI (Ferrari 412 T2) 1m 54.631s	**BERGER** (Ferrari 412 T2) 1m 54.392s
HERBERT (Benetton B195) 1m 56.085s	**HÄKKINEN** (McLaren MP4/10B) 1m 55.435s
BLUNDELL (McLaren MP4/10B) 1m 56.622s	**COULTHARD** (Williams FW17) 1m 56.254s
HILL (Williams FW17) 1m 57.768s	**IRVINE** (Jordan 195) 1m 57.001s
FRENTZEN (Sauber C14) 1m 58.148s	**PANIS** (Ligier JS41) 1m 58.021s
BARRICHELLO (Jordan 195) 1m 58.293s	**SALO** (Tyrrell 023) 1m 58.224s
BOULLION (Sauber C14) 1m 58.356s	**BRUNDLE** (Ligier JS41) 1m 58.314s
SCHUMACHER (Benetton B195) 1m 59.079s	**KATAYAMA** (Tyrrell 023) 1m 58.551s
INOUE (Footwork FA16) 2m 00.990s	**LAMY** (Minardi M195) 1m 59.256s
PAPIS (Footwork FA16) 2m 01.685s	**BADOER** (Minardi M195) 2m 01.013s
MORENO (Forti FGP01) 2m 03.817s	**MONTERMINI** (Pacific PR02) 2m 02.405s
DINIZ (Forti FGP01) 2m 09.537s	**LAVAGGI** (Pacific PR02) 2m 06.407s

RACE CLASSIFICATION

Pos	Driver	Nat	Car	Laps	Time
1	Michael Schumacher	D	Benetton B195-Renault	44	1h 36m 47.875s
2	Damon Hill	GB	Williams BW17-Renault	44	1h 37m 07.368s
3	Martin Brundle	GB	Ligier JS41-Mugen Honda	44	1h 37m 12.873s
4	Heinz-Harald Frentzen	D	Sauber C14-Ford Zetec-R	44	1h 37m 14.847s
5	Mark Blundell	GB	McLaren MP4/10B-Mercedes	44	1h 37m 21.647s
6	Rubens Barrichello	BR	Jordan 195-Peugeot	44	1h 37m 27.549s
7	Johnny Herbert	GB	Benetton B195-Renault	44	1h 37m 41.923s
8	Mika Salo	SF	Tyrrell 023-Yamaha	44	1h 37m 42.423s
9	Olivier Panis	F	Ligier JS41-Mugen Honda	44	1h 37m 54.045s
10	Pedro Lamy	P	Minardi M195-Ford ED	44	1h 38m 07.664s
11	J-C Boullion	F	Sauber C14-Ford Zetec-R		1 lap behind
12	Taki Inoue	J	Footwork FA16-Hart		1 lap behind
13	Pedro Diniz	BR	Forti FGP 01-Ford ED		2 laps behind
14	Roberto Moreno	BR	Forti FGP 01-Ford ED		2 laps behind

Retirements	Nat	Car	Laps	Reason
Ukyo Katayama	J	Tyrrell 023-Yamaha	28	Spin
Giovanni Lavaggi	I	Pacific PR02-Ford ED	27	Gearbox
Luca Badoer	I	Minardi M195-Ford ED	23	Accident
Gerhard Berger	A	Ferrari 412 T2-Ferrari	22	Electrics
Eddie Irvine	GB	Jordan 195-Peugeot	21	Refuelling fire
Massimiliano Papis	I	Footwork FA16-Hart	20	Spin
Andrea Montermini	I	Pacific PR02-Ford ED	18	Out of fuel
David Coulthard	GB	Williams FW17-Renault	13	Gearbox
Jean Alesi	F	Ferrari 412 T2-Ferrari	4	Suspension
Mika Häkkinen	SF	McLaren MP4/10B-Mercedes	1	Spin

Fastest lap				
David Coulthard	Williams FW17-Renault	lap 11	1m 53.412s (137.561mph)	

DRIVERS' CHAMPIONSHIP

Michael Schumacher	66
Damon Hill	51
Jean Alesi	32
David Coulthard	29
Johnny Herbert	28
Gerhard Berger	25
H-H Frentzen	10
O Panis & R Barrichello	8
M Blundell & M Brundle	7
Eddie Irvine	6
Mika Häkkinen	5
J-C Boullion	2
G Morbidelli & A Suzuki	1

CONSTRUCTORS' CUP

Benetton-Renault	84
Williams-Renault	74
Ferrari	57
Ligier-Mugen Honda	16
Jordan-Peugeot	14
McLaren-Mercedes & Sauber-Ford	12
Footwork-Hart	1

Italy

10 September 1995
Circuit: Monza

If someone used the 1995 Italian Grand Prix as the basis for a film script it would be rejected as ludicrously contrived. Act one, the young star, grimly determined after being rejected by his team, takes brilliant pole position, goes off on parade lap but is able to race thanks to restart triggered by multiple pile-up. Looking certain to win for first time, spins out through no fault of his own.

Act two,the tremendously popular veteran, in last Monza drive for charismatic local team, takes over the lead, pursued by the two World Championship rivals, who collide and spin off. Veteran star now closely followed by team-mate, another darling of the crowd, and also having his last Monza drive, who takes lead after pit stop.

Act three, the two heroes are on target for storybook one-two in front of wildly cheering crowd...but camera breaks loose from lead car and takes out the respected veteran, who could have been killed. Darling of crowd races on alone for emotional victory only to retire with eight laps to go. Cries in arms of team manager.

Act four, team-mate of world champion, who had retired in act two, who has fiercely criticised his German sidekick and his team after being fired, comes through to win. All top six finishers are a refreshing surprise, but Britain's championship contender given suspended one-race ban after rival's team protests his driving.

Chaotic, but true. So now let's put some names to this unlikely situation. If anything like this was going to happen it would be at Monza, the world's most historic and dramatic Grand Prix circuit. Situated in a heavily-wooded park on the outskirts of Milan, it has been the scene of almost every Italian GP since 1922. It was a slightly different, but safer, Monza this year after the removal of some one hundred trees (to the understandable fury of the local Green Party, although for every tree removed five more were to be planted) in order greatly to increase run-off areas at the main corners. Monza is the spiritual home of the fanatical Ferrari-loving Tifosi, whose passionate excitement was heightened by the facts that their heroes Gerhard Berger and Jean Alesi would be representing them in Italy for the last time and that world champion Michael Schumacher would be joining Ferrari in 1996. Firstly, though, Schumacher and his British rival Damon Hill were again fighting for the World Championship.

Lots of drivers who had jobs lined up for 1996 failed to finish. Johnny Herbert, who hadn't, did. And he scored his second win of the year, to boot (top).

An Alesi/Ferrari (left) win appeared to be on the cards for the second year in succession at Monza. Incorrect...

Rumour had it that David Coulthard might sign for Ferrari (above). The Scot did his best to satisfy the locals, just in case...

David Coulthard was the young star who brilliantly took pole position, and convincingly so. Fastest on Friday and faster still on Saturday – a very impressive 0.6s quicker than Michael Schumacher, who was followed on the grid by Berger, Hill, Alesi and Jordan's Rubens Barrichello. With a seat to win for 1996 after being dropped by Williams, and there was a vacancy at Ferrari, David had a point to prove.

But he certainly didn't enhance his reputation when he spun his Williams on the parade lap to the grid! "Oil on the track," said David as a delighted Michael Schumacher shot off from what was now effectively pole position. On lap two he lost his lead to a forceful Gerhard Berger, but on that same lap the red flag went out to stop the race after a multiple pile-up at the Ascari bends, triggered by the spinning Arrows of Massi Papis. Which was David Coulthard's reprieve.

Since the race had run less than two laps, he was able to restart from pole position in Damon Hill's reset spare car. Not ideal, but a lot better than being out. This time David got it right by rocketing away and steadily building a lead over Berger, who had again passed Schumacher. Then came Hill, Alesi and Johnny Herbert, who was soon demoted by Rubens Barrichello and Mika Häkkinen's further improved McLaren-Mercedes.

But it was the battle for the lead which got people's attention. As Coulthard steadily drew away, only three seconds covered Berger, Schumacher, Hill and Alesi. It was great to watch as the two Ferraris, the Benetton and the Williams matched each other rev for rev. By lap 12 of 53, Coulthard had built a lead of nearly three seconds without putting a wheel wrong. At last, in his 20th Grand Prix, it looked as though he was going to achieve a well-deserved first victory.

Wrong! Out went the young Scot as, on lap 14, his Williams spun across the Roggia chicane's gravel trap. David surprisingly managed to struggle out of the loose

Having passed the audition for Saturday Night Fever, Heinz-Harald Frentzen (above) went on to finish third.

Every time you looked up, there was a Minardi going off somewhere. Lamy takes his turn (top).

Back on course? Häkkinen's second place gave McLaren a welcome fillip (right).

gravel (which isn't supposed to be possible) and got back to the pits, but his race was over. A failed wheel bearing was diagnosed.

So now a Ferrari was in the lead – Gerhard Berger's. The Tifosi erupted. It was to get even better for them when, on lap 24, Schumacher and Hill again collided as they lapped Taki Inoue's wandering Arrows at the Roggia. As usual the blame, if blame there was, was difficult to apportion. Schumacher, the man in front, blamed Hill. Hill blamed Inoue for being "all over the track", but was also puzzled by the fact that Schumacher was "suddenly going at nought miles per hour". Unsurprisingly their viewpoints didn't match, but whoever was to blame (and the stewards subsequently gave Hill a suspended one-race ban after Benetton had protested his driving), the rivals were both out, with Hill still 15 championship points behind Schumacher and only five races to go.

Ferraris were first and second!

So was this going to be a longed-for Ferrari one-two, as in 1988? It certainly seemed like it for both the 412 T2s looked and sounded fine. When the one-stop leaders (only the Tyrrell team stopped twice) had completed their refuelling and tyre changing on lap 30, the positions of the two scarlet Maranello cars had been reversed, thanks to Alesi making a quicker stop (lap 25) than Berger. This overcame the fact that Gerhard had set the fastest lap of the race on lap 24 (1m 26.419s, 149.361mph). They were followed by a new third-placed combination – Johnny Herbert and his Benetton. Johnny and his team had decided on a late-stop strategy and their plan had paid off, for now he was ahead of Häkkinen's McLaren, Barrichello's Jordan and the excellent Heinz-Harald Frentzen's Sauber, which was to make a lot more progress before the race ended.

For three more glorious laps the two Ferraris raced at the front, nose-to-tail, with no team orders as team manager Jean Todt said that Ferrari's points position did not merit such intervention. "I was very upset to lose the lead at the stop," said Berger, "but then I said, 'OK let's fight'. I was pushing but not overdoing it. I knew the last five laps would be the most important

ones so I was waiting for them. I know Monza – there are always some strange things in the last few laps."

But a strange, and potentially horrific, thing was to happen to Gerhard long before then. On lap 33, racing at some 180mph, he saw the rear wing-mounted camera on Alesi's car, right in front of him, detach itself and fly through the air towards him. Unable to swerve, he could do nothing. Fortunately it smashed into his left front suspension; if it had hit Gerhard's head it would have killed him.

Now he was out of the race which had meant so much to him, leaving Jean Alesi to carry the torch for Ferrari. Which he did with honour. For another 13 laps he led the field from Johnny Herbert and Mika Häkkinen, and although Herbert closed the gap to seven seconds, Jean looked in no real danger of losing his second Grand Prix win. Then, in this amazing race, out went Alesi with, like Coulthard, a wheel bearing failure. "For over three years we have had no problems with them," wails Jean Todt. The Tifosi started leaving, though there was joy for Johnny Herbert, who now led. With a 17s lead over Häkkinen, he could concentrate on finishing. Which is exactly what he did, to win his second GP in five races and cock a metaphorical snook at the team which had dropped him. An inherited victory, true, but to win you have to finish.

It was a very different looking top six, after a day which had been filled with drama from the start of the parade lap to the end. A great race for McLaren-Mercedes with Mika Häkkinen second and Mark Blundell fourth. Even better for Sauber-Ford, for whom Heinz-Harald Frentzen took his and the team's first-ever podium position with a fine third place, only 6.5s behind Häkkinen, and for whom Jean-Christophe Boullion finished sixth. It was a good day for Tyrrell, too, Mika Salo scoring his first-ever points in fifth place. That also gave his team its first points of the season.

It's an unpredictable life in Formula One. "Today should help me get something else for next year," said Herbert.

He certainly deserved it.

Benetton-Renault

Schumacher goes off at Lesmo Two on Friday and has problems setting up car before qualifying second on Saturday. "I have never pushed so hard," says Michael, who is passed by inspired Berger at start and runs third until Coulthard spins out of race. Battles for second with Damon Hill, nearly three seconds behind Gerhard, until lap 24 when controversial collision after passing Taki Inoue's Arrows removes both drivers. But then, as at Silverstone, Johnny Herbert comes good after starting eighth. Up to sixth, laps one and two, but passed by Barrichello and Häkkinen. After retirements of Coulthard, Hill, Schumacher and Barrichello, and with late one-stop strategy which takes him past Häkkinen, Johnny is third behind Alesi and Berger on lap 30. To second after Berger retires, lap 33, and into lead, lap 46, when Alesi out. Increases lead over Häkkinen to 18s and wins second GP. Moves up to third in drivers' championship. Benetton, now 20 points ahead of Williams in constructors' contest, protest Hill's driving as a result of which Damon receives one-race suspended ban. Uneasy atmosphere after pre-race criticism by Herbert.

Tyrrell-Yamaha

New electronic throttle, further suspension mods and revised aerodynamics, but both drivers complain of lack of grip. Salo starts 16th, Katayama 17th. Tyrrell only team to adopt two-stop strategy. Mika spins down to last in first lap confrontation with Panis, but recovers to finish fifth (one lap down) and score his first World Championship points (and team's first of 1995), despite losing time with sticking fuel nozzle at first stop. Katayama to pits after engine stops (lap 29, sensor problem) and has to wait as Salo is already there. Rejoins last but classified 10th, six laps down. First time all season that team has got both cars to flag.

Williams-Renault

A gloomy Monza. No points. A totally-focused, fully fit David Coulthard drives brilliantly to top times in both qualifying sessions and take second career pole position. Amazingly spins out at Ascari bends on parade lap, but is reprieved by lap two race stoppage which permits restart from pole position in Damon Hill's spare car. Settles down rapidly in strange car and builds 3s lead over Berger, only to spin off and retire, lap 14, when front wheel bearing fails. Hill starts less than happy fourth after late start in Saturday qualifying (engine change). Battles for second with Schumacher, but hits the Benetton at Roggia chicane, lap 24, as he and Michael lap wandering Inoue. Benetton protests Hill's driving; Damon gets one-race suspended ban, to outrage of Schumacher, who is under suspended four-race ban for his vigorous driving against Hill in Belgium. Hill blames Inoue. Schumacher blames Hill. Whatever, Damon now has only five races to overcome 15-point deficit.

McLaren-Mercedes

A heartening Monza. Häkkinen goes off in both Friday sessions (steering breakage in afternoon) before qualifying seventh, two places ahead of Blundell, who has to give car to Mika at end of Saturday session. Mika leads on lap 27 during fuelling stops. Down to third behind Alesi and Herbert, laps 33-45, but to second when Alesi retires. Finishes contented second, delighted with reliability of car. Blundell drives fine race, too, finishing fourth. McLaren lifted to fourth in constructors' championship.

Arrows-Hart

Papis 15th on grid despite gearbox selection and software problems. Inoue 20th after several offs. After triggering multi-car pile-up by spinning at Ascari bends following first start, Massi drives sound race on home track, nearly scoring his first point. Sixth with seven laps to go, but passed by Boullion on last lap but one. Finishes seventh, one lap down. Inoue blamed by Hill for incompetence which, in Damon's view, caused him to collide with Schumacher. Taki nevertheless soldiers on to finish eighth, only one lap down. Hart engine performs outstandingly well at Monza.

Jordan-Peugeot

With revised differential, set-up, exhaust system and aerodynamics, Rubens Barrichello qualifies fine sixth, 1.46s off Berger and six places ahead of Irvine, who has a brake problem on Saturday. But another

heart-breaking race. With 13laps to go Rubens and Eddie are fourth and sixth (Rubens having led on lap 26 during fuel stops). But...Irvine out on lap 41 (oil pressure), Rubens on lap 44 (brakes, steering, hydraulics and exploded clutch!). Team still to achieve reliability.

Pacific-Ford

Montermini starts 21st, but hits Papis's car in lap two Ascari bends pile-up and is out. In last race, Giovanni Lavaggi qualifies 24th but spins out, lap six.

Forti-Ford

Moreno and Diniz start 22nd and 23rd. Diniz spins into gravel trap during lap one Ascari fracas and breaks driveshaft. Takes spare and finishes ninth, three laps down. Moreno hits Papis in Ascari pile-up and, with no spare, is out.

Minardi-Ford

An eventful race. Badoer rolls car heavily at Ascari bends on Saturday; Lamy also goes off. Luca 18th on grid, Pedro 19th. In rebuilt cars, Lamy has differential seize on first lap whilst Badoer again goes off when 13th, lap 27.

Ligier-Mugen Honda

Driving Ligier with electronic throttle and low-downforce set-up for first time, Martin Brundle happy with 13th on grid, but unimpressed at being harpooned by Andrea Montermini's Pacific at the end of Sunday warm-up. Gets away well in rebuilt car and runs 10th behind Irvine, laps 2-8. Grapples with handling imbalance which turns out to be slow puncture. Tours in on three wheels as flailing tyre destroys bodywork. Retires and is given reprimand by stewards for leaving debris on track. Olivier Panis goes off in both Friday sessions and on Saturday morning before qualifying 13th. Spins and beaches car on kerb at Goodyear chicane when 11th, lap 21.

Ferrari

Emotional last GP in Italy for current Ferrari drivers. Team brings four cars to Monza, together with two evolutions of V12 engine after four-day test at the track. Weekend starts well with Berger and Alesi second and fifth on Friday, despite brake problem for Gerhard and loss of power for Jean. No better for Alesi on Saturday, still fifth on grid with inconsistent engine; worse for Berger, who drops to third after only seven laps due to electrical problem. After Coulthard goes off on parade lap, Berger passes Schumacher to lead before race stoppage. Runs second to Coulthard after restart and leads, lap 14, after David retires. Alesi up to second after Schumacher/Hill collision lap 24, and takes lead from Berger with faster stop on lap 25. Alesi/Berger now first and second for Ferrari, laps 30-32, to euphoric joy of Tifosi. Gerhard out, lap 33, when camera from Alesi's car comes off and smashes his left-front suspension. It could have been worse...Then, as in 1994, distraught Alesi retires from lead when rear wheel bearing fails with only eight laps to go. "In all my long professional career I have never known such bitter disappointment," says team manager Jean Todt.

Sauber-Ford

After a three-day test at Monza, Sauber well pleased with results. Heinz-Harald Frentzen re-signs for 1996 before qualifying 10th with higher-revving version of Ford Zetec V8. Drops to 12th after poor start and fights with Mark Blundell until lap 25 tyre/refuelling stop. Passes Mark to take seventh, lap 27, and gets by Irvine two laps later. Gains further places from Berger, Barrichello and Alesi retirements to finish well- deserved third, 6.5s behind Häkkinen. First-ever podium finish for team and driver. Jean-Christophe Boullion goes off in Friday qualifying when throttle sticks open. Qualifies 14th on Saturday and takes second start from pit lane after being involved in lap two pile-up. Drives cautious race and does very well to pass Massi Papis's Arrows to take sixth place, one lap down.

ITALY
10 SEPTEMBER 1995

Monza

Curva di Lesmo · Curva del Serraglio · Seconda Variante · Variante Ascari · Curva Grande · Parabolica · Variante Goodyear

Circuit length
3.604 miles/5.799 km

STARTING GRID

COULTHARD (Williams FW17) 1m 24.462s	**SCHUMACHER** (Benetton B195) 1m 25.026s
BERGER (Ferrari 412) 1m 25.353s	**HILL** (Williams FW17) 1m 25.699s
ALESI (FERRARI 412) 1m 25.707d	**BARRICHELLO** (Jordan 195) 1m 25.919s
HÄKKINEN (McLaren MP4) 1m 25.902s	**HERBERT** (Benetton B195) 1m 26.433s
BLUNDELL (McLaren MP4) 1m 26.472s	**FRENTZEN** (Sauber C14) 1m 26.541s
BRUNDLE (Ligier JS41) 1m 27.067s	**IRVINE** (Jordan 195) 1m 27.271s
PANIS (Ligier JS41) 1m 28.870s	**BOULLION** (Sauber C14) 1m 28.741s
PAPIS (Footwork FA16) 1m 28.870s	**SALO** (Tyrrell 023) 1m 29.028s
KATAYAMA (Tyrrell 023) 1m 29.287s	**BADOER** (Minardi M195) 1m 29.559s
LAMY (Minardi M195) 1m 29.936s	**INOUE** (Footwork FA16) 1m 30.515s
MONTERMINI (Pacific PR02) 1m 30.721s	**MORENO** (Forti FGP01) 1m 30.834s
DINIZ (Forti FGP01) 1m 32.102s	**LAVAGGI** (Pacific PR02) 1.32.470s

RACE CLASSIFICATION

Pos	Driver	Nat	Car	Laps	Time
1	Johnny Herbert	GB	Benetton B195-Renault	55	1h 18m 27.916s
2	Mika Häkkinen	SF	McLaren MP4/10B-Mercedes	55	1h 18m 45.695s
3	Heinz-Harald Frentzen	D	Sauber C14-Ford Zetec-R	55	1h 18m 52.237s
4	Mark Blundell	GB	McLaren MP4/10B-Mercedes	55	1h 18m 56.139s
5	Mika Salo	SF	Tyrrell 023-Yamaha		1 lap behind
6	J-C Boullion	F	Sauber C14-Ford Zetec-R		1 lap behind
7	Massimiliano Papis	I	Footwork FA16-Hart		1 lap behind
8	Taki Inoue	J	Footwork FA16-Hart		1 lap behind
9	Pedro Diniz	BR	Forti FGP 01-Ford ED		3 laps behind
10	Ukyo Katayama	J	Tyrrell 023-Yamaha		6 laps behind

Retirements	Nat	Car	Laps	Reason
Jean Alesi	F	Ferrari 412 T2- Ferrari	45	Wheel bearing
Rubens Barrichello	BR	Jordan 195-Peugeot	43	Hydraulics
Eddie Irvine	GB	Jordan 195-Peugeot	40	Engine
Gerhard Berger	A	Ferrari 412 T2-Ferrari	32	Suspension
Luca Badoer	I	Minardi M195-Ford ED	26	Accident
Michael Schumacher	D	Benetton B195-Renault	23	Accident
Damon Hill	GB	Williams FW17-Renault	23	Accident
Olivier Panis	F	Ligier JS41-Mugen Honda	20	Spin
David Coulthard	GB	Williams FW17-Renault	13	Wheel bearing
Martin Brundle	GB	Ligier JS41-Mugen Honda	10	Puncture
Giovanni Lavaggi	I	Pacific PR02-Ford ED	6	Spin
Pedro Lamy	P	Minardi M195-Ford ED	0	Differential
Andrea Montermini	I	Pacifid PR02-Ford ED		Did not take restart
Roberto Moreno	BR	Forti FGP 01-Ford ED		Did not take restart

Fastest lap

Gerhard Berger	Ferrari 412 T2-Ferrari	lap 24	1m 26.419s (149.361mph)

Results and Data © FIA 1995

DRIVERS' CHAMPIONSHIP

Michael Schumacher	66
Damon Hill	51
Johnny Herbert	38
Jean Alesi	32
David Coulthard	29
Gerhard Berger	25
H-H Frentzen	14
Mika Häkkinen	11
Mark Blundell	10
R Barrichello & O Panis	8
Martin Brundle	7
Eddie Irvine	6
J-C Boullion	3
Mika Salo	2
G Morbidelli & A Suzuki	1

CONSTRUCTORS' CUP

Benetton-Renault	94
Williams-Renault	74
Ferrari	57
McLaren-Mercedes	21
Sauber-Ford	17
Ligier-Mugen Honda	16
Jordon-Peugeot	14
Tyrrell-Yamaha	2
Footwork-Hart	1

24 September 1995
Circuit: Estoril

Portugal

"It's great. You spend all year qualifying eighth, and you might pick up a couple of wins if you're lucky." Johnny Herbert paints his view of Benetton life to 1996 Enstone recruits Berger and Alesi (above).

Pole position, fastest lap, a dominant victory...and Williams let him go. Coulthard (above left) finally secures his first F1 victory, after a faultless performance.

He's good at that too...Mr and Mrs Schumacher Jnr play Mr and Mrs Schumacher Snr at table football (left). In the tournament proper, the world champion was knocked out at the semi-final stage. By his dad...

And so to Portugal for the first of two races, 1500 miles apart, on successive weekends – a tough schedule. The 2.71-mile circuit near Estoril, at practically the most westerly point of mainland Europe, is well worth the trip. It has some dauntingly fast bends, a pleasant change from the usual diet of second and third gear corners, a 185 mph straight and some gradient. The drivers like it, if you exclude the 30mph chicane which was introduced in 1994 for safety reasons, but tyres do not. It is very hard on the Goodyears.

Portugal was going to be another crucial race for Damon Hill, who was 15 points behind Michael Schumacher in the championship. With five races to go and 50 points to be won it was by no means an impossible challenge, but Damon needed at least to finish ahead of Michael to reduce the gap. On the face of it, it looked as though he would be the stronger at Estoril. Not only had he won there in 1994, but both he and his team-mate David Coulthard had a much-revised Williams-Renault to drive. A new rear suspension allied to a new gearbox had produced some impressive testing times at Silverstone.

The Benettons, meanwhile, had a new front

suspension, while the two McLaren-Mercedes were practically all-new after their lack of success thus far. New front and rear suspension, new gearbox and new aerodynamics – but they'd gone backwards not forwards. Mark Blundell was 12th on the grid and his forceful team leader Mika Häkkinen was a totally dispirited 13th.

The two qualifying sessions had belonged to Williams all the way. Hill was fastest on Friday, a mere 0.1s quicker than Coulthard, with Schumacher third. On Saturday, however, the Scot lapped nearly 0.4s faster than Hill and nearly a full second quicker than Schumacher to take his second successive pole position. That meant it was the third all-Williams front row of the season, with a concerned Schumacher third ahead of Gerhard Berger's Ferrari – and Heinz-Harald Frentzen's Sauber! The Swiss team had been testing at Mugello and seemed to have found a few solutions.

Neither McLaren nor Williams were to race the cars they'd qualified. Working all Saturday night, McLaren rebuilt its disappointing MP4/10C as an MP4/10B for Häkkinen and a hybrid 10B/C for Blundell. Williams decided to play safe with its well-tried and successful FW17 rear end. The team wasn't to regret it.

There was very nearly a disaster at the start. From row eight of the grid, Ukyo Katayama tangled with Luca Badoer's Minardi. In a flash, at well over 100 mph, Ukyo's Tyrrell flew into the air, barrel-rolled and crashed to the ground minus wheels and suspension. The race was immediately stopped so that the Japanese could be taken to hospital where, miraculously, he was found to have nothing worse than a very stiff neck.

The grid reformed only for Heinz-Harald Frentzen, who had been nerfed off the track at the first start, to stall his car on the parade lap. He would now have to start from the back.

Coulthard had led the first start and made no mistake second time around. However, this time Hill was out-

As Inoue trundles towards the first corner, the mangled remains of Katayama's inverted Tyrrell lie between the distorted Pacific of Montermini and Badoer's stranded Minardi. The race was stopped, and the Japanese driver was lucky to be extracted without serious injury (top).

We had rolling Tyrrells on the grid, Rolling Stones in the pits (above). Jerry Hall looks on as Mick Jagger offers Frank Williams odds that the Stones will still be going in the year 2095.

With that bloke who sometimes wears a kilt disappearing from view, Schumacher holds off Hill, Berger, Herbert, Alesi and just about everybody else in the opening stages (right).

dragged by Schumacher who was up to second before the first corner. With his championship rival ahead of him on a track where passing was more than difficult, Hill's plight was now almost as bad as Frentzen's.

Coulthard's second lap was the fastest of the race (1m 23.220s, 117.26 mph), and by then Frentzen was already up to 14th having passed nine of his rivals. David drew away to a 6s lead by lap 18, but Hill could do nothing about Schumacher as the three of them raced away from Berger, Herbert and Alesi. As ever, pit strategies were going to be vital and now Williams and Hill decided to alter their original intentions. With Damon stuck behind Schumacher and three stops planned, they decided to stop twice in the hope that one fewer stop would enable him to get past and stay ahead.

On lap 18 Schumacher and Hill came in together, but Damon lost two places to Alesi and Herbert due to his longer stop. Coulthard came in on lap 19 and rejoined still first, 4.5s ahead of Schumacher. And by now Frentzen was up to ninth, behind Mika Häkkinen's McLaren. On lap 26 he passed Mika, and his next target was Martin Brundle, going very well in his Ligier.

Berger and Alesi were on different strategies: three stops for Gerhard, two for Jean. On lap 34, the Ferraris were nose to tail, with Berger looking for a way past but Alesi refusing to yield. In the end, Berger got by when Jean made his second stop but he had lost a lot of time.

As cars poured in and out of the pits, with most of then stopping three times, Hill's modified strategy appeared to be paying off. He ascended to second when Schumacher stopped again and then into the lead, on lap 39, as Coulthard made his second stop. There were 33 laps still to go though. How would the tyre-wear versus time-saved equation work out after Hill had come in again?

On lap 44, Häkkinen retired. Mighty McLaren had fallen even further. Simultaneously, Hill made his final stop. Coulthard retook the lead and Schumacher moved back to second, but he was seemingly unable to do anything about closing the gap. Their third stops would decide the issue and show, too, whether or not Hill's bold gamble was going to pay off.

Lap 54 was the one which saw the leaders pit for the last time. Coulthard rejoined still in the lead as Hill passed Schumacher, stationary in the pits. He was up to second, but only 3s ahead of the Benetton with 16 laps still to go. Would Damon, on worn rubber, be able to stay ahead of the freshly-shod Schumacher?

No, he would not. On lap 62 Michael squeezed by at the new chicane. Damon's gamble had failed.

At the end of an intriguing race Scotland's David Coulthard at last took a well deserved first Grand Prix win – and highly popular it was too. Six points for Schumacher extended his championship lead to 17 points with only four races to go, but with Berger fourth, half a second ahead of the smouldering Alesi, the man of the race for me had been Heinz-Harald Frentzen. He finished sixth after starting last in a race which had only seen five retirements, and on a track where passing is difficult.

The next race, the Grand Prix of Europe at the Nürburgring, was close to his home and to Schumacher's. Germany would be agog for its heroes in only seven days – assuming everybody got there in time!

PORTUGUESE GRAND PRIX – TEAM ANALYSIS

Benetton-Renault

Schumacher qualifies third with Herbert sixth. Both follow three- stop strategy. Michael passes Hill at second start but cannot get by Coulthard. Passed by Damon at third stop but catches and passes Hill on lap 62 to finish second and increase championship lead to 17 points. Herbert reaches fourth during pit stops but finishes seventh, one lap down.

Tyrrell-Yamaha

Both drivers unhappy with balance and grip. Salo 15th on grid, Katayama 16th. Ukyo collides with Badoer at start and is taken to hospital after the race is consequently stopped. Happily, no lasting damage. Salo stops twice before finishing 13th, two laps down, after suffering from lack of grip.

Williams-Renault

New rear suspension and gearbox help Coulthard and Hill occupy front row with David on pole. Back to standard FW17 spec for race. Coulthard dominates brilliantly to win first GP and set fastest lap. Hill loses second to Schumacher at start and cannot pass Michael. Switches to two-stop strategy which enables him to run second to David, laps 55-61, but on worn tyres and with gearbox problem has to yield to Schumacher and finishes third, another two points behind in the championship. A total of 14 points for William lifts team to within 12 of Benetton in constructors' championship.

McLaren-Mercedes

Virtually new car with different front and rear suspension, gearbox and aerodynamics proves to be a crushing disappointment with Blundell and Häkkinen 12th and 13th on grid. Saturday all-nighter returns Mika's car to MP4/10B and Mark's to hybrid B/C spec. Häkkinen third fastest in warm-up but retires from eighth, lap 45 (engine). Blundell finishes unhappy ninth, one lap down, suffering from wrenched back. Worried team stays on to test for two days prior to long journey to the Nürburgring.

Arrows-Hart

After qualifying 20th, Papis breaks gearbox at first start. There is insufficient time to reset spare car, so he has to sit race out. Inoue starts 19th and finishes reliable 15th, three laps down.

Jordan-Peugeot

With much-needed reliability, both cars finish after Barrichello and Irvine start eighth and 10th on grid. Rubens has to stop three times due to tyre wear but finishes 11th, one lap down. Two-stop Irvine takes 10th, also a lap down. "We didn't get it right," says Eddie Jordan.

Pacific-Ford

Swiss rent-a-driver Jean-Denis Deletraz replaces Giovanni Lavaggi and qualifies 24th, 12s slower than pole. Retires with cramp, lap 15. Andrea Montermini starts 21st, suffers car damage from Katayama/Badoer collision and restarts from pit lane. Climbs to 16th before 10s penalty for pit lane speeding. Retires from 16th, lap 54 (gearbox).

Forti-Ford

Pedro Diniz and Roberto Moreno qualify 22nd and 23rd. Both involved with Katayama/Badoer first-start collision and Roberto has to restart in spare car. Both handicapped by transmission problems but finish 16th (Diniz, five laps down) and 17th (Moreno, seven laps adrift).

Minardi-Ford

For his home GP Pedro Lamy qualifies 17th, but unhappily retires from 16th with gearbox hydraulic pressure problem on only lap seven. From 18th on grid Luca Badoer hit by swerving Katayama and has to start from pit lane in spare car set up for Lamy. Finishes 14th, three laps down.

Ligier-Mugen Honda

Disappointed ninth on grid for Brundle. Panis 11th. Martin further disappointed with eighth place, one lap down, after setting fourth fastest lap. But Olivier penalised (again!) for jumping start. Spins out on dirty tyres after receiving penalty, lap 11.

Ferrari

Berger satisfied with fourth on grid but fed-up Alesi starts seventh. Gerhard opts for three-stop strategy, Jean goes for two. Neither can match Schumacher and the two Williams drivers, but race each other for fourth place from lap 37 with Berger, on superior strategy, trying to get past Alesi. Despite repeated radio instructions from Jean Todt, Alesi refuses to move over but is passed by Gerhard at Jean's second stop. Their race resumes and Gerhard finishes a full-distance fourth, 0.5s ahead of a furious Jean, who says: "I may not finish the season with Ferrari." No one believes him.

Sauber-Ford

A superb performance by Heinz-Harald Frentzen, benefiting from the results of post-Monza testing at Mugello. Further enhances reputation in both qualifying and the race. After being in about his usual place (11th) on Friday, H-H improves to a best-yet fifth (for team and himself) on Saturday. As result of this switches from usual one-stop strategy to two. Is punted off at first start and then has to take second start from back of grid after stalling an parade lap. Charges superbly past Blundell, Häkkinen and Irvine to seventh on lap 37 and finishes a lapped but delighted sixth on a hard-to-pass track where there were only five retirements. J-C Boullion starts 14th and finishes 12th, one lap down.

RACE 13 PORTUGAL

24 SEPTEMBER 1995

PORTUGAL RESULTS AND STATISTICS

Estoril

Circuit length
2.709 miles/4.359 km

STARTING GRID

COULTHARD (Williams FW17) 1m 20.537s	**HILL** (Williams FW17) 1m 20.905s
SCHUMACHER (Benetton B195) 1m 21.301s	**BERGER** (Ferrari 412) 1m 21.970s
FRENTZEN (SAUBER C14) 1m 22.226s	**HERBERT** (Benetton B195) 1m 22.322s
ALESI (Ferrari 412) 1m 22.391s	**BARRICHELLO** (Jordan 195) 1m 22.538s
BRUNDLE (Ligier JS41) 1m 22.588s	**IRVINE** (Jordan 195) 1m 22.831s
PANIS (Ligier JS41) 1m 22.904s	**BLUNDELL** (McLaren MP4) 1m 22.914s
HÄKKINEN (McLaren MP4) 1m 23.064s	**BOULLION** (Sauber C14) 1m 23.934s
SALO (Tyrrell 023) 1m 23.936s	**KATAYAMA** (Tyrrell 023) 1m 24.287s
LAMY (Minardi M195) 1m 24.657s	**BADOER** (Minardi M195) 1m 24.788s
INOUE (Footwork FA16) 1m 24.883s	**PAPIS** (Footwork FA16) 1m 25.287s)
MONTERMINI (Pacific PR02) 1m 26.172s	**DINIZ** (Forti FGP) 1m 27.292s
MORENO (Forti FGP) 1m 27.523s	**DELETRAZ** (Pacific PRO2) 1m 32.769s

RACE CLASSIFICATION

Pos	Driver	Nat	Car	Laps	Time
1	David Coulthard	GB	Williams FW17-Renault	71	1h 41m 52.145s
2	Michael Schumacher	D	Benetton B195-Renault	71	1h 41m 59.393s
3	Damon Hill	GB	Williams FW17-Renault	71	1h 42m 14.266s
4	Gerhard Berger	A	Ferrari 412 T2-Ferrari	71	1h 43m 17.024s
5	Jean Alesi	F	Ferrari 412 T2-Ferrari	71	1h 43m 17.574s
6	Heinz Harald Frentzen	D	Sauber C14-Ford Zetec	1 lap behind	
7	Johnny Herbert	GB	Benetton B195-Renault	1 lap behind	
8	Martin Brundle	GB	Ligier JS41-Ts-Ferrari	1 lap behind	
9	Mark Blundell	GB	McLaren MP4/10B-Mercedes	1 lap behind	
10	Eddie Irvine	GB	Jordan 195-Peugeot	1 lap behind	
11	Rubens Barrichello	BR	Jordan 195-Peugeot	1 lap behind	
12	J-C Boullion	F	Sauber C14-Ford Zetec	1 lap behind	
13	Mika Salo	SF	Tyrrell 023-Yamaha	2 laps behind	
14	Luca Badoer	I	Minardi M195-Ford	3 laps behind	
15	Taki Inoue	J	Footwork FA16-Hart	3 laps behind	
16	Pedro Diniz	BR	Forti FGP 01-Ford	5 laps behind	
17	Roberto Moreno	BR	Forti FGP 01-Ford	7 laps behind	

Retirements	Nat	Car	Laps	Reason
Andrea Montermini	I	Pacific PR02-Ford	53	Gearbox
Mika Häkkinen	SF	McLaren MP4/10B-Mercedes	44	Engine
Jean-Denis Deletraz	CH	Pacific PR02-Ford	14	Cramp
Olivier Panis	F	Ligier JS41-Mugen Honda	10	Spin
Pedro Lamy	P	Minardi M195-Ford	7	Hydraulics
Ukyo Katayama	J	Tyrrell 023-Yamaha	0	Accident
Massmiliano Papis	I	Footwork FA16-Hart	0	Accident

Fastest lap			
David Coulthard	GB	Williams FW17-Renault 1m 23.220s (117.188mph)	

Results and Data © FIA 1995

DRIVERS' CHAMPIONSHIP

Michael Schumacher	72
Damon Hill	55
David Coulthard	39
Johnny Herbert	38
Jean Alesi	34
Gerhard Berger	28
H-H Frentzen	15
Mika Häkkinen	11
Mark Blundell	10
Rubens Barrichello & Olivier Panis	8
Martin Brundle	7
Eddie Irvine	6
J-C Boullion	3
Mika Salo	2
G Morbidelli & A Suzuki	1

CONSTRUCTORS' CUP

Benetton-Renault	100
Williams-Renault	88
Ferrari	62
McLaren-Mercedes	21
Sauber-Ford	18
Ligier-Mugen Honda	16
Jordan-Peugeot	14
Tyrrell-Yamaha	2

1 October 1995
Circuit: Nürburgring

Let's rock and roll (above). A one, a two, a one-two-three-four...On lead vocals, all the way from Kerpen, please welcome...Michael Schumacher.

Pass me if you can (above left). It took a considerable effort for Hill to pass Schumacher...and yards later he ran wide and ceded his advantage. The German never looked back.

"You know that house you've just bought? That can go for starters." Jean Todt tells Eddie Irvine a few facts of Ferrari life, while Eddie Jordan tries to look unhappy about the amount Ferrari had to pay him to buy out the Ulsterman's 1996 contract (left).

Estoril had seen a great race in great weather. Now, just a week later in a state of apprehensive gloom, the Formula One scene reformed at the Nürburgring, near Cologne, for the season's last Grand Prix in Europe. It had been a frantic dash for the teams to rebuild their cars, rush them some 1500 miles from Portugal and then ready them for another race. There was no expectation that the Grand Prix of Europe would justify such toil, for we remembered the 'new" Nürburgring from the races that had been held there in 1984 and 1985 as being a bland replacement for the fabulous, 14-mile Nordschleife circuit which had been dropped for safety reasons.

We hadn't looked forward to returning, especially in October when the temperature, amidst the inevitable rain and fog of the Eifel mountains, would be some 20 degrees lower than Estoril. Yes, the weather was dull, wet and cold but the circuit generated one of the best races for years, full of incident from before the start to the finish. And Michael Schumacher proved beyond doubt that he was the finest driver of his day.

"It's a great circuit," said Damon Hill, and compared to many of today's emasculated tracks he was right.

The facilities are superb and the atmosphere is very special. It may be a pale shadow of the breathtaking old 'Ring, but somehow you are very conscious of the fact that Nuvolari, Caracciola, Rosemeyer, Fangio, Moss, Stewart and other greats drove some of their finest races just yards away.

It was anorak and woolly-hat time on Friday. Seven degrees! But it was sunny and dry. There was extra practice since it was a new track for nearly everyone, but Damon Hill missed a lot of it due to a broken oil pipe. In spite of that he was second fastest to David Coulthard in the qualifying session – faster than Michael Schumacher, who had done hundreds of laps there. "It's not a difficult place to learn," said Damon, and he was quietly pleased with both himself and the revised Williams rear suspension and gearbox which was to be used for its first race.

On Saturday the Eifel area gave us a taster of what it could do: wet in the morning, damp and greasy in the afternoon. Of the top 10 only an inspired Schumacher, Jean Alesi and Heinz-Harald Frentzen went quicker, but none of them improved on their Friday grid positions. So it was a fourth all-Williams front row with David Coulthard on pole for the third race in succession, ahead of Hill, Schumacher, Gerhard Berger, Eddie Irvine (who Ferrari had sensationally signed for 1996) and Alesi. It wasn't as good as Damon had hoped for but, 17 points behind Schumacher in the championship, at least he was ahead of the Benetton.

Race morning was foul, with driving rain and fog so thick that the warm-up was delayed. The rain stopped and the weather cleared but the Nürburgring is notoriously slow to dry, and it was still largely wet as the start approached. So, rain tyres or slicks?

Everyone went for rain tyres except Ferrari and

Ligier presents a solution to one of the dafter ideas on the calendar (above). Will anybody admit to having suggested a race at the Nürburgring in October?

David Coulthard took pole (again), fell off before the start of the race (again) and eventually finished third (top).

Irvine heads Herbert and Barrichello. The two Britons would switch positions after Herbert ran into the Jordan, but both scored points (right).

McLaren, and for Jean Alesi that was to be a brilliant decision. Almost unbelievably Coulthard again spun off before the race had even started. He ran back to take Hill's adjusted spare and just scrambled on to the grid in time...only for the start to be aborted when Massimiliano Papis stalled his Arrows.

Then away they went with Coulthard in the lead and, horror of horrors for Hill, Schumacher and Irvine both ahead of him while Berger slid back after making an even worse start. Damon got past Irvine on the first lap but Schumacher, whom he had to beat, was still ahead. By lap five he was right behind the Benetton and only

1.4s behind race leader Coulthard. And now a dry line was emerging; the slick-shod Alesi was charging.

He passed Herbert on lap six to take fifth, and overtook Irvine on lap nine. By lap 10 he was two seconds faster than Coulthard. It was time for everyone except the Ferraris and the embarrassingly outclassed McLarens of Häkkinen and Blundell (20th and 21st, and both passed by Pedro Diniz!) to switch to slicks.

Schumacher and Hill, second and third, came in together an lap 11. Michael, on what turned out to be a three-stop strategy, rejoined fourth but Hill, on two stops, dropped to seventh. Then in came

115

Coulthard...and into the lead went Alesi. Jean's progress was nothing less than astounding as he drew away, reeling off fastest lap after fastest lap. On lap 15, he was 19s ahead of Coulthard, who was racing nose-to-tail with Schumacher, Hill and Berger. In a no-holds-barred struggle, Damon fought past Schumacher, only to run wide at the next corner and be repassed. On lap 18 the championship contenders came within an ace of another collision as Schumacher ruthlessly, but fairly, chopped Hill at the chicane. "We didn't touch," said Michael. "It was close, but that's what racing is all about."

Not long afterwards Mika Häkkinen, struggling with appalling handling, held up Coulthard, who had got two seconds clear of Schumacher. Immediately, the following three-way battle was right back with him and on lap 21 Michael forced his Benetton past the Williams to second place. All four got past Häkkinen and Schumacher eased away, but on lap 22 Alesi was an incredible 34s up the road.

It was to get even better for Jean, who was on a one-stop strategy and making the most of the dry line that was now all around the circuit. Coulthard, not wishing to interfere with the battle for the championship, let Hill through to third (3.75s behind Schumacher) on lap 23. Six laps later, with Alesi a daunting 43.5s ahead, Hill was right with Schumacher again. This was turning out to be a fantastic race.

Finally, as we were beginning to wonder if Alesi was going to stay out there for ever, in came the Ferrari on lap 34, three laps after Johnny Herbert had rammed Eddie Irvine's Jordan and stopped for a new nose. As Alesi rejoined in came Schumacher for his second (and, he thought, last stop). Hill rose to second, 4.6s behind

Tyrrell recruited Gabriele Tarquini from the Ministry of Silly Hats to deputise for Katayama (top).

Closing in for the kill: Alesi finds his mirrors full of Benetton with only three laps to go (above right).

Salo passes the stricken Sauber of Frentzen, who mistook Diniz's canary yellow Forti for a strip of dull grey tarmac (below).

the Ferrari, with Coulthard third and Michael down to fourth thinking that all was now lost.

But it wasn't. Not by a long way.

New tyres or not, Alesi was losing time to a grimly determined Hill, who had yet to make his second stop. On lap 38 Damon had wiped out the 4.6s gap and was right behind the Ferrari as he radioed to his pit that he was now being held up and must come in. But Coulthard was already there, and Hill would have to stay out for an extra lap. Which may well have cost him the race and the 1995 World Championship. Desperate to get past Alesi, Damon lunged inside the Ferrari, went on to the grass as Jean held his line, hit the kerbing and lost his front wing. He pitted for repairs, which took 57s, and dropped down to fourth behind Schumacher and Coulthard. Disaster.

Now Schumacher and Hill really got their heads down. On lap 51 Michael had reduced the gap to Alesi from 16s to nothing – in 10 laps! On lap 52, to his consternation, he was told to come in for a third stop. When he exited he was 22s behind Alesi with 15 laps to go. And Hill was over seven seconds behind Coulthard, but gaining.

Steadily and brilliantly, Schumacher and his new tyres gained on Alesi and his old rubber as Damon did the same to Coulthard. But on lap 59 Hill's race ended. Three seconds behind Coulthard and with an apparently certain third place in sight to keep his increasingly slim championship hopes alive (David would have yielded, surely?), he lost the Williams on a damp patch and thumped heavily into the tyre-lined Armco. "After I hit Alesi I had something wrong with the steering and couldn't feel properly what the car was doing. I'm not going to be world champion this year, but I put up a good fight and did everything I could to win the race today." It was a bitter pill, as usual he took

it like the sportsman that he is.

"When I saw Damon in the wall I had to decide whether to stay second or push to win, and my fans pushed me to try and win," said Schumacher. Indeed they did, with flags, banners, cheering, air-horns, gestures and rocket-firing all round the track. And he went with a vengeance. On lap 54, the gap was 20s. On lap 57, with the fastest lap of the race (1m 21.180s, 125.55 mph), it was down to 13.7s. On lap 60 it was 7.8s, and two laps later it was less than a second, after Alesi had run wide across the grass at the chicane. Could Alesi hold the Benetton back for just another five laps?

No sir. Three laps later, with a passing move around the outside, something I could hardly believe even as I watched it, Schumacher slipped inside the slithering Ferrari and into the lead, interlocking wheels as he did so. The place erupted, and Michael raced on to win his seventh Grand Prix of the year by 2.7s. It was spell-binding drive of outstanding brilliance which will be talked about for years to come, and it virtually guaranteed him his second successive World Championship. He was now 27 points ahead of Hill with only 30 to be won from the last three races. He had only to finish fourth or higher in any one of them to be assured of the crown.

Ferrari was already getting the cherished 'Number One' ready for his 1996 car.

For the record David Coulthard was third in the spare Williams, with a displeased Frank Williams waiting to interview him about his second pre-race-departure from the track. Rubens Barrichello finished a worthy fourth after a run of bad luck. Johnny Herbert recovered well from his incident with Irvine to finish fifth and Eddie came home sixth to give Jordan their second double-points finish of the season.

Benetton-Renault

A truly great team performance. Schumacher third fastest behind both Williams men in Friday qualifying and starts there (on rain tyres), despite being fastest in generally slower wet Saturday session. On drier line passes Hill at start and races nose-to-tail with Damon and Coulthard until lap 11 stop. Resumes thrilling battle, albeit now for second as slick-shod Alesi has taken lead, almost colliding with Hill as he blocks the Williams on lap 18. Passes Coulthard to second, lap 21, but loses place to Hill at second tyre/fuel stop, lap 34. Second again, lap 41, after second stops for Coulthard and Hill, but now 16s behind race leader Alesi. Charges brilliantly, closes to within 0.8s and then stops for third time, lap 52. Rejoins, still second, 22s behind Alesi with only 15 laps to go. With series of fastest laps, catches Alesi on lap 63 and audaciously squeezes into lead at chicane on lap 65 with only two laps to go. Superbly wins his seventh GP of year by 2.7s after spell-binding drive in front of over 100,000 euphoric country-men, virtually to clinch his second successive World Championship. Johnny Herbert starts disappointing seventh in "still very nervous car", Collides with Irvine on lap 31 and drops to 13th after stopping for new nose. Makes fine recovery to finish fifth, 3.5s ahead of Irvine, for two points which help Benetton to increase constructors' champi-onship lead over Williams to 20 points.

Tyrrell-Yamaha

Team test driver and touring car ace Gabriele Tarquini replaces Ukyo Katayama for one race only whilst Ukyo recovers from Portuguese crash. Qualifies 19th and finishes 14th (six laps down), despite a spin. Salo starts 15th and is running 10th on lap 45 when hit by Boullion. Pits with puncture, but still finishes 10th (three laps down).

Williams-Renault

A very disappointing race. Coulthard superbly takes third successive pole with Hill alongside, both using revised FW17B rear suspension and gearbox. Both start on wets, but Coulthard again spins off track before start of race, this time on out lap. Takes start in Damon's hastily reset spare car. David and Damon race first and third, tightly sandwiching Schumacher, until first stops for slicks (DH lap 11, DC lap 12). Three-way battle resumes, now behind slick-tyred Jean Alesi. Fourth-placed Hill nearly collides with defensive Schumacher, lap 18. Damon and Michael both pass Coulthard to second and third (laps 21 and 23). Hill takes second when Michael stops again, lap 34, and closes 4.6s gap to Alesi by lap 38. Tries to pass Jean at chicane, lap 40, but squeezed on to grass, hits kerb and has to stop for new nose. Rejoins fourth behind Coulthard and reduces 9s gap to 3.3s but spins out on wet patch, lap 59, effectively to destroy his World Championship hopes. Sportingly applauds Schumacher from track-side on Michael's slowing-down lap. Coulthard finishes distant third. Williams now 20 points behind Benetton in championship.

McLaren-Mercedes

Dreadful weekend on Mercedes-Benz home ground. Team stays at Estoril, testing until Tuesday evening, and then makes non-stop 1500 mile trip to Nürburgring…where things are no better. Using high mid-wing Häkkinen qualifies ninth with Blundell 10th, both over two seconds off pace. Starting on slicks on damp track, Mika/Mark drop to 20th and 21st in "impossible" cars and are both passed by Pedro Diniz! Blundell spins out of 19th, lap 14. Häkkinen improves as track dries but finishes two laps down in eighth place. Team announces that David Coulthard will join Häkkinen in 1996.

Arrows-Hart

Papis qualifies 17th, Inoue 21st. Massi causes start to be aborted by stalling. Finishes 12th, three laps down, after 10s penalty for not starting at rear of grid. Faulty ECU prevents Inoue starting at all.

Jordan-Peugeot

After trying high mid-wing extension, Irvine qualifies fifth. Passes Berger to fourth, laps 1-8. On rain tyres passed by slick-shod Alesi, lap 9. Runs second to Jean during early tyre stops but down to sixth after his own, lap 15. Rammed by Herbert when seventh, lap 31, but finishes sixth, one lap down, 1.2s ahead of Brundle despite spinning on lap 52. Rubens starts 11th but gains four places on first lap and has trouble-free race to finish fourth, one lap down, for fourth points finish of year. With both cars in top six, Jordan moves up two places

in constructors' championship. Paddock flabbergasted by news that Irvine drives for Ferrari in 1996, with Martin Brundle taking his place at Jordan.

Pacific-Ford

Montermini and Deletraz start 20th and 24th. Andrea overtakes both McLarens (!) but retires from 13th, out of fuel due to rig fault (lap 46), having unwittingly hit refueller Paul Summerfield and broken his leg. Deletraz finishes pedestrian 15th and last, seven laps down.

Forti-Ford

Diniz and Moreno line up 22nd and 23rd. Roberto retires after 22 laps (gearbox). Pedro finishes leisurely 13th, five laps down.

Minardi-Ford

Portugal's Pedro Lamy (16th) again outqualifies Luca Badoer (18th). Both race reliably to finish ninth (Lamy) and 11th. Gian Carlo Minardi again understandably proud of the fact that, with Ford ED V8s, they are once more the top non-works engine finishers.

Ligier-Mugen Honda

Martin Brundle causes dismay by announcing that he will drive for Jordan in 1996, in place of Eddie Irvine. After problems setting up car (in common with nearly everybody else), qualifies 12th before another good tactical race. On two-stop strategy up to eighth in "too stiff" car before first stop, lap 12. Back to eighth before second stops lap 38, and then, as track dries and car improves, pushes hard from seventh in closing stages behind Irvine and Herbert. Finishes 1.2s behind sixth-placed Irvine. With his future at Ligier in doubt, Olivier Panis goes off heavily in Friday qualifying when throttle jams open. Qualifies 14th in new chassis an Saturday. Stops for slicks, lap 13, when 10th, but spins off and stalls, lap 15.

Ferrari

Already tense atmosphere after Alesi fined $200,000 by team for his Portuguese outburst. Then Gerhard Berger criticises PR manager Giancarlo Bacchini in front of the press! Alesi spins into Armco on Friday morning and only manages nine laps in afternoon, qualifying sixth. Is one of few to improve time on wet Saturday, but still starts two places behind Berger. In view of grid places, team gambles on starting both drivers on slick tyres on damp-to-wet track. Berger makes poor start and drops to ninth but Alesi passes Herbert and then Irvine to fourth by lap six. Jean to second, lap 12, when Schumacher and Hill stop and then into lead, lap 13, when Coulthard stops for slicks. On inspired one-stop strategy, Alesi races away to build amazing 43.6s second lead over Schumacher on lap 29. Makes sole stop on lap 34 and rejoins, still first, now only 4.6s ahead of Hill as Schumacher also stops. Is caught by Hill on lap 38 but Damon goes off, lap 40, trying to pass. From 17s ahead, Jean then caught by charging Schumacher who has to take third stop, lap 52. With 15 laps to go, Alesi is 22.4s ahead of Michael…who then reels off succession of fastest laps to catch Alesi again on lap 64. On worn tyres Jean resists the inevitable but Schumacher brilliantly passes at the chicane on lap 65. Alesi finishes second, 2.8s down, complaining about being held up by Häkkinen but convinced he had done his best with the right strategy. Berger recovers to fifth, lap 13, and has long and exciting fight with Coulthard, Schumacher and Hill. Tyre-stops lap 24 and retains fifth place. Up to fourth during tyre stops, lap 40, but then retires in pits after 41 laps, following long delay unsuccessfully trying to locate and correct electronic problem.

Sauber-Ford

With the Nürburgring close to his Monchengladbach home, Heinz-Harald Frentzen naturally hopes to do well in further improved Sauber (mainly aerodynamics). Does not do so. On track he knows intimately, he goes off several times trying too hard. Qualifies eighth on Friday and is one of few to improve an wet Saturday. In from eighth on lap six to take 10s jump-start penalty which drops him to 15th. Charges to seventh by lap 16 but collides with Diniz as he is lapping the Forti and is out of race. Jean-Christophe Boullion qualifies best-yet 13th using development engine, but cannot put power down during race. Nevertheless is eighth at lap 16 stop. Slides down to 14th but recovers to 11th as tyres come in. Retires, lap 45, after hitting Salo's Tyrrell and breaking his Sauber's nose.

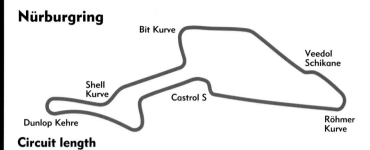

RACE 14

EUROPE

1 OCTOBER 1995

Nürburgring

Bit Kurve

Veedol Schikane

Shell Kurve

Castrol S

Dunlop Kehre

Röhmer Kurve

**Circuit length
2.831 miles/4.556 km**

STARTING GRID

COULTHARD (Williams FW17) 1m 18.738s	**HILL** (Williams FW17) 1m 18.972s
SCHUMACHER (Benetton B195) 1m 19.150s	**BERGER** (Ferrari 412) 1m 19.821s
IRVINE (Jordan 195) 1m 20.488s	**ALESI** (Ferrari 412) 1m 20.521s
HERBERT (Benetton B195) 1m 20.653s	**FRENTZEN** (Sauber C14) 1m 20.749s
HÄKKINEN (McLaren MP4) 1m 20.866s	**BLUNDELL** (McLaren MP4) 1m 20.909s
BARRICHELLO (Jordan 195) 1m 21.211s	**BRUNDLE** (Ligier JS41) 1m 21.541s
BOULLION (Sauber C14) 1m 22.059s	**PANIS** (Ligier JS41) 1m 22.062s
SALO (Tyrrell 023) 1m 23.058s	**LAMY** (Minardi M195) 1m 23.328s
PAPIS (Footwork FA16) 1m 23.689s	**BADOER** (Minardi M195) 1m 23.760s
TARQUINI (Tyrrell 023) 1m 24.286s	**MONTERMINI** (Pacific PR02) 1m 24.696s
INOUE (Footwork FA16) 1m 24.900s	**DINIZ** (Forti FG01) 1m 25.157s
MORENO (Forti FG01) 1m 26.098s	**DELETRAZ** (Pacific PR02) 1m 27.853s

RACE CLASSIFICATION

Pos	Driver	Nat	Car	Laps	Time
1	Michael Schumacher	D	Benetton B195-Renault	67	1h 39m 59.044s
2	Jean Alesi	F	Ferrari 412 Ts-Ferrari	67	1h 40m 01.728s
3	David Coulthard	GB	Williams FW17-Renault	67	1h 40m 34.426s
4	Rubens Barrichello	BR	Jordan 195-Peugeot		1 lap behind
5	Johnny Herbert	GB	Benetton B195-Renault		1 lap behind
6	Eddie Irvine	GB	Jordan 195-Peugeot		1 lap behind
7	Martin Brundle	GB	Ligier JS41-Mugen Honda		1 lap behind
8	Mika Häkkinen	SF	McLaren MP4/10B-Mercedes		2 laps behind
9	Pedro Lamy	P	Minardi M195-Ford		3 laps behind
10	Mika Salo	SF	Tyrrell 023-Yamaha		3 laps behind
11	Luca Badoer	I	Minardi M195-Ford		3 laps behind
12	Massimilliano Papis	I	Footwork FA16-Hart		3 laps behind
13	Pedro Diniz	BR	Forti FGP 01-Ford		5 laps behind
14	Gabriele Tarquini	I	Tyrrell 023-Yamaha		6 laps behind
15	J-D Deletraz	CH	Pacific PR02-Ford		7 laps behind

Retirements	Nat	Car	Laps	Reason
Damon Hill	GB	Williams FW17-Renault	59	Accident
Andrea Montermini	I	Pacific PR02-Ford	46	Out of Fuel
J-C Boullion	F	Sauber C14-Ford Zetec	45	Collision
Gerhard Berger	A	Ferrari 412 T2-Ferrari	41	Electrics
Roberto Moreno	BR	Forti FGP 01-Ford	23	Driveshaft
Heinz-Harald Frentzen	D	Sauber C14-Ford Zetec	18	Collision
Olivier Panis	F	Ligier JS41-Mugen Honda	15	Accident
Mark Blundell	GB	McLaren MP4/10B-Mercedes	15	Spin

Fastest lap

Michael Schumacher	D	Benetton B195-Renault	57	1m 21.180s (125.547mph)

DRIVERS' CHAMPIONSHIP

Michael Schumacher	82
Damon Hill	55
David Coulthard	43
Johnny Herbert/Jean Alesi	40
Gerhard Berger	28
H-H Frentzen	15
Mika Häkkinen/Rubens Barrichello	11
Mark Blundell	10
Martin Brundle/Eddie Irvine	7
J-C Boullion	3
Mika Salo	2
Gianni Morbidelli/Aguri Suzuki	1

CONSTRUCTORS' CUP

Benetton Renault	112
Williams Renault	92
Ferrari	68
McLaren Mercedes	21
Jordan Peugeot/Sauber Ford	18
Ligier Mugen-Honda	16
Tyrrell Yamaha	2
Footwork Hart	1

22 October 1995
Circuit: TI International – Aida

In April 1995, a horrific earthquake hit Japan in the Kobe area, destroying countless buildings, roads, railways and communications and putting paid to the Pacific Grand Prix at the Aida circuit, in the vicinity of ravaged Okayama. In the circumstances it seemed unlikely that the race would be held at all, but with typical Japanese application, dedication and efficiency everything was rebuilt in time for a rescheduled date in October – an astounding achievement.

So Aida became the first race in a Japanese double-header, coupled with the national GP at Suzuka the following weekend. A very tough schedule, but worth the effort. Aida is an incredible place. Set high in glorious hills and a long way from any sizeable city, it was created and paid for (£65m!) by one man, Hajime Tanaka, a stupefyingly wealthy golf-course constructor who also has a passion for motor racing.

The drivers regard it as a challenge, but like so many modern tracks it offers few overtaking opportunities. Everyone expected that Aida would see Michael Schumacher clinch three points and his second successive World Championship, to take the coveted Number One to Ferrari with him for 1996; and they weren't wrong.

Schumacher's drive was almost as awe-inspiring as his virtuoso performance at the Nürburgring had been three weeks earlier, but that's a lot more than could be said for his qualifying efforts. The Benettons had a revised rear suspension and aerodynamic changes, but for the whole weekend they were visibly nervous and looked likely to fly off the track at any moment.

That's the way Schumacher likes his cars, but the two Williams-Renaults of David Coulthard and Damon Hill were superior. Coulthard was quickest on Friday and Saturday to take his fourth successive pole position, despite never having seen the track before. Quickest again in the warm-up, he looked unbeatable. This certainly wasn't good news for Damon Hill, who simply had to win to have any chance of sustaining his brittle title hopes.

Schumacher wasn't exactly beside himself with pleasure, for the best he could do was third on the grid and in Sunday's warm-up he spun off, damaged his race car and then had an engine vibration problem on the grid itself. Experience has shown that you should never expect Benetton to falter in the race, but it really wasn't looking good for Michael. We should have known better!

A star in the making? Jan Magnussen was called up to replace Mika Häkkinen, after the latter had been required to have his appendix ripped out. The young Dane gave a good account of himself (above).

Party on! Benetton commences celebration of the first of Michael Schumacher's parting gifts (left). Next stop: the constructors' title...

Being third on the grid was actually a bonus for Schumacher, for it was on the clean side of the track, behind pole-sitter Coulthard. Hill had to contend with a dusty and slippery surface which was almost certain to affect his start adversely. Indeed it did, and Schumacher's too… As Hill moved across to block his rival, fast-starting Jean Alesi rocketed his Ferrari past both of them into second place whilst Berger, from fifth on the grid, also passed Michael to demote the world champion to fifth place.

Meanwhile, with a clear track ahead of him, the excellent David Coulthard got the hammer down and calmly pulled away from Alesi. His lead on lap five was over eight seconds as Schumacher got ahead of Berger and set about catching Hill. Before long we had the sight of Alesi, Hill and Schumacher racing each other for second place and, as they got in each other's way, Coulthard extended his lead. On lap 18, as his Ferrari, Williams and Benetton pursuers swept into the

pits together for their first pit stop, which was to transform the race, he was nearly 15s up the road

Schumacher entered the pit lane last but, after a superb turn round by his team, he departed first, now in fourth place, and ahead of both Alesi and Hill, now ninth and embroiled in time-consuming traffic. Damon did his best to extract himself, but in his anxiety he ran into the back of Eddie Irvine and nearly ended both their races. By lap 25 he was fourth, but his was a lost cause.

In a seemingly dominant situation, David Coulthard had decided to change his planned strategy from three stops to two. After his first, on lap 24, he still led, some five and a half seconds ahead of Schumacher. But now, lap by lap, Schumacher closed the gap until, on lap 33, he was right behind the Williams. Could Coulthard stave him off until Michael took the second of what we now knew were going to be three stops? He could and did. In came Schumacher on lap 38 of 83, rejoining

"People never used to take pictures of me before I met you." David Coulthard reflects on life with Andrea Murray (left).

Hill elbowed Schumacher aside at the start, and allowed Alesi to get ahead of him (top). He would be growing fairly tired of the sight of the Ferrari's gearbox before long.

Pedro Diniz's girlfriend discovers that it's possible to get a Forti in focus while shooting at 1/30th of a second (above).

second, 21s down on Coulthard – but on fresh tyres.

By now Hill was history. After his second of three stops on lap 39 he was 55s behind Coulthard and 37s behind Schumacher, whose 40th lap would be the race's fastest (1m 16.374s, 108.462 mph).

When Coulthard left the pits after his second and last stop, Michael was in the lead after an incredible effort. Now David had to do 33 laps on his last set of Goodyears, knowing that Schumacher was going to come in again and that he had got to stop Michael from building enough of a lead to be able to stop, change tyres and still retain the lead. He tried, but failed.

The Benetton strategy, which the team had formulated during the race, worked brilliantly as Schumacher confidently exploited it. He needed an advantage of some 20s when he made his third stop: on lap 51 he led by 14s; on lap 55 he led by 20. Coulthard fought like a tiger to hold it at that level, but on lap 60, when Michael made his final stop, he was 22s ahead of the Williams. It was enough. As he left the pit lane he was some four seconds ahead of Coulthard.

David was on increasingly tired rubber, Michael on a brand new set of Goodyears. Schumacher's insistence on preserving his tyres during Friday and Saturday so that he would have three sets of new Goodyears for the race had well and truly paid off. He reeled off his last 24 laps, with Coulthard powerless to stop, and won his eighth Grand Prix of 1995 by 15s to secure his second World Championship title with two races still to go.

For all that, he was very lucky to finish at all. For the last nine laps he had been experiencing downshift

Olivier Panis fails to understand the subtleties of the Anglo-Japanese joke being told over his left shoulder, as Ligier returnee Aguri Suzuki exchanges pleasantries with Tom Walkinshaw (above).

It was all change at Aida. Gianni Morbidelli was recalled by Arrows, after Massimiliano Papis fell short of lire (left).

Jean-Denis Delétraz having defaulted on a payment ("We're not about to run him on talent alone," disclosed Pacific boss Keith Wiggins), Bertrand Gachot reclaimed his seat. For two laps...(right)

problems, and on the last lap he was jammed in one gear. Overjoyed, Michael's next target for 1995 was to beat Nigel Mansell's 1992 record of nine wins in a season.

Aida was a scene of crushing disappointment for Damon Hill. After vicious criticism by the media (it's easy to criticise when you've neither driven a Formula One car, nor can even dream of the skill required to do so), he had desperately hoped to do well, despite knowing that his chances of pulling off the championship were almost nil. Now he had not only lost all chance of the championship for the second year in succession, but was going to have to fight equally hard to prevent his team-mate David Coulthard to pip him for second place.

Aida was not kind to Ferrari, either, for Berger and Alesi took fourth and fifth, both a lap down, leaving no doubt that they were still well off the pace.

McLaren was even more at sea. Despite increasingly desperate efforts to make the unloved MP4/10B competitive, their two drivers had finished ninth and 10th, two laps down. Even so, one of them had every

reason to feel very pleased indeed with himself. McLaren's 22-year-old Danish test driver Jan Magnussen had been hastily pressed into service for his first Grand Prix, only days before the event, when Mika Häkkinen had gone down with appendicitis.

With only seven short test sessions behind him and absolutely no experience of starts and pit stops, Magnussen responded magnificently. From a creditable 12th on the grid he drove like a veteran and didn't put a wheel wrong before finishing 10th, only 2.4s behind experienced team-mate Mark Blundell.

Although Michael Schumacher had won the 1994 championship with only 12 scores from the 16 races, he had undoubtedly felt unhappy about having done so in an atmosphere of recrimination and the accusations of cheating which had surrounded his team. Now, however, he had won the title fair and square after a series of superb drives. All that was left for him before he went to Ferrari was to help Benetton clinch its first constructors' championship. A handy 21 points ahead with two races to go, it seemed very likely that he could do just that.

Benetton-Renault

Another brilliant drive by Schumacher, plus superior strategy, gives him his second successive World Championship and puts team within reach of its first constructors' title. New rear suspension and revised aerodynamics on B195, but Michael off the pace in very twitchy car during qualifying. Starts third after going off during warm-up. Baulked by Hill at start (angry words after race) and drops to fifth. Passes Berger to fourth and takes first of three stops, with Alesi and Hill, lap 18. Enters pit lane last of the three, but exits it first, now second to Coulthard. Superb teamwork, again. Catches David on lap 33 after Coulthard's first stop, but cannot pass. Retains second at stop, lap 38, sets fastest lap of race and takes lead when Coulthard stops, lap 50. Races away from two-stop Coulthard to take eighth win of year and clinches championship with two races to go. But is lucky to finish, jammed in gear, after having had downshift problems for last nine laps. Johnny Herbert starts seventh, still not at ease with car, and finishes disappointed sixth, one lap down. Only 0.5s behind Alesi after a great fight with the Ferrari in the closing laps.

Tyrrell-Yamaha

Neither driver able to get car set up properly for important home race for Yamaha and Katayama. Ukyo starts 17th for first race since big off in Portugal, Salo 18th. Both have trouble-free races with two stops to finish 12th (Salo) and 14th (Katayama), both three laps down.

Williams-Renault

Desolation for Damon and disappointment for Williams, despite another fine qualifying performance by both drivers. Coulthard takes superb fourth successive pole for first race at Aida with Hill second, 0.2s slower. Hill, on dirty side of track, has poor getaway, baulks Schumacher and, with Coulthard in lead, drops to third behind Alesi. Down to ninth amongst traffic after delay at first stop, lap 19. Recovers to third, hitting Irvine on way, with forceful drive after second stop, lap 39, but championship hopes destroyed. Coulthard retains lead at first stop, but his two-stop plan is inferior to Schumacher's. Finishes second, now only 10 points behind Hill in championship with two races to go. Team now 21 points behind Benetton in constructors' championship.

McLaren-Mercedes

At short notice, 22-year-old Danish test driver Jan Magnussen replaces appendicitis-stricken Mika Häkkinen and starts impressive 12th on grid, two places and 0.6s behind Mark Blundell. Both race reliably in woefully inadequate car, with three stops, to finish ninth (Mark Blundell) and 10th (Jan Magnussen), two laps down. Magnussen's debut marks him as a man of the future, but the MP4/10B continues greatly to disappoint.

Arrows-Hart

Massimiliano Papis ousted by returnee Gianni Morbidelli, who starts a "rusty" 19th, with Taki Inoue 20th. Neither goes race distance. Inoue out on lap 39 when engine "just stopped". Morbidelli retires from 14th, lap 54, when Hart V8 unusually fails.

Jordan-Peugeot

Eddie Irvine takes excellent sixth on grid, but passed by Herbert at start. Spends most of race battling with Frentzen. Stops twice, and is hit by charging Hill on lap 24, but is still eighth when collects puncture, lap 72. After extra unscheduled stop, finishes 11th (two laps down). Rubens Barrichello qualifies five places behind Irvine, although only 0.2s slower. Races with impressive Magnussen for 39 laps before retiring from ninth, lap 68 (electronics).

Pacific-Ford

Jean-Denis Delétraz fails to come up with money for drive and is replaced by returnee Bertrand Gachot, who is admittedly rusty after three-month lay off. Bert qualifies 24th, three places behind Andrea Montermini, who keeps his place after the FIA refuses to grant Katsumi Yamamoto the necessary Superlicence. Neither goes far. Gachot out lap three (gearbox hydraulics); Montermini out from 18th, lap 15 (transmission failure).

Forti-Ford

Amidst rumours that team will not be able to afford to continue in 1996, Pedro Diniz (said to be making $8m payment to drive for Ligier next season) qualifies 21st. Roberto Moreno, who would have lost his seat to Hideki Noda, had the latter been granted a Superlicence, starts 22nd. Both stop three times. Moreno finishes 16th, five laps down, Diniz 17th, six laps adrift.

Minardi-Ford

By taking 14th (Lamy) and 16th (Badoer) places on the grid, ahead of a Sauber, both Tyrrells and both Arrows, all with "works" engines, Minardi again proves the worth of its chassis. Both drivers finish: Lamy 13th, three laps down; Badoer 15th, also three laps adrift, despite overshooting his pit and later losing both mirrors.

Ligier-Mugen Honda

Team uses new C-spec engine for first of two home races for the Japanese engine builder. After much negotiation and discussion, believed to involve 1996, Aguri Suzuki replaces Jordan-bound Martin Brundle. Suzuki outqualifies Panis on Friday but Oliver takes ninth on grid on Saturday, four places ahead of Aguri. Panis even better fourth fastest during Sunday warm-up, prior to two-stop race. Drops to 13th on lap one after being delayed by Herbert. After strong drive, finishes relieved eighth (in view of recent poor performances), two laps down. Suzuki spins out of 13th, lap 11.

Ferrari

A disappointing meeting. Jean Alesi suffers from nasty attack of 'flu prior to his 100th Grand Prix and his first race at Aida (a back problem after a Mugello testing accident forced him to step down in 1994). Fourth in Friday qualifying, and stays there. Gerhard Berger takes fifth on grid. Both have three stops and both race reliably – but too slowly. On new tyres Alesi makes demon start to pass Schumacher and Hill, grabbing second. Stays there until lap 19 stop when 15s behind leader Coulthard. Resumes third, now behind Schumacher, but subsequently drops back due to less grippy sets of tyres. Finishes fifth, one lap down, only just ahead of Johnny Herbert after a fierce fight in the closing stages.
The two points gained move Jean up to fourth place in championship. Berger finishes fourth, also one lap down, despite engine misfire.

Sauber-Ford

Heinz-Harald Frentzen satisfied with eighth on grid. Makes good start and passes Herbert, but immediately passed by Irvine. Stops twice and spends most of race in close company with Irvine until Eddie punctures on lap 73. H-H finishes just out of points in seventh, one lap down. Jean-Christophe Boullion spins out of Saturday qualifying and loses three places to start 15th. Then spins out of race on lap eight whilst trying to pass obstructive Pedro Lamy.

PACIFIC RESULTS AND STATISTICS

22 OCTOBER 1995

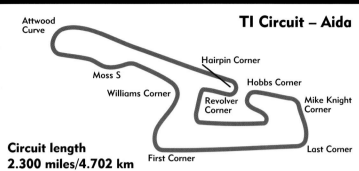

TI Circuit – Aida

Attwood Curve · Moss S · Williams Corner · Hairpin Corner · Revolver Corner · Hobbs Corner · Mike Knight Corner · First Corner · Last Corner

**Circuit length
2.300 miles/4.702 km**

STARTING GRID

COULTHARD (Williams FW17) 1m 14.013s	**HILL** (Williams FW17) 1m 14.213s
SCHUMACHER (Benetton B195) 1m 14.284s	**ALESI** (Ferrari 412 T2) 1m 14.919s
BERGER (Ferrari 412 T2) 1m 14.974s	**IRVINE** (Jordan 195) 1m 15.354s
HERBERT (Benetton B195) 1m 15.556s	**FRENTZEN** (Sauber C14) 1m 15.561s
PANIS (Ligier JS41) 1m 15.621s	**BLUNDELL** (McLaren MP4/10C) 1m 15.652s
BARRICHELLO (Jordan 195) 1m 15.774s	**MAGNUSSEN** (McLaren MP4/10C) 1m 16.339s
SUZUKI (Ligier JS41) 1m 16.519s	**LAMY** (Minardi M195) 1m 16.596s
BOULLION (Sauber C14) 1m 16.646s	**BADOER** (Minardi M195) 1m 16.887s
KATAYAMA (Tyrrell 023) 1m 17.014s	**SALO** (Tyrrell 023) 1m 17.213s
MORBIDELLI (Footwork FA16) 1m 18.114s	**INOUE** (Footwork FA16) 1m 18.212s
DINIZ (Forti F601) 1m 19.579s	**MORENO** (Forti F601) 1m 19.745s
MONTERMINI (Pacific PR02) 1m 20.093s	**GACHOT** (Pacific PR02) 1m 21.405s

RACE CLASSIFICATION

Pos	Driver	Nat	Car	Laps	Time
1	Michael Schumacher	D	Benetton B195-Renault	83	1h 48m 49.972s
2	David Coulthard	GB	Williams FW17-Renault	83	1h 49m 04.892s
3	Damon Hill	GB	Williams FW17-Renault	83	1h 49m 28.305s
4	Gerhard Berger	A	Ferrari 412T2		1 lap behind
5	Jean Alesi	F	Ferrari 412T2		1 lap behind
6	Johnny Herbert	GB	Benetton B195-Renault		1 lap behind
7	Heinz-Harald Frentzen	D	Sauber C14-Ford Zetec		1 lap behind
8	Olivier Panis	F	Ligier JS41-Mugen Honda		2 laps behind
9	Mark Blundell	GB	McLaren MP4/10C-Mercedes		2 laps behind
10	Jan Magnussen	DK	McLaren MP4/10C-Mercedes		2 laps behind
11	Eddie Irvine	GB	Jordan 195-Peugeot		2 laps behind
12	Mika Salo	SF	Tyrrell 023-Yamaha		3 laps behind
13	Pedro Lamy	P	Minardi M195-Ford ED		3 laps behind
14	Ukyo Katayama	J	Tyrrell 023-Yamaha		3 laps behind
15	Luca Badoer	I	Minardi M195-Ford ED		3 laps behind
16	Roberto Moreno	BR	Forti FG01-Ford ED		5 laps behind
17	Pedro Diniz	BR	Forti FG01-Ford ED		6 laps behind

Retirements	Nat	Car	Laps	Reason
Rubens Barrichello	BR	Jordan 195-Peugeot	67	Engine
Gianni Morbidelli	I	Footwork FA16-Hart	53	Engine
Taki Inoue	J	Footwork FA16-Hart	38	Engine
Andrea Montermini	I	Pacific PR02-Ford ED	14	Gearbox
Aguri Suzuki	J	Ligier JS41-Mugen Honda	10	Spun off
Jean-Christophe Boullion	F	Sauber C14-Ford Zetec	7	Spun off
Bertrand Gachot	F	Pacific PR02-Ford ED	2	Hydraulics

Fastest lap

Michael Schumacher D Benetton B195-Renault lap 40   1m 16.374s (108.4567mph)

DRIVERS' CHAMPIONSHIP

Michael Schumacher	92	Jean-Christophe Boullion	3
Damon Hill	59	Mika Salo	2
David Coulthard	49	Gianni Morbidelli	1
Jean Alesi	42	Aguri Suzuki	1
Johnny Herbert	41		
Gerhard Berger	31		
Heinz-Harald Frentzen	15		
Mika Hakkinen	11		
Rubens Barrichello	11		
Mark Blundell	10		
Olivier Panis	8		
Martin Brundle	7		
Eddie Irvine	7		

CONSTRUCTORS' CUP

Benetton-Renault	123
Williams-Renault	102
Ferrari	73
McLaren-Mercedes	21
Jordan-Peugeot	18
Sauber-Ford	18
Ligier-Mugen Honda	16
Tyrrell-Yamaha	2
Footwork-Hart	1

29 October 1995
Circuit: Suzuka

Fanaticism for the Prancing Horse is not restricted to the suburbs of Milan (above).

Another one in the bag (top): Schumacher and Herbert celebrate clinching the constructors' title for Benetton – the first time since 1983 that anyone bar Williams or McLaren had won the crown. The new, lighter Häkkinen looks on, having proved that loss of an appendix is no handicap.

Damon Hill gets out of shape (left). By Sunday evening, he'd be out of favour, too.

Two weeks in Japan was something different. No communication with the locals because of the language problem; very different food; a very different culture. It made it hard to take for a lot of people, but I must say that I find the place absolutely fascinating.

Suzuka is about as different from Aida, scene of the previous weekend's Pacific GP, as it could be. Owned by Honda and situated close to one of the company's enormous motor cycle factories on the edge of the bustling modern city, it is without doubt the finest purpose-built circuit in the world, with its own excellent hotel, restaurants, shops, leisure complex and amusement park. Not for Suzuka a joined-up succession of second and third gear bends, typical of so many of today's tracks. It has a unique figure-of-eight configuration, with gloriously fast sweeping, undulating corners and 190 mph straights which really challenge both car and driver. Some 62 per cent of the lap is spent at full throttle (more than Hockenheim), and the drivers are subjected to over 2g for more than 30s per lap. Only the ridiculous chicane, where Prost and Senna controversially collided in 1989, mars it.

To the delight of Benetton's Japanese sponsor Mild Seven, which had already seen Michael Schumacher clinch his second successive World Championship at Aida, Suzuka was where he guaranteed his team's first ever victory in the constructors' championship. And he did it in commanding style. Frankly, it never looked as

though he was going to be challenged. He was fastest in Friday and Saturday's qualifying sessions, and dominated the race. He notched up his eighth fastest lap and ninth win of the season, equalling Nigel Mansell's 1992 record.

It was a demoralising defeat for his rivals, especially Williams and Ferrari, none of whose four drivers even finished the race. It was dry on both Friday and Saturday, when Michael was truly in charge, over 0.8s faster than Alesi, with Häkkinen next up. The significant thing was that Mika Häkkinen, back after his appendix operation, had been up there on both days in a McLaren with yet another update of the Mercedes-Benz V10.

But where were David Coulthard and last year's winner Damon Hill, who had occupied the front row of the grid for the last three Grands Prix? Answer: fourth (Hill) and sixth, sandwiching Gerhard Berger's Ferrari, and under a cloud having both gone off on Saturday morning. With Benetton only needing a few extra points for the prestigious constructors' championship, it didn't look as though Williams was going to deny them.

Qualifying had seen two big accidents. Mark Blundell, off at some 170mph on Friday, was bravely going to start the race in a rebuilt McLaren, last on the grid after missing Saturday's session. But Aguri Suzuki, who was again replacing Martin Brundle for Ligier, failed to start after crashing heavily on Saturday and breaking a rib. After two days the prediction for Sunday was that it would be wet. Not another ghastly day like 1994, surely?

Fortunately not, although the track was indeed wet for the start, with everyone on rain tyres after heavy rain in the warm-up four hours earlier. However, the skies were clear, albeit grey and threatening.

Schumacher is a meteoric starter and Suzuka was no exception. He moved straight into the lead, followed by Alesi, Häkkinen and Hill with Eddie Irvine up from seventh on the grid to take fifth, in front of Coulthard and Alesi. With years of Japanese F3000 racing behind him, Eddie knows Suzuka. It showed.

"Sixth?" Mika Salo expresses surprise as his Tyrrell troubles the scorers for the second time in 16 races (above).

Schumacher converts pole position into the lead, while Alesi prepares for another brief outburst of total heroism. Häkkinen and Hill lead the murky chase (top).

Mark Blundell had a torrid time in qualifying, starting last after a 170-plus mph practice accident. He overcame his bruises to finish seventh (right).

There was no change at the top for five laps, but then in came Jean Alesi to take a 10s penalty for jumping the start. He was 29s behind Schumacher and down to 10th when he rejoined, and on the very next lap his team-mate Gerhard Berger swept into the pits for the same reason. He dropped to 15th, so surely Ferrari's race was over already? Not a bit of it!

With the track now drying rapidly, Alesi was the first to stop for slick tyres, on lap seven. It was an inspired decision. Now down to 15th, a massive 51s behind race leader Schumacher, Alesi began a spell-binding charge. Maximising his advantage as his rivals followed his tyre-changing example, Jean scythed his way forwards. Ninth on lap nine, sixth on lap 10, fourth on lap 11 and second on lap 12, only 6.8s behind Schumacher! Absolutely incredible. He had taken over 44s off Michael in just four laps and had shot past Hill at the chicane as though Damon was paralysed.

Awestruck, we watched Jean press on in that inimitable, head-down style of his as he sliced into Schumacher's lead with a searing succession of fastest laps with the rest, led by Damon Hill, falling away behind him. By lap 19, with Hill third, Häkkinen fourth and Coulthard past Irvine to fifth, Jean was just one second behind the Benetton. But Schumacher had his measure and pulled away to stabilise the gap at some two seconds. And then, yet again, a heartbreaking retirement for Alesi. With smoke pouring from the back of his Ferrari, he pulled off with broken transmission.

So now, with Schumacher 21s ahead of Hill, it looked as though the 53 lap race was effectively over. But it wasn't. Damon took the lead as Schumacher came in for his second stop on lap 31. When Michael rejoined he set about regaining his lead on new Goodyears with the fastest lap of the race (1m 42.976s, 127.388 mph). On lap 35, as Hill pitted, Schumacher regained control. The German led from Hill, Coulthard, Häkkinen, Herbert and Irvine.

Now the drama began again! Lap 37: Hill off! He slipped up at the tricky Spoon Curve, as rain made it greasy. He pitted for a new nosecone and slipped to fifth, with Coulthard now three places ahead of him.

Then Coulthard spun off. Same place. Same reason. Although he rejoined he was off again at the next corner as he spun, terminally, on gravel he had dropped. Potentially good news for Damon, but he had to come in for a 10s penalty for speeding in the pit lane. He never did though, for on lap 41 he was incredibly off again at the Spoon Curve, this time for good. Both Williams drivers out, no points for the team, absolutely no chance of the constructors' championship and an incandescent atmosphere in the garage.

With Gerhard Berger long gone after retiring in the pits with yet another broken sensor, it was joy bells all the way for Benetton as Schumacher, now 30s ahead of Häkkinen, calmly paced himself to his record-equalling ninth win of the season.

There were just four men on the same lap: Schumacher, Häkkinen, Herbert and Irvine. With Olivier Panis fifth for Ligier, to the delight of the team's engine supplier Mugen Honda, which had never scored a point in its homeland, attention switched to the battle for the last point between Tyrrell-Yamaha's Mika Salo and McLaren's Mark Blundell, who had risen from last on the grid. Mika took the point in the end, but it was close.

There was euphoria for Benetton, sealed with a first constructors' title after 10 years of effort. There was misery for Williams and Ferrari, and dejection for poor Ukyo Katayama, so anxious to do well at home, who had to retire his Tyrrell in agony with a broken thumb. But there were smiles for Hakkinen, Blundell, McLaren and Mercedes, who at least seemed to be climbing out of their pit of despair. And Johnny Herbert now had a chance of finishing third in the drivers' championship.

Renault? They drew enormous satisfaction from having won 15 out of the year's 16 races. Now for the nine-hour flight to Australia for the emotion-laden last race of the year, sadly the last likely to be held in Adelaide, where we had all had such marvellous times over the years. Could Schumacher win a record 10th race there? No one was going to bet against it!

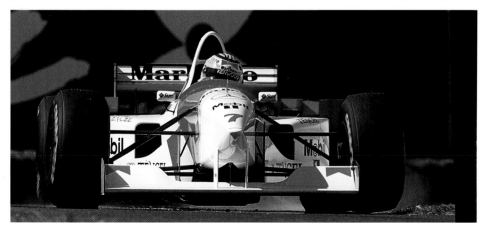

Benetton-Renault

The best day in Benetton's 10-year history. Michael Schumacher equals Nigel Mansell's 1992 record of nine wins in a season and, with Johnny Herbert's help, clinches team's first-ever constructors' championship. Schumacher dominates qualifying to start from 10th career pole. Takes lead at start and, although strongly challenged by Alesi until lap 25, holds it for all bar four laps during tyre/fuel stops. Sets fastest lap and beats Häkkinen by 19.34s. JH also drives fine race from ninth on grid. With three-stop strategy, is up to fifth on lap 27. Profits from Hill and Coulthard retirements to finish third, retaining chance of taking third place in drivers' championship.

Tyrrell-Yamaha

At Yamaha's home track, Mika Salo and Ukyo Katayama start 12th and 14th – Katayama with dislocated left thumb after trapping hand in steering wheel during warm-up. Bitterly disappointed Ukyo retires from 12th, lap 11, unable to control car. Salo drives strong race on track he knows well. Held up by Inoue for "15 laps" but finishes sixth (one lap down) after battling with Mark Blundell for last 10 laps.

Williams-Renault

Appalling weekend for team. Both drivers go off on Saturday morning, before qualifying fourth (Hill) and sixth (Coulthard)... to outspoken dismay of team bosses. Hill to third behind Häkkinen after Alesi takes 10s penalty, but caught and repassed by Jean, lap 11. Up to second after Alesi's retirement, lap 25. Coulthard third by lap 29. Damon leads, laps 32-35, when Schumacher stops, but he goes off at Spoon Curve, lap 37. In for new nose and drops to fifth. Coulthard now second, but he runs wide at Spoon Curve, lap 40. Rejoins but spins out at next corner on gravel which sprays from his own sidepods. Hill given 10s penalty for pit lane speeding, but he spins off on lap 41 before he can serve his punishment. Fined $10,000. Team loses constructors' championship; both drivers in bad odour.

McLaren-Mercedes

Success at last. With further-revised engine Häkkinen, fully recovered from appendectomy, starts third. Drives "my best race ever" with one stop to finish strong second after Alesi/Hill/Coulthard retirements. Mark Blundell has heavy 160 mph off on Friday; starts courageous last. Races through field to seventh place, one lap down, after battling with Salo for last 10 laps.

Arrows-Hart

Morbidelli rammed out of race by Wendlinger at first corner after starting 15th. Inoue finishes 12th, two laps down.

Jordan-Peugeot

After generally trouble-free qualifying, Irvine starts excellent seventh and passes Coulthard and Berger at start to lie fifth at a circuit he knows well. Goes for wet set-up which creates understeer as track dries. Passed by Coulthard, lap 15, after first of three stops, then hit by Barrichello lap 16. Then hit by Frentzen, lap 20, but retains sixth place. Spins at Spoon Curve, lap 40, but takes fine fourth to maintain 100 per cent points-scoring record at Suzuka. Barrichello 10th on grid. Up to seventh after changing to slick tyres (lap 11), but spins out, lap 16, after hitting Irvine.

Pacific-Ford

Throat-infected Montermini qualifies 20th, Gachot 23rd. Bertrand out lap six (driveshaft bearing). Andrea spins out of 15th, lap 24.

Forti-Ford

Roberto Moreno returns to the scene of best-ever GP finish (second with Benetton in 1990). Qualifies 22nd after unsuccessfully trying to get semi-automatic gearbox to work. Fails again on parade lap and starts from pit lane. Retires lap one, stuck in fourth. Pedro Diniz starts 21st and spins out, lap 33.

Minardi-Ford

Gian Carlo Minardi continues to eulogise about performance of his "non works-engined" cars. Pedro Lamy takes 17th on grid, one place ahead of Badoer. Badoer overcomes brake problem to finish ninth, two laps down; Lamy 11th with wrong set-up for wet.

Ligier-Mugen Honda

Aguri Suzuki again replaces Martin Brundle for second home race. Sadly fails to start after high-speed off in Saturday qualifying which leaves him with a broken rib. Also precludes expected announcement of his retirement from F1. Olivier Panis starts 11th and runs strong two-stop race. Finishes lapped fifth to give Mugen first GP points on home soil.

Ferrari

Lack of reliability again overcomes seemingly strong team effort and deals cruel blow to Alesi. At track which suits car Jean qualifies excellent second, 0.86s slower than Schumacher. Berger fifth on grid in new car, built up after he destroyed original monocoque on kerb on Friday. Alesi starts well and hangs on to Benetton, some 2.8s down, until having to take 10s penalty for jump start, lap five. Rejoins 10th, now 29s down, as Berger also takes penalty stop from sixth, lap six, which drops him to 15th. Alesi first in for slick tyres as track starts to dry, lap seven. Now down to 15th, 51s behind Schumacher. With sensational series of fastest laps is up to incredible second on lap 12, only 6.8s behind Michael. Closes gap to 2.2s, lap 17, only to retire with broken transmission, lap 25. "I am convinced I did not jump the start. The grid slopes downhill and if the car moved a few centimetres it certainly was not intentional. The desire to win again for Ferrari is still there. I will try once more in Australia." Meantime, Berger retires from ninth with broken sensor, lap 16.

Sauber-Ford

Jean-Christophe Boullion dropped to give Karl Wendlinger "last chance" drives at Suzuka and Adelaide. Karl, rusty from lack of race driving, fails to impress. Starts 16th, 4.9s off pace, and races to 10th, two laps down after hitting Morbidelli at start and having to stop on two successive laps for slick tyres due to misunderstanding. Circuit specialist Heinz-Harald Frentzen is sixth on Friday, but drops to eighth on Saturday due to morning engine problem which costs set-up time. Loses two places at start when engine dies. Hits Irvine on lap 20. In for new nose and down to 10th. Spins at slippery Spoon Curve lap 40 and in for another nose. Still finishes eighth, one lap down.

JAPAN

29 OCTOBER 1995

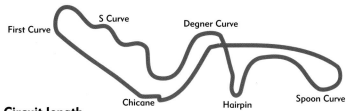

Suzuka

First Curve · S Curve · Degner Curve · Chicane · Hairpin · Spoon Curve

Circuit length
3.641 miles/5.859 km

STARTING GRID

SCHUMACHER (Benetton B195) 1m 38.023s	**ALESI** (Ferrari 412 T2) 1m 38.888s
HÄKKINEN (McLaren MP4/10B) 1m 38.954s	**HILL** (Williams FW17B) 1m 39.032s
BERGER (Ferrari 412 T2) 1m 39.040s	**COULTHARD** (Williams FW17B) 1m 39.155s
IRVINE (Jordan 195) 1m 39.621s	**FRENTZEN** (Sauber C14) 1m 40.010s
HERBERT (Benetton B195) 1m 40.439s	**BARRICHELLO** (Jordan 195) 1m 40.381s
PANIS (Ligier JS41) 1m 40.838s	**SALO** (Tyrrell 023) 1m 41.355s
KATAYAMA (Tyrrell 023) 1m 41.977s	**MORBIDELLI** (Footwork FA16) 1m 42.059s
WENDLINGER (Sauber C14) 1m 42.912s	**LAMY** (Minardi M195) 1m 43.102s
BADOER (Minardi M195) 1m 43.542s	**INOUE** (Footwork FA16) 1m 44.074s
MONTERMINI (Pacific PR02) 1m 46.097s	**DINIZ** (Forti FG01) 1m 46.654s
MORENO (Forti FG01) 1m 48.267s	**GACHOT** (Pacific PR02) 1m 48.289s
BLUNDELL (McLaren MP4/10B) 16m 42.640s	

RACE CLASSIFICATION

Pos	Driver	Nat	Car	Laps	Time
1	Michael Schumacher	D	Benetton B195-Renault	53	1h 36m 52.930s
2	Mika Häkkinen	SF	McLaren MP4/10B-Mercedes	53	1h 37m 12.267s
3	Johnny Herbert	GB	Benetton B195-Renault	53	1h 38m 16.734s
4	Eddie Irvine	GB	Jordan 195-Peugeot	53	1h 38m 35.066s
5	Olivier Panis	F	Ligier JS41-Mugen Honda		1 lap behind
6	Mika Salo	SF	Tyrrell 023-Yamaha		1 lap behind
7	Mark Blundell	GB	McLaren MP4/10B-Mercedes		1 lap behind
8	Heinz-Harald Frentzen	D	Sauber C14-Ford Zetec		1 lap behind
9	Luca Badoer	I	Minardi M195-Ford ED		2 laps behind
10	Karl Wendlinger	A	Sauber C14-Zetec		2 laps behind
11	Pedro Lamy	I	Minardi 195-Ford ED		2 laps behind
12	Taki Inoue	J	Footwork FA16-Hart		2 laps behind

Retirements	Nat	Car	Laps	Reason
Damon Hill	GB	Williams FW17B-Renault	40	Spin
David Coulthard	GB	Williams FW17B-Renault	39	Accident
Pedro Diniz	BR	Forti FG01-Ford ED	32	Spin
Jean Alesi	F	Ferrari 412 T2	24	Transmission
Andrea Montermini	I	Pacific PR02-Ford ED	23	Spin
Gerhard Berger	A	Ferrari 412 T2	16	Engine sensor
Rubens Barrichello	BR	Jordan 195-Peugeot	15	Accident
Ukyo Katayama	J	Tyrrell 023-Yamaha	12	Accident
Bertrand Gachot	B/F	Pacific PR02-Ford ED	6	Driveshaft bearing
Roberto Moreno	BR	Forti FG01-Ford ED	1	Gearbox
Gianni Morbidelli	I	Footwork FA16-Hart	0	Spin
Aguri Suzuki	J	Ligier JS41-Mugen Honda		Did not start – accident

Fastest lap

Michael Schumacher   Benetton B195-Renault   lap 33   1m 42.976s (127.976mph)

DRIVERS' CHAMPIONSHIP

Michael Schumacher	102	Jean-Christophe Boullion	3
Damon Hill	59	Mika Salo	3
David Coulthard	49	Gianni Morbidelli	1
Johnny Herbert	45	Aguri Suzuki	1
Jean Alesi	42		
Gerhard Berger	31		
Mika Häkkinen	17		
Heinz-Harald Frentzen	15		
Rubens Barrichello	11		
Mark Blundell	10		
Olivier Panis	10		
Eddie Irvine	10		
Martin Brundle	7		

CONSTRUCTORS' CUP

Benetton-Renault	137
Williams-Renault	102
Ferrari	73
McLaren-Mercedes	27
Jordan-Peugeot	21
Sauber-Ford	18
Ligier-Mugen Honda	18
Tyrrell-Yamaha	3
Footwork-Hart	1

Australia

12 November 1995
Circuit: Adelaide

Despite doing a fair impression of a Stanley Steamer for the last few laps, Olivier Panis's second-placed Ligier somehow lasted long enough to have a chance of running over the bloke in the yellow jacket with the chequered flag (above).

As all around him were driving into each other, or the pit wall, Damon Hill (left) drove faultlessly in Adelaide's last scheduled Grand Prix. Williams even had time for a flunked pit stop, yet still he won by over two laps.

Adelaide 1995 was a bitter-sweet occasion for Formula One. Sweet because it is always a treat to return to the lovely City of Churches on the coast of South Australia, but bitter because this was the last time that we would be doing so.

When the Grand Prix scene arrived Down Under for the first time in 1985, it didn't really know what to expect. Few of us had been to Australia, but everybody knew that it had never held a World Championship Grand Prix and we expected it all to be a bit ragtime. Nothing could have been further from the truth. Adelaide, we found, was a calm and beautiful city of parks, with its Torrens river, fine buildings and wide, open streets, which had taken the idea of a Grand Prix to its heart. Everything there seemed to revolve around the race. The organisation and administration were a model of calm perfection, and nothing was too much trouble for some of the most friendly, cheerful and hospitable people we had ever had the good fortune to meet.

A seemingly limitless number of superb restaurants;

the fabled South Australian wines; great weather and a laid-back attitude. It made the social scene a joy, and to top it all the circuit, comprising specially-closed everyday streets, was a driver- and car-challenging delight. We all proceeded to have a ball for 10 years and the Australian GP, the last of the year, became the one to which we all looked forward as the climax of the season, irrespective of whether or not the championships had already been decided.

There had been some great races and vivid memories: Nigel Mansell failing to win the championship in 1986, when a rear tyre on his Williams burst at some 190mph on the Jack Brabham straight with only a few laps to go; Keke Rosberg's victory at the first race in 1985; Thierry Boutsen's win for Williams in the wet, wet 1989 event; the shortest-ever, even wetter Grand Prix in 1991, which was literally washed-out after only 24 minutes and 14 laps of frighteningly dangerous misery; the historic 500th F1 GP in 1990, won by Ayrton Senna; the great Brazilian's last-ever win in 1993; Nigel Mansell's victory in 1994, after the drama of the collision between Michael Schumacher and Damon Hill, which ended their championship battle.

In all its 10 years, Adelaide hadn't produced a dull race. And 1995 was to be no exception, before the race moves to the rebuilt Albert Park facility, in Melbourne.

Adelaide wasn't going out with a whimper. It was going out with a gigantic bang and a non-stop buzz of fun, activity and on-track happenings which ensured that we'd never forget it. Both the World

There were some strange things to be seen in Adelaide. A member of the Alesi Liberation Front breaks cover (above).

Arrows of outrageous good fortune: Gianni Morbidelli heads Mark Blundell on his way to third place (top).

Damon Hill receives a warm reception from his team, who couldn't prevent him from winning by two clear laps, despite one mildly chaotic pit stop (right).

Championships had been decided, but there were plenty of reasons why everyone would be straining every nerve and sinew to win. No less than eight of the top drivers were going to be moving to different teams in 1996, and they all wanted to do so as winners. Michael Schumacher could become the most successful F1 driver in one season by beating Nigel Mansell's 1992 record of nine wins. Damon Hill, who was staying with Williams, needed a fourth 1995 victory to silence his vociferous media critics and raise his spirits after a barren spell. Berger and Alesi wanted to end their Ferrari careers on a high and David Coulthard, Johnny Herbert, Mark Blundell, Martin Brundle and Eddie Irvine were similarly determined to finalise the list of Adelaide victors.

It wasn't going to be easy for any of them though. With its heat, its 190 mph straight, its succession of brake-sapping 90-degree bends and its 1h 45m duration, Adelaide is a notorious car-breaker. On average less than half the entry had finished every year since 1985 and it was by no means unusual for only single numbers to go the distance. As we were to see again!

It all started badly, though. On Friday afternoon Mika Häkkinen, approaching the right-handed Malthouse Bend at some 140 mph, had a piece of debris slice into his left rear tyre which instantly deflated.

Pitched into a lightly protected concrete barrier with enormous impact. Mika suffered head injuries which would have killed him had it not been for the lightning response of the track's medics. In the nearby Royal Adelaide Hospital, Häkkinen made encouragingly rapid progress over the next few days, but the very popular Finn's racing future remained sadly uncertain.

Back at the track, the two Williams drivers were dominating, as they had so very often during 1995 qualifying sessions. Looking steady and totally in command Damon Hill was fastest on Friday, Saturday and again in Sunday's warm-up. In pole position for the seventh time in 1995, he was only 0.1s faster than team-mate David Coulthard and, as ever, there were to be no team orders. With Schumacher third after a troubled time getting his Benetton set up properly, the top three in the championship were again the fastest on the grid, followed by the Ferraris of Gerhard Berger and Jean Alesi, Frentzen's Sauber, Barrichello's Jordan and Johnny Herbert's Benetton.

Under blue skies and in blazing sunshine, before the largest crowd in the history of Formula One (over 205,000), David Coulthard's start was meteoric as he catapulted his Williams-Renault past Damon Hill's into the lead. So were those of Berger and Alesi – both past Schumacher to demote the double world champion to

fifth – a very rare occurrence for fast-starting Michael, who rapidly got past Alesi to take fourth on the first lap. But as Coulthard and Hill, separated by only a second or so, drew away, Schumacher found Berger a much tougher proposition.

By the time he found a way past the Austrian's Ferrari, the two Williams men were nearly 11s up the road as Alesi, Frentzen and Herbert fought for fifth place behind Gerhard. As ever we exercised our brains about strategy. Was Schumacher so far behind because he was carrying a heavier fuel load than the two Williams men ahead? No he wasn't. They were just quicker than him. So much so that when second-place Damon Hill stopped for fuel and tyres on lap 18, he was a massive 16s ahead of the Benetton.

As Damon rejoined, now third, it was time for race-leader David Coulthard to come in and he did – into the pit wall! Hardly believing our eyes we watched him enter the pit lane, lock up his brakes and thump straight into the concrete divider between the track and the pits. Front-running Coulthard had gone off for the third time in 1995 in very strange circumstances (remember those pre-race offs at Monza and the Nürburgring?). "With my foot on the brake the engine still drove me forward and pushed me into the wall," he said. Whatever, David's fine drive was over and Schumacher now led Hill – until his pit stop on lap 21.

As Damon raced by into the lead, Alesi shot past the pit lane exit a whisker before Schumacher emerged, now third. Down the 190mph Jack Brabham straight the Ferrari and the Benetton raced as one until Schumacher

peeled out from under Alesi's rear wing and boldly took back second. But Jean turned in as he did so, and for the second year in succession at Adelaide, Schumacher was involved in a controversial collision. As Alesi's front wing shredded, Michael drove over the debris moments before Jean shot into the pits for a new nosecone. To no avail though. The Ferrari's handling was destroyed and Alesi was out of his last Grand Prix for the Prancing Horse team. Then in came Schumacher for a check-up, as the rear end "felt funny". A 27s stop dropped Michael to seventh. Two laps later he was in again to retire, his hopes of that 10th win shattered.

As Schumacher grimly strode down to his future employer's garage for a furious discussion with Alesi, Hill had seen three of his main rivals removed in four laps. He was now 32s ahead of Johnny Herbert, who had yet to stop, with Berger third, Frentzen fourth, Brundle fifth and Irvine sixth. Surely all Damon had to do now was to keep it steady to win for the first – and last – time at Adelaide? Exactly so. And he did as, one by one, his remaining opponents fell by the wayside while he reeled off the laps with metronomic precision. First to go was Martin Brundle. Out of seventh place after driving into the back of Blundell's McLaren. Then Gerhard Berger, an enormous 50s behind Damon but in second place, when his engine blew up for the second time in as many days. Frentzen superbly took second for Sauber only to have his gearbox fail on lap 40. Eddie Irvine was next. Out from third on lap 63, when his Peugeot engine's air pressure system gave up.

Ahead of him Johnny Herbert had been second, and he would have finished third in the drivers' championship if he had stayed there. But he didn't. Broken driveshaft, lap 70 with only 11 to go. Adelaide was certainly living up to its reputation. How many were going to finish?

Hill was now at least a lap ahead of everyone with Olivier Panis second in a Ligier which looked and sounded as though it was more than ready for retirement. But, popping and banging and with a thick plume of smoke pouring out behind him, Olivier soldiered on. Damon lapped him for the second time on the last lap, but Panis finished second, just over 10s ahead of Gianni Morbidelli who had never been on the podium before in his 59 Grands Prix (it was the first time that an Arrows driver had been there since Phoenix 1989). Only eight drivers were classified as finishers, with Mark Blundell, Mika Salo and Pedro Lamy taking the remaining points-scoring places for McLaren, Tyrrell and Minardi (the team's first point of the season).

A great win for Damon Hill, and thoroughly deserved. It sent the gigantic crown home very happy indeed, sadly realising that they had been present while history was made at the grand finale of the Adelaide Australian Grand Prix. For them and for us the next Grand Prix was going to be in Australia, too, but this time it would be the first of the year – Melbourne 1996. If its debut was as good as Adelaide's swansong, it was going to be well worth looking forward to.

Stranger still. In the middle of this lot, somebody really is wearing a Manchester City shirt (above).

Alesi and Schumacher practise for their post-race argument (top).

Benetton-Renault

Not a fairy tale ending to a wonderful year. Michael Schumacher only sixth fastest in twitchy car on Friday morning and, shocked by Häkkinen's heavy crash, reluctant to go out in qualifying. Nevertheless does so and is fourth fastest. Improves to third on grid by going second fastest on Saturday after major changes to set-up. Makes bad start and is passed by Berger and Alesi. Takes Alesi on first lap but does not go past Berger until lap five, by which time Coulthard and Hill are well clear. Cannot stop the two close-running Williams from increasing their lead, but up to first, lap 20, following Hill's pit stop and Coulthard's dramatic retirement. Down to third, immediately behind Alesi, after own stop, lap 21. Passes Jean at hairpin but Alesi tries to repass and hits Benetton. Schumacher to pits for check after running over Alesi front-wing debris. Rejoins seventh but retires in pits, lap 26, with rear suspension damage. Visits Ferrari garage for angry confrontation with Alesi after failing to win hoped-for record 10th GP in one season. Johnny Herbert starts eighth but improves to fourth in warm-up. Up to seventh at start but then stuck behind Frentzen until H-H pit-stops from fourth, lap 21. Johnny takes first of two stops on lap 30 when second, after missing slippery pit lane entry on lap 29. Rejoins behind Frentzen again, but back to second after H-H retires, lap 40, and looking good for third in championship, only to retire, with driveshaft failure. But still a great year for Benetton after winning both championships.

Tyrrell-Yamaha

Fourteenth on grid for Salo, three seconds off pace. Races with Morbidelli to 11th at first of two stops, lap 26. Eighth at second stop, lap 51, and benefits from Herbert and Irvine retirements to finish contented fifth, three laps down (third points finish from last six races). Katayama starts 16th after usual spins. Suffers from engine and tyre problems and runs into Minardi pit lane area, injuring two mechanics. Retires from seventh on lap 71 with low oil pressure. Team looks forward to more competitive 1996 with new Yamaha V10.

Williams-Renault

A happy ending to a troubled 1995. Damon Hill and David Coulthard dominate both days of qualifying with Hill taking seventh pole of season and circuit rookie Coulthard starting superb second, 0.1s slower. David makes dynamic start, passes Hill and surges ahead. Damon pit stops from close second, lap 18, and rejoins third behind Schumacher. Coulthard then unbelievably slides into pit lane wall when making stop, lap 19, and immediately retires. An embarrassing end to his Williams career. Hill leads on lap 22 and destroys opposition as field diminishes. Takes fourth 1995 win by amazing two laps with fastest lap of race (1m 17.943s, 108.709mph), justifiably elated at his turn of fortune after an immaculate drive.

McLaren-Mercedes

A very troubled finish to an awful season. Cut rear tyre slams Mika Häkkinen into wall at some 125 mph during Friday qualifying. Only magnificent immediate action by medical team saves Mika's life before he is taken to Royal Adelaide Hospital with head injuries. Makes heartening progress during Saturday/Sunday, but racing future sadly unpredictable. Mark Blundell pitches in for last race with team. Qualifies 10th, and is up to sixth by lap 27, but hit by Martin Brundle and forced into spin. Resultant damage destroys aerodynamic balance but Mark soldiers on to finish fourth of eight, two laps down.

Arrows-Hart

Great finish to season after Gianni Morbidelli starts 13th and Taki Inoue 19th. Gianni races with Salo, up to seventh before first stop, lap 27. Back into points lap 35 and is fifth at second stop, lap 53. Benefits from Irvine and Herbert retirements to take first-ever podium finish, two laps down (team's first podium since 1989). A real fillip for Arrows and for Brian Hart's engine men at Harlow. Inoue unsurprisingly spins out of race from 17th, lap 16.

Jordan-Peugeot

Continued unreliability again frustrates potential success. Seventh on grid for Barrichello and ninth for Irvine. Rubens blocked at start and down two places. Races ninth behind Irvine but into tyre wall, lap 21, when throttle sticks open. In last race for Jordan, Irvine up to third at first stop, lap 25. Third again at second stop, lap 40. Retains place after third stop, lap 57, but has to pit again, lap 61, with loss of air pressure. Retires lap 63. After 18 retirements from 34 starts season ends very disappointingly for Jordan.

Pacific-Ford

Team tries to replace Andrea Montermini with 1995 British F3 Champion Oliver Gavin. Effort founders due to Superlicence problem. After usual lack of track time caused by financial limitations Montermini starts 22nd with Bertrand Gachot 23rd. Andrea up to 17th, lap one, but gearbox fails lap three. Bertrand drives carefully to finish eighth and last, five laps down. Now team gets down to producing better car for 1996.

Forti-Ford

After abandoning semi-automatic gearbox development at race tracks, Roberto Moreno starts trouble-free 20th with Pedro Diniz 21st. Gap to pole position down to five seconds but still far too close for comfort with 107 per cent qualifying rule looming in 1996. Moreno spins into pit wall at lap 21 stop and retires. Diniz best-ever seventh, four laps down, with team frustrated by fact that sixth and one point would have earned them valuable FOCA travel benefits for 1996.

Minardi-Ford

A happy ending at last for Gian Carlo Minardi's hard-trying team after 17 races of non-stop endeavour. Luca Badoer improves two places on grid on Saturday to qualify 15th. All his efforts come to nought on grid, however, when engine management problems prevent him even starting race. Much better fortune for Pedro Lamy who starts 17th. Up to 13th by first stop, lap 24. Seventh of 11 still running on lap 52 when Ukyo Katayama runs into Minardi area, destroying compressed air system and injuring two mechanics. In danger of running out of fuel, Lamy delays second stop until lap 59. Rejoins eighth and is in points at sixth, lap 70, after Irvine and Herbert retire. Finishes sixth, three laps down, for his first-ever point and also team's first of 1995.

Ligier-Mugen Honda

A great, if lucky, result for the Flavio Briatore/Tom Walkinshaw/Tony Dowe-headed team. Martin Brundle returns for his last drive for Ligier before joining Jordan in 1996. Despite Japanese two-race layoff in favour of Aguri Suzuki, Martin again outqualifies team-mate Olivier Panis to start 11th, two seconds off the pace. Passes Mark Blundell on lap one and races 10th behind Irvine and Barrichello for 19 laps. Pit stops from fifth, lap 26, and rejoins eighth. Runs into back of Mark Blundell, lap 30, stalls engine and retires. But Panis saves the day. Starts 12th and battles with Blundell before taking early pit stop, lap 24. Into points at sixth, lap 33, and is lapped fourth at second stop, lap 54. Up to impressive second, lap 70, after Herbert and Irvine retirements and brought in for unscheduled "safety-first" fuel stop, a lap ahead of third-placed Morbidelli. Major Mugen engine problem develops three laps from end but Olivier presses on with smoke pouring from engine bay. Lapped by Hill for second time on last lap but finishes second to equal previous best finish. Olivier's six points move Ligier to fifth in constructors' championship.

Ferrari

A truly dismal end to a patchy season marred by continued unreliability despite substantial performance improvements. After post-Japan work to overcome engine sensor problems which had affected him several times, Gerhard Berger qualifies third for his last race for Ferrari before joining Benetton with team-mate Jean Alesi in 1996. But is lucky to do so after doing 13 laps, one more than permitted, in Friday qualifying and having times cancelled before being reinstated on appeal. With two previous wins and most points for any driver at Adelaide (33), Gerhard hopes for third victory at his 11th Adelaide race. Passes Schumacher to third at start but caught and passed by Michael, lap five. Pit stops from fourth, lap 18, rejoins seventh and climbs to second, lap 31, as others stop. Is 48s behind Hill but intends to pace himself until last 30 laps. But engine blows on lap 35, as it had during Saturday morning free practice, and Gerhard is out. Jean Alesi, grimly determined to do well in last Ferrari race, loses most of Friday qualifying when engine sensor cable fails but qualifies fifth with Saturday time. Like Berger passes Schumacher to fourth at start but loses place to Michael before end of first lap. To third during first round of stops between lap 22. Passes Schumacher to second, lap 23, as Michael exits pit lane but is forcefully repassed at first hairpin. Alesi tries to regain place at exit of corner but collides with the Benetton and shreds Ferrari front wing. Into pits for new nose but car handling ruined and retires from seventh lap 34. Irate Schumacher visits his 1996 team's garage to remonstrate with unrepentant Jean.

Sauber-Ford

It could have been the team's highest-ever second place, but it wasn't. As usual the enormously impressive Heinz-Harald Frentzen shines in qualifying to go faster than the car seems able to by qualifying sixth. Starts race with intended three-stop strategy and races with Alesi and Herbert. Is fourth at first scheduled stop, lap 21, and rejoins seventh. After retirements and pit stops is superb second and looking good, lap 35 (albeit a massive 63s behind Hill, after being persistently blocked by Mark Blundell to H-H's plainly demonstrated fury), but then gearbox fails, lap 40. Karl Wendlinger, on the second of his two end-of-season "last chance" races does badly. Crashes heavily on Friday morning but qualifies provisional 11th. Cannot drive during Saturday qualifying due to whiplash pain and starts 18th. Retires after eight laps troubled by pain from circuit bumps. Sadly it seems that Karl's second comeback attempt had failed.

12 NOVEMBER 1995

Adelaide

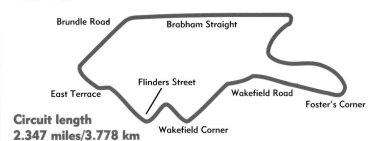

Brundle Road
Brabham Straight
Flinders Street
East Terrace
Wakefield Road
Foster's Corner
Wakefield Corner

**Circuit length
2.347 miles/3.778 km**

STARTING GRID

HILL (Williams FW17B) 1m 15.505s	**COULTHARD** (Williams FW17B) 1m 15.628s
SCHUMACHER (Benetton B195) 1m 15.839s	**BERGER** (Ferrari 412 T2) 1m 15.932s
ALESI (Ferrari 412 T2) 1m 16.305s	**FRENTZEN** (Sauber C14) 1m 16.647s
BARRICHELLO (Jordan 195) 1m 16.725s	**HERBERT** (Benetton B195) 1m 16.950s
IRVINE (Jordan 195) 1m 17.116s	**BLUNDELL** (McLaren MP4/10B) 1m 17.348s
BRUNDLE (Ligier JS41) 1m 17.624s	**PANIS** (Ligier JS41) 1m 18.033s
MORBIDELLI (Footwork FA16) 1m 18.391s	**SALO** (Tyrrell 023) 1m 18.604s
BADOER (Minardi M195) 1m 18.810s	**KATAYAMA** (Tyrrell 023) 1m 18.828s
LAMY (Minardi M195) 1m 18.875s	**WENDLINGER** (Sauber C14) 1m 19.561s
INOUE (Footwork FA16) 1m 19.677s	**MORENO** (Forti FG01) 1m 20.657s
DINIZ (Forti FG01) 1m 20.878s	**MONTERMINI** (Pacific PR02) 1m 21.659s
GACHOT (Pacific PR02) 1m 21.998s	

RACE CLASSIFICATION

Pos	Driver	Nat	Car	Laps	Time
1	Damon Hill	GB	Williams FW17B-Renault	81	1h 49m 15.946s
2	Olivier Panis	F	Ligier JS41-Mugen Honda		2 laps behind
3	Gianni Morbidelli	I	Footwork FA16-Hart		2 laps behind
4	Mark Blundell	GB	McLaren MP4/10B-Mercedes		2 laps behind
5	Mika Salo	SF	Tyrrell 023-Yamaha		3 laps behind
6	Pedro Lamy	P	Minardi M195-Ford ED		3 laps behind
7	Pedro Diniz	BR	Forti FG01-Ford ED		4 laps behind
8	Bertrand Gachot	F/B	Pacific PR02-Ford ED		5 laps behind

Retirements	Nat	Car	Laps	Reason
Ukyo Katayama	J	Tyrrell 023-Yamaha	70	Oil pressure
Johnny Herbert	GB	Benetton B195-Renault	69	Driveshaft
Eddie Irvine	GB	Jordan 195-Peugeot	62	Air pressure loss
Heinz-Harald Frentzen	D	Sauber C14-Ford Zetec	39	Gearbox
Gerhard Berger	A	Ferrari 412 T2	34	Engine
Martin Brundle	GB	Ligier JS41-Mugen Honda	29	Accident
Michael Schumacher	D	Benetton B195-Renault	25	Collision
Jean Alesi	F	Ferrari 412 T2	23	Collision
Roberto Moreno	BR	Forti FG01-Ford ED	21	Pit lane accident
Rubens Barrichello	BR	Jordan 195-Peugeot	20	Accident
David Coulthard	GB	Williams FW17B-Renault	15	Pit lane accident
Taki Inoue	J	Footwork FA16-Hart	15	Spin
Karl Wendlinger	A	Sauber C14-Ford Zetec	8	Neck injury
Andrea Montermini	I	Pacific PR02-Ford ED	2	Gearbox
Luca Badoer	I	Minardi M195-Ford ED	0	ECU problem
Mika Häkkinen	SF	McLaren MP4/10B-Mercedes		Did not start

Fastest lap				
Damon Hill	Williams FW17B-Renault	16	1m 17.943s (108.419mph)	

DRIVERS' CHAMPIONSHIP

Michael Schumacher	102
Damon Hill	69
David Coulthard	49
Johnny Herbert	45
Jean Alesi	42
Gerhard Berger	31
Mika Häkkinen	17
Olivier Panis	16
Heinz-Harald Frentzen	15
Mark Blundell	13
Rubens Barrichello	11
Eddie Irvine	10
Martin Brundle	7

Gianni Morbidelli	5
Mika Salo	5
Jean-Christophe Boullion	3
Aguri Suzuki	1
Pedro Lamy	1

CONSTRUCTORS' CUP

Benetton-Renault	137
Williams-Renault	112
Ferrari	73
McLaren-Mercedes	30
Ligier-Mugen Honda	24
Jordan-Peugeot	21
Sauber-Ford	18
Footwork-Hart	5
Tyrrell-Yamaha	5
Minardi-Ford	1

With his sideburns and natural affinity for the guitar, Damon Hill (above) could have been confused for a rock star, and often elicited the sort of crowd reaction normally reserved for REM.

Trading places (top): Jean Alesi might have been disappointed when his Ferrari stranded him at the Hungaroring, but at least it gave him the opportunity to observe the reliability of Michael Schumacher's Benetton, aka the car he'll be driving in 1996.

If Jean Alesi got a nice, warm feeling from watching the Schumacher's Benetton in action, the reverse was not necessarily true. Michael studies his destiny via the small screen (left).

In 1994 Formula One suffered. Two tragic deaths, accusations of cheating, political manoeuvring, bans, suspensions and a potentially disastrous pit lane fire marred the season and left everybody relieved when it ended.

Thankfully, 1995 was largely different. There were several truly exciting races, a very worthy world champion in Michael Schumacher, a first-ever constructors' championship for Benetton and another stunning year for Renault, whose fine V10 blew everybody else away. And when it all looked to have gone horribly wrong in Adelaide, where Mika Häkkinen was transferred to the intensive care unit of the local hospital after a serious practice accident, the paddock was swiftly cheered by the news that the talented Finn's injuries were not as serious as had first been feared.

Due to the repercussions of the awful Kobe earthquake in Japan, there were 17 Grands Prix instead of the traditional 16, and many of them were blockbusters. There were three first-time winners in Jean Alesi, Johnny Herbert and David Coulthard, and nine victories for Michael Schumacher, who equalled Nigel Mansell's seasonal record. At 26, with many years of racing

before him if he so desires, the German could well become the most successful F1 racer of all time.

Some of his 1995 wins will long be talked about. Monaco, where superior driving and a better strategy destroyed Damon Hill; winning from 16th on the grid in Belgium; his successful pursuit of Jean Alesi in the Grand Prix of Europe at the Nürburgring; and his title-clinching win at Aida were amongst them.

The rest were pulped, in a different class altogether.

There were only four wins for Damon Hill, compared with six in 1994, but that was enough to give him second place in the championship for the second year in succession. Justified or not, he was the subject of frequent criticism for the number of times he was involved in collisions or spun out of the action. Damon is a good man and an accomplished driver who has had much well-deserved success, but he must have been very disappointed with most of a season which had started – and, in Australia, ended – so well.

His team-mate David Coulthard had a patchy year, too. Dragged down by tonsillitis in the opening races of the season, which affected him

more than he was prepared to admit, his was a very commendable first full year of Grand Prix racing with a first- ever win in Portugal and a string of podium places. But that was not enough to stop him from being dropped for 1996 in favour of Indycar champion Jacques Villeneuve, son of the late, great French-Canadian Gilles.

Car reliability problems affected David more than is usual for a Williams driver, but so too did driving lapses like his surprising pre-race excursions at Monza and the Nurburgring. Nevertheless, Williams could well rue Coulthard's departure to McLaren for 1996, given that he did not want to go.

In a situation where Benetton was the class of the field and Williams failed to get it all together, Ferrari was equally disappointing. With only one win, and a lucky one at that, they had been expected to do much better. It was a case of so near and yet so far. Alesi in particular deserved more than his Canadian win, but was denied it by virtue of poor reliability. With the vastly expensive Schumacher bringing his Number One status to Maranello, thanks to Benetton, and an all-new V10 to replace the traditional V12, Italy expects the Prancing Horse to deliver in 1996.

And what of McLaren, once upon a time seemingly invincible? This was surely the most degrading year since Ron Dennis took over the then-failing organisation in 1980. With the very public Nigel Mansell debacle, a demeaning first year with mighty Mercedes-Benz and an intractable chassis that no amount of development and testing seemed able to improve, it was not until the end of the season that things started to come right. And then Mika Häkkinen had his accident in Adelaide, fortunately with less serious consequences than was initially feared.

With so much to lose in the way of prestige, sponsorship and self-respect, not to mention the potential of two fine drivers in Hakkinen – assuming he recovers in time for the start of the season – and Coulthard, it will

be a very busy winter at Woking.

As it will at Jordan's Silverstone headquarters. Its first year with Peugeot power was much the same as McLaren's in 1994, with repeated reliability problems. The learning curve in Formula One is fearsomely steep but, as with Ferrari and McLaren, 1996 will be a year when Eddie's team has to improve by finishing consistently and winning races. If they don't, it won't be for a lack of trying or, with Martin Brundle and Rubens Barrichello, a lack of driving experience.

After the golden years leading to 1994, when legendary greats like Prost, Senna, Piquet, Lauda and Mansell competed against each other, 1995 was a year of fresher talent. Schumacher had more than made his mark already, but I was mighty impressed too with Heinz-Harald Frentzen (as was Frank Williams, to the extent of trying to get him into his team), Mika Salo, David Coulthard, Johnny Herbert (two wins in a car he was unhappy with, and he still got the bullet - amazing), Mika Häkkinen, Rubens Barrichello and Eddie Irvine (Ferrari-bound, need I say more?).

How many of them will reach the summit remains to be seen, but there is a lot of talent there.

There were controversies in 1995, of course. With the ever- present hazard of fire and all its implications, is it wise to continue with refuelling, even if it creates strategic interest? Were all those jump-start penalties, which spoilt so many races, really merited? Should heavily-funded 'no-hopers' be allowed to compete at the pinnacle of motor sport at the expense of talented drivers who have no money? And if not, what can be done about it? Is it right to make it even more difficult for new teams to enter Formula One by introducing the new '107 per cent' qualifying requirement? How do you stop highly motivated drivers running into each other with so much at stake?

Whatever, 1995 was an excellent year all in all. Here's to 1996!